CONTENTS

89757

MISSIONARY Conquest

PREFACE

Two separate, if related, concerns generated this volume. First was a graduate seminar on Indian mission history that I taught on some three times over a four-year period at Iliff School of Theology. The seminar involved students in intensive primary research in a field that is nearly boundless in terms of archival materials, denominational involvement, complexities of tribal differentiation, and the interweaving of discrete mission history with the general history of the European invasion and occupation of what today is known as North America. Each student was asked to take on a piece of this whole and critically analyze the sources, reporting the results back to the seminar where we all read enough to engage in constructive dialogue with each other. Two things emerged repeatedly in the course of each seminar. One was the remarkable uniformity in motivations, strategies, and results of the missionary endeavor across the broad diversity of topics, tribes, denominations, time periods, and geographical regions. The other was the extent to which the research itself seemed to effect change in individual students, particularly white American students.

The second concern was the growing apprehension many of us have had over the then-impending celebration of the Columbus Quincentenary and the extent to which it seemed destined to strengthen and validate the unhealthy mythological illusion that white U.S. citizens have about themselves and their role in the world. The year 1492 seems to have triggered the "Western world" mythology that has come to dominate the entire globe's economics, politics, and academics, imposing itself as the natural, unquestionable norm of human existence. This illusion of Western world superiority has functioned implicitly, and at times brutally explicitly, to facilitate the conquest and enslavement of native peoples, the exploitation of their labor and the natural resources, and the genocidal destruction of whole cultures and peoples. The religious institutions of the "West" (that is, the churches of Europe and then the immigrant churches of the Americas) have been closely associated with this history of colonialism and conquest and have consistently lent legitimacy to those acts. At some level the church has ultimately functioned to provide theological justification for acts of conquest, even when it has protested to the contrary or interceded at the surface level on behalf of the conquered.

The church or missionary responses to European/American colonialism exhibited two general patterns. One pattern, which viewed immigrant America as the New Israel, overtly helped build the theological base for the doctrine of Manifest Destiny. The other pattern may have been very critical of white American dealings with Indians or Blacks, but lived its own Manifest Destiny agenda. Indeed, these critics were opposed to the brutal military conquest of native peoples. They preferred the conquest of conversion instead. For them this meant conversion to what they assumed were a superior culture and set of values and societal structures every bit as much as it meant conversion to the gospel of Jesus Christ. For instance, both Bartolomé de Las Casas and Henry Benjamin Whipple in different ways earned great reputations as defenders of Indian people, yet both are implicated in the cultural destruction of Indian tribes. Las Casas first devised the famed "reduction" paradigm for missionary conquest. Whipple engineered the U.S. government's theft of the Black Hills from the Sioux people, which finally broke the back of Sioux resistance.

Perhaps the most fearful aspect of the church's complicity in the conquest of native peoples in this latter sense is that it always happened with the best of intentions, both verbally expressed and, I believe, heartfelt. Las Casas wrote tomes criticizing the atrocities committed by his countrymen against Indian people in the Caribbean, Mexico, and the rest of Latin America. Yet, out of his heartfelt need to protect these Indian people, he was the author of the infamous "reduction" system, which dislocated Indian people from their families and from their culture and inculturated them into European values and social systems. More than three hundred years later, Whipple was sure that he had acted in the best interests of the Sioux and that their only hope of survival was a reduced land base where European-style agriculture and a sedentary existence could more effectively be imposed on them. Neither Las Casas nor Whipple could possibly foresee the long-term demoralizing effects his missions would have on Indian people. Neither understood his role in a process of pacification that enabled, simplified, and enhanced the ultimate conquest of those tribes. Thoroughly blinded by their own inculturation and their implicit acceptance of the illusion of European superiority, these apostles of the church, and indeed virtually every missionary of every denomination, functioned one way or another as a participant in an unintended evil. Las Casas and Whipple served two different denominations, derived from two different European ancestries, had genuine good intentions for the fate of Indian peoples, and yet participated in what I will call the cultural genocide of those same peoples.

The implicit agenda of this book, perhaps most clearly apparent in the final chapter, is to raise a critical question for us to consider in our own historical and theological context, namely, What is our blindness today? With the best of intentions and with the full support of our best theologies and intellectual capabilities, do we continue to fall into the same sorts of traps and participate in unintended evils? My presupposition is that without confronting and owning

MISSIONARY
Conquest

THE GOSPEL AND NATIVE AMERICAN CULTURAL GENOCIDE

GEORGE E. TINKER

FORTRESS PRESS ✝ MINNEAPOLIS

MISSIONARY CONQUEST
The Gospel and Native American Cultural Genocide

The excerpt from *Ceremony* by Leslie Marmon Silko, copyright © Leslie Silko, is used by permission of Viking Penguin, a division of Penguin Books USA, Inc.

Interior design: James Brisson
Cover design: Spangler Design Team
Cover art: Thomas Hart Benton (1889–1975), *Aggression (American Historical Epic)*, ca. 1919–24, courtesy of The Nelson-Atkins Museum of Art, Kansas City, Missouri (Bequest of the artist) F75–21/3.

Library of Congress Cataloging-in-Publication Data

Tinker, George E.
   Missionary conquest : the Gospel and Native American cultural
genocide / George E. Tinker.
     p. cm.
   Includes bibliographical references.
   ISBN 0-8006-2576-5 :
   1. Indians of North America—Missions.   2. Indians, Treatment of—
North America—History.   3. Missions—North America—History.
4. Missionaries—North America—Biography.   5. Serra, Junípero,
1713–1784.   6. Eliot, John, 1604–1690.   7. Smet, Pierre-Jean de,
1801–1873.   8. Whipple, Henry Benjamin, 1822–1901.   I. Title.
E98.M6T56   1993
266'.0089'97—dc20
                                                            93-22388
                                                                  CIP

Manufactured in the U.S.A.   AF 1-2576

97   96   95   94   93   1   2   3   4   5   6   7   8   9   10

our past, as white Americans, as Europeans, as American Indians, as African Americans, and so forth, we cannot hope to overcome that past and generate a constructive, healing process, leading to a world of genuine, mutual respect among peoples, communities, and nations.

I must acknowledge my indebtedness to and gratitude for the help and support of many people, not least of all my family. They have patiently endured the usual neglect generated by the demands of the academy and the commitment of time needed to write even a small volume. Iliff School of Theology and particularly Jane Smith, my dean, gave strong encouragement and, more than that, a quarter's research and writing leave to begin the project. Finally, I owe a very special word of thanks to my research aides, who with great dedication and expertise kept me nourished with a steady diet of primary source material. Lowell Uda, Bill Witt, and Loring Abeyta were not only consistently attentive to details, directing my attention to bits and pieces in the sources that I might otherwise have overlooked, but also engaged me in ongoing debate about the issues even as I wrote. The Reverend Linda Seracuse, along with these assistants, gave close attention to questions of style and syntax, thereby enhancing my own writing skills.

CHAPTER 1

Missionary Intentions, Missionary Violence

Tayo, the protagonist in Leslie Silko's 1977 novel *Ceremony*,[1] struggles through-out the story to regain his health and well-being, which had been shattered by a complex set of cultural dislocations. These dislocations include the memory of generations of oppression of Indian peoples by the invading Europeans and the imposition of their social, economic, and political structures. Both the memory of this oppression and its continuation have resulted in a residual dysfunctionality in his family as in so many Indian families. Tayo's status in his own community as a mixed blood is another source of dislocation, but the coup de grace is the total cultural and spiritual dislocation resulting from his expe-riences in the jungles of the Pacific during World War II. His journey to health is quintessentially spiritual and is to be understood in its entirety as a "ceremony," a traditional Indian spiritual rite. But in the best Indian sense of spiritual, the ceremony includes social, psychological, and even political dimensions. As part of his link to his pre-war past, Tayo comes to understand that he must recover a small herd of wild, Mexican range cattle purchased years earlier by a late uncle and now enclosed behind a very stout and expensive fence on the ranch of a wealthy white landowner. We are not told, nor does Tayo know, how or why the cattle are where they are.

As Tayo cuts through the fence to free the cattle, he finds himself making excuses for a respected white man's thievery of these economically useless cu-riosities of the bovine nation:

> The strands of wire were four inches apart and a quarter of an inch thick. He had to stop to shake the muscle cramps from his hands. The moon was rising early. He worked on his knees, cutting away the wire at ground level, where it continued under the surface six inches deep to discourage coyotes and wolves from digging under it. He tried to clear a place to kneel, but the ground was almost solid with pebbles and rocks. After the first ten feet of cutting and bending back wire, his knees went numb; he felt cold air on his skin and knew that his Levis were worn through at both knees. He was thinking about the cattle and how they had ended up on Floyd Lee's land. If he had seen the cattle on land-grant land or in some

Acoma's corral, he wouldn't have hesitated to say "stolen." But something inside him made him hesitate to say it now that the cattle were on a white man's ranch. He had a crazy desire to believe that there had been some mistake, that Floyd Lee had gotten them innocently, maybe buying them from the real thieves. Why did he hesitate to accuse a white man of stealing but not a Mexican or an Indian? He took off his gloves and stuck his hands inside his jacket to wipe the broken blisters on his shirt. Sweat made the raw skin sting all the way up both arms, leaving his shoulders with a dull ache. He knew then he had learned the lie by heart—the lie which they had wanted him to learn: only brown-skinned people were thieves; white people didn't steal, because they always had the money to buy whatever they wanted.

The lie. He cut into the wire as if cutting away at the lie inside himself. The liars had fooled everyone, white people and Indians alike; as long as people believed the lies, they would never be able to see what had been done to them or what they were doing to each other. He wiped the sweat off his face onto the sleeve of his jacket. He stood back and looked at the gaping cut in the wire. If the white people never looked beyond the lie, to see that theirs was a nation built on stolen land, then they would never be able to understand how they had been used by the witchery; they would never know that they were still being manipulated by those who knew how to stir the ingredients together: white thievery and injustice boiling up the anger and hatred that would finally destroy the world: the starving against the fat, the colored against the white. The destroyers had only to set it into motion and sit back to count the casualties. But it was more than a body count: the lie devoured white hearts, and for more than two hundred years white people had worked to fill their emptiness; they tried to glut the hollowness with patriotic wars and with great technology and the wealth it brought. And always they had been fooling themselves, and they knew it.[2]

The "lie" that Tayo names here is a reality he stumbles upon, almost accidentally, and he discovers it deeply embedded within himself as an Indian person. On the lips of a white adversary Tayo would have recognized the lie immediately for what it is: a self-serving illusion of white superiority, an illusion undergirded by what Rollo May calls America's pseudoinnocence,[3] an illusion that damages the health and well-being of both white and Indian peoples. The truth is, however, that Indian people have internalized this illusion just as deeply as white Americans have, and as a result we discover from time to time just how fully we participate today in our own oppression. Implicitly, in both thought and action, we too often concede that the illusion of white superiority is an unquestionable factual reality. One part of the illusion, a part that the denominations of American churches live with too comfortably, is the historical interpretation of their missionary outreach to the native peoples of this continent.

This book, then, is about Indian people in North America and the Christian missionaries who devoted their lives to Indian evangelization. It is a story filled with pathos, energy, suffering, and even romance, when told by the missionaries and their biographers or historians. All too often in telling this story, well-meaning authors hyperbolize the romantic aspects of a missionary's work but include little of critical substance. The biographies of missionaries tend to be much closer in form to that medieval genre of hagiography (that is, the life of a saint) than to post-Enlightenment analytical historiography.

Told from an Indian perspective, the story is far less entertaining and much less endearing. Pain and devastation become dominant elements as Indian anger erupts to the surface. Indeed, today the white missionary, both in the historical memory of Indian people and in the contemporary experience, has become a frequent target of scorn in most segments of the Indian world. Many implicitly recognize some connection between Indian suffering and the missionary presence, even as they struggle to make sense not only of past wrongs, but also of the pain of contemporary Indian existence. The pain experienced by Indians today is readily apparent in too many statistics that put Indians on the top or bottom of lists. For instance, Indian people suffer the lowest per capita income of any ethnic group in the United States, the highest teenage suicide rate, a 60 percent unemployment rate nationally, and a scandalously low longevity that remains below sixty years for both men and women.

Yet even in the contemporary Indian world, there is no common understanding of this history. On the one hand, the old traditional ways have enjoyed a revival over the past twenty years. This revival has been fueled in part by anger over generations of oppression suffered at the hands of white civilization and its institutions. The latter include Christian churches as well as educational, economic, and political institutions. As a part of this larger movement, the return to traditional Indian religions is an exercise in self-determination and not just a product of anger at memories or current experiences of missionary history as a cultural imposition. Most Indian people in North America have been Christianized, however, even if only nominally. A good portion of Indian people have been Christian for several generations, and more than a few are very faithful to the denominations into which they have been evangelized. Furthermore, Indian congregations quite commonly remain faithful not only to the denomination, but to the very missionary theology that was first brought to them, even when the denomination has long ago abandoned that language for a more contemporary articulation of the gospel. One must at least suspect that the process of Christianization has involved some internalization of the larger illusion of Indian inferiority and the idealization of white culture and religion. Some have called it internalized racism, and as such it surely results in a praxis of self-hatred.[4]

What I am describing should surprise no one. The phenomenon is part of a much broader process that can be seen in other aspects of human existence. Just as an abused child slowly but inevitably internalizes a parent's abuse as a consistent demonstration of the child's own shortcomings and may even regard the life of the abusive parent as exemplary, so communities of oppressed peoples internalize their own oppression and come to believe too many of the stereotypes, explicit and implicit, spoken by the oppressor.

Methodology

This study attempts to bring greater clarity to American Indian mission history by critically analyzing that history. I take four of the churches' most loved and respected historical missionary figures and present synopses of these different mission contexts. Although I hope to achieve some objective validity in this study, I have pursued the research unabashedly and without apology from an American Indian point of view. If this approach should seem unduly biased, then I plead for some understanding that I am writing to counter a perceived bias. That is, what has been published about Indians and missionaries too often has been written with an implicit and sometimes explicit bias toward Euroamerican culture. The result has been a predisposition to favor and even heroize the missionaries at the cost of depreciating Indian peoples, sometimes as savage and sometimes as innocent but childish, yet always as culturally (and, hence, spiritually) less than the European-Christian norm.

The primary objectives of the study are to demonstrate the inevitable confusion of virtually every missionary between the gospel he, or occasionally she,[5] proclaimed to Indian people and the missionary's own European or Euroamerican culture, and to trace the resulting devastation of Indian peoples and their cultures. The motivation and the theoretical basis for the missionary endeavor, apparent both from the actual practice of the missionaries and from their writings, will demonstrate that they not only preached a new gospel of salvation, but also just as energetically imposed a new cultural model for existence on Indian people. The evidence will show that these two tasks became nearly indistinguishable in practice.

To state the case baldly and dramatically, my thesis is that the Christian missionaries—of all denominations working among American Indian nations—were partners in genocide. Unwittingly no doubt, and always with the best of intentions, nevertheless the missionaries were guilty of complicity in the destruction of Indian cultures and tribal social structures—complicity in the devastating impoverishment and death of the people to whom they preached.[6] I will explore the extent to which each of these missionary heroes implicitly blurred any distinction between the gospel of salvation and their own culture. This blurring invariably resulted in the missionary's culture, values, and social and political structures, not to say political hegemony and control, being imposed on tribal peoples, all in the name of the gospel. That is to say, the kerygmatic content of the missionary's Christian faith became confused with the accoutrements of the missionary's cultural experience and behavior. It is important to my thesis that my selections are among the churches' most remembered and most revered missionaries, who have been the subjects of countless hagiographies and continue to serve as models. They have, I would argue, been elevated implicitly to the status of sainthood. My examples include John Eliot in Puritan New England, Pierre-Jean De Smet in the Northwest, soon to be officially "Saint" Junípero Serra in California, and Henry Benjamin Whipple, Episcopal bishop of Minnesota during the latter half of the nineteenth century.

I must stress that my point is not simply to criticize these departed heroes nor to punish their memory; nor do I wish to impose a burden of guilt on their existing denominations or heirs today.[7] Rather, I intend to expose the illusion, the covert "lie" of white self-righteousness as it was internalized and acted out by the missionaries themselves. I do this out of a sense that this is part of America's unfinished business. Tangentially, it becomes a contribution to our understanding of why Native American peoples have generally failed to enter the American mainstream and continue to live in poverty and oppression, marginalized on the periphery of society. By and large, Indian people have not found liberation in the gospel of Jesus Christ, but, rather, continued bondage to a culture that is both alien and alienating, and even genocidal against American Indian peoples.[8] Finally, in a conclusion I will bring many of these things together to try to explore their contemporary significance.

Cultural Genocide

To accuse Whipple, De Smet, or any of these missionaries of genocide will require some preliminary discussion of the concept at stake. Most importantly, it will require a broader definition of genocide than is generally used.[9] In addition to the straightforward executions of military conquest or police action, such a broader definition must include the notion of cultural genocide and the interrelated subcategories of political, economic, social, and religious genocide. When people are killed as a military tactic or as part of a police action, intended to systematically exterminate a people in the service of some political end, genocide's violence and bloodshed are readily apparent, especially when a policy of genocide is clearly articulated by the perpetrating political entity, as it was in Nazi Germany. That Native American peoples were also subjected to genocide should be self-evident, although it was rarely articulated as policy.[10]

In 1948, in response to the systematic murder of Jews and others in Nazi Germany, the United Nations Genocide Convention began the process of broadening our understanding by defining genocide as "any of several kinds of acts committed with intent to destroy, in whole or in part, a national, ethnic, racial or religious group, as such."[11] The definition proposed here moves beyond the United Nations definition in one critical respect. Namely, I am arguing that the conscious intent to destroy a people is not necessary for an act to be genocidal or for it to succeed in destroying. What I call cultural genocide functions at times as conscious intent, but at other times at such a systemic level that it may be largely subliminal. In such cases, the good intent of some may be so mired in unrecognized systemic structures that they even remain unaware of the destruction that results from those good intentions.

Cultural genocide is more subtle than overt military extermination, yet it is no less devastating to a people. Although the evidence is clear that Serra's missionary empire engaged in severe corporal punishment, there is certainly no evidence that missionaries ever engaged in the systematic killing of Indian people (with the exception, of course, of "Col." John Chivington at Sand Creek, who was a former missionary and the Methodist district superintendent in Denver when he volunteered for military service). Nevertheless, the Native American population of coastal California was reduced by some 90 percent during seventy years under the sole proprietorship of Serra's mission system.[12] Imported diseases, especially "virgin soil" epidemics, are usually cited as the cause for such dev-astating statistics.[13] Yet the effects of the European invasion on the culture, political structure, and economics of the people call for a thorough analysis of all the effects of the missions in California, including the extent to which the evangelizing effort weakened the native cultures so as to imperil the very survival of the people.

Cultural genocide can be defined as the effective destruction of a people by systematically or systemically (intentionally or unintentionally in order to achieve other goals) destroying, eroding, or undermining the integrity of the culture and system of values that defines a people and gives them life. First of all, it involves the destruction of those cultural structures of existence that give a people a sense of holistic and communal integrity. It does this by limiting a people's freedom to practice their culture and to live out their lives in culturally appropriate patterns. It effectively destroys a people by eroding both their self-esteem and the interrelationships that bind them together as a community. In North American mission history, cultural genocide almost always involved an attack on the spiritual foundations of a people's unity by denying the existing ceremonial and mythological sense of a community in relationship to the Sacred Other. Finally, it erodes a people's self-image as a whole people by attacking or belittling every aspect of native culture.

At least four interrelated vehicles can be used in coming to some under-standing of cultural genocide. These four categories are patently artificial and certainly overlap extensively, but they may be helpful in understanding the complexities of cultural genocide. It needs to be repeated that cultural genocide is never the ultimate goal and quite often not the overt intention but results from the pursuit of some other goal of economic gain and political dominance.

1. The *political* aspects of cultural genocide involve the use of political means and political power, always with the threat of military or police intervention, by a more powerful political entity in order to control and subdue a weaker, culturally discrete entity. This constitutes genocide because it results in the loss not only of a people's political viability but also of their cultural viability.[14] The treaties signed by the United States with Indian nations were indeed a form of political genocide. They were invariably forced on Indian peoples who were offered little choice or alternative. Moreover, missionaries often aided govern-ment officials in these processes. The consistent failure of the United States to keep those treaty agreements is a further act of political/cultural genocide.[15] The "Civilization" Act passed by the U.S. Congress in 1819 was clearly an attempt to co-opt the churches and their missionaries to serve the government's political ends with respect to Indian peoples.[16] And the missionaries were only too glad to be co-opted for the sake of federal land grants and funding for mission schools. The so-called Grant Peace Policy of the 1870s delegated to the denominations the responsibility for filling the positions of Indian agent, parceling out particular nations or reservations to various denominations.[17] The missionaries of all the churches came to Indian nations with the firm support of the political authorities.

In Utah, for instance, the Mormon leader, Brigham Young, was called on to serve as U.S. Indian agent for the territory.[18] Even missionaries of the most revered memory regularly fell into complicity with the political impetus to conquest. In 1539 the governor of Guatemala, Alonso de Maldonado, wrote in great praise of the missionary outreach of Bartolomé de Las Casas and his value to the interests of the crown:

> Father Bartolome de Las Casas and other religious here are succeeding in the peaceful conquest of this warlike territory. To this end they have been carrying on negotiations with the Indians, unknown to any Spaniard save themselves and me.[19]

Here a secular political authority acknowledges that the great friend of Indian people in the early Spanish conquest of the Americas also had conquest on his mind, even if he hoped to accomplish it without the brutality and bloodshed he witnessed on the part of his countrymen.

2. The *economic* aspects of genocide involve using or allowing the economic systems, always with political and even military support, to manipulate and exploit another culturally discrete entity that is both politically and economically weaker. The results can range from enslavement and the direct exploitation of labor to the pillaging of natural economic resources that leaves a people unable to sustain themselves. The eradication of the buffalo and the coincident federal establishment of the reservation system is an example of economic and political forms of cultural genocide functioning together to destroy the viability of Plains Indian cultures.[20] When Kit Carson destroyed the entire agricultural production of the Navajo people, he used an economic strategy to win a military victory and achieve their final subjugation.[21] The destruction of the crops caused immediate hunger; destruction of whole orchards meant long-term devastation.

3. *Religious* aspects of genocide involve the overt attempt to destroy the spiritual solidarity of a people. Sometimes this was done by outlawing ceremonial forms, as in the 1890 legislation that made performance of the plains Sun Dance and the Hopi Snake Dance, among others, a punishable crime.[22] At other times, military suppression was used, as in the case of the Ghost Dance. This resulted on one occasion in the massacre of some 350 people at Wounded Knee (December 29, 1890), including a great many women, children, and old people.[23] Most typically, however, the missionaries, emboldened by their sense of political and economic superiority, used preaching and the promised bliss of conversion to denounce or belittle native forms of prayer and argue their own spiritual superiority. Moreover, they used their influence to promote the 1890 legislation limiting freedom of religion for Indian peoples and implicitly "establishing" Christianity.[24]

4. The *social* aspects of cultural genocide involve a wide variety of social changes that have been imposed on Indian nations with disruptive consequences. These

include seemingly minor changes in personal behavior as well as changes that are fundamental to group cohesion. The latter may be obvious attacks on the relationships that bind a community together, such as the missionary proclivity for imposing the nuclear family ideal and displacing the extended kinship system upon which an Indian nation and individuals depend for their identity. The former can be just as dislocative. When conversion to the gospel of Jesus Christ is measured by the length of one's hair, cutting a man's hair is more than a symbolic change in personal behavior. It immediately changes his status within the group. Indeed, it effectively separates him from the group and generates a fundamental social shift from the independence of a healthy interdependent community to a dysfunctional co-dependent relationship between an alienated remnant of a conquered people and their conquerors.

The Ideology of White Superiority and Cultural Genocide

The missionaries were people of their own times and especially of their own cultural heritage. As a result, they came to Indian country with a particular frame of reference for understanding the Indian context and formed notions for the solution of Indian problems out of their own European cultural perception of the world. Because of their own cultural self-understanding, the missionaries, like the U.S. government, did not hesitate to impose their solutions or their culture on Indian people. The prevailing and thoroughly entrenched philosophical presupposition that fueled all European attitudes toward Indians was one of pronounced cultural and intellectual superiority.[25] The notion of European superiority over native peoples goes back to the very beginnings of the European invasion, as Columbus's own diary entry for October 12, 1492, documents. His immediate reaction to his first encounter with western hemisphere peoples included thoughts of domination and enslavement:

> [October 12, 1492] They ought to make good and skilled servants, for they repeat very quickly whatever we say to them. I think they can easily be made Christians, for they seem to have no religion. If it pleases Our Lord, I will take six of them to Your Highnesses when I depart. . . . [October 14] . . . these people are very unskilled in arms. Your Highnesses will see this for yourselves when I bring to you the seven that I have taken. After they learn our language I shall return them, unless Your Highnesses order that the entire population be taken to Castile, or held captive here. With 50 men you could subject everyone and make them do what you wished.[26]

Indeed, differentiation by race seems to have gathered impetus at the time of the Renaissance under Aristotelian pressure for ever-greater classification and taxonomy.[27] After surviving and then successfully repelling the Muslim invasion, the European mind-set, with an air of finality, became entrenched in the basic presupposition of the inherent superiority of its own culture and its own religion, combining both in its notion of civilization.

This European/Euroamerican notion of superiority works its way out in at least two general branches of a historical trajectory—a trajectory that used inherent superiority as a rationalization for conquest and even genocide. It became a justification for slavery and the *encomienda* system among Spanish immigrants and, later, an excuse for punishing the "hostiles" in the western United States in order to tame their perceived savagery. The other branch of the same trajectory led to a much more sympathetic concern for "the Indians," but one that saw the resolution of "the Indian problem" in the replacement of Indian culture with European culture, sometimes blatantly referred to as "Christian culture" or "Christian civilization."[28] It was this second branch of the trajectory that energized the missionary endeavor, but around an arrogance that never questioned its clear goal of Christianizing and civilizing the savages, whom Whipple called "wild Indians."[29]

My point is not just to chastise the missionaries. Not only would that serve little purpose, but it would be asking these forebears in the faith to have done the impossible—namely, to have demonstrated an awareness beyond what was culturally possible at that time. Instead, my investigation has a primary objective and two closely related subordinate objectives. First, this analysis is part of an ongoing process of owning our history, honestly knowing our past, so that our future may be freed from living in a cover-up mode and our decisions for the future may be most creative and life-giving. It is equally crucial for white Americans to recognize occasions of oppressing others in their past and for Native American peoples to identify the sources of the oppression they have experienced and continue to experience. Both Indian and white must confront the lie that Tayo discovered—the lie that finally results in both the oppressor and the oppressed blaming the oppressed for their own oppression. Naming the oppression suffered by Indian peoples is easy. Las Casas wrote in the sixteenth century to expose Spanish atrocities, and, in *A Century of Dishonor* (1881), Helen Hunt Jackson described the ongoing evil perpetrated against Indian people in the United States. Modern writers continue to expose the past and present oppression and exploitation of Native Americans in ways that call into question the whole process of modern political systems.[30] Yet the churches have somehow avoided recognition of their participation in this history of destruction and oppression.

My second objective is to provide a better understanding of what is at stake in the evangelization process. If we concede good intentions to the missionaries in general, we also must be careful to recognize them as people of their own times, incapable of the hindsight of critical analysis with which we are more likely to be blessed. That they confused their spiritual proclamation of the gospel of Jesus Christ with the imposition of new and strange cultural models for daily life is today inexcusable. But a century and more ago, the distinction between gospel and Euroamerican culture was far less clear. Add to that the apparent cultural superiority, in the European mind at least, of wearing clothes, using a fork, and other seeming technological wonders. Moreover, the missionaries most often came to an Indian nation after the effects of conquest had already become visible, increasing the missionaries' sense of their own cultural superiority. De

Smet's criticism of the squalor of some Indian nations is an example. In his rather devastating critique of the Potawatomis, for instance, De Smet seemed blind to the fact that he was witnessing a people in postconquest depression and not the independent, self-sufficient nation they must have been before European contact. As he moved west among nations that had been less affected at that point by the European invasion, he was invariably more impressed. In the nineteenth century, the widespread notion of divinely appointed Manifest Destiny, along with convictions that America was God's "New Israel" and the European immigrants its chosen people, infected the missionaries as much as it did others. Even today the distinction becomes blurred on occasion.[31] Thus, it would have been impossible for these earlier missionaries to see and acknowledge their own sin in this regard. Unfortunately, the results were inevitably devastating for Indian people, utterly contradicting the intentions of the missionaries themselves.

As a third, related objective, I hope to trace the connection between each mission effort and the governing social institutions of which the missionary's church was a part, to show that the mission presence inadvertently or self-consciously facilitated the disruptive incursion of Euroamerican military, political, economic, and social power into an Indian nation's existence. This pattern becomes blatantly apparent in the government's reforms of Indian affairs during the Grant administration, when the churches were intentionally and explicitly recruited to participate in the government's pacification efforts, the so-called peace policy. For instance, at this time the government divided the reservations among the denominations, giving the churches primary responsibility for the Indian nations. Thus, for a time, the federal government even delegated the responsibility for selecting Indian agency superintendents to the churches.[32]

It is crucial to our understanding of the missionary enterprise to recognize that John Eliot engaged in Indian evangelization at the request of the civil, albeit theocratic, government of Massachusetts, and that his work began as an act of political expediency on the part of John Winthrop. Likewise, none should forget that "Saint" Junípero Serra entered California as the cutting edge of Spanish colonization, and that he came with a contingent of military troops. His most bitter struggles did not involve the relief of Indian suffering or even the salvation of their souls but rather whether the missions or a secular governing structure would ultimately control those troops.

Our understanding is certainly deficient if we overlook the close relationship between the missions and Euroamerican economic interests. It was in the self-interest of the fur trading companies, for example, to support the missionary enterprise, since the missionaries contributed to the pacification of Indian nations, thereby aiding and abetting the companies' exploitation of Indians, Indian lands, and Indian resources. Hence, we should not be surprised that John McLoughlin, director of the Hudson Bay Company's trading enterprise in the Oregon Territory, contributed generously and repeatedly to both Protestant and Catholic mission efforts. Instead, what cries out for clarification and understanding is the unthinking reciprocity provided by the missionaries, who seldom questioned the exploitation, but rather implicitly validated it. Of course, occasional but notable exceptions to this broad generalization can be found. Even those who voiced objections, however, continued the missionary's implicit function of validating white economic interests. De Smet kept secret his knowledge of the existence of gold ore in the Black Hills, because he feared the rank exploitation of those Indian peoples.[33] Yet he is a prime example of a missionary functioning in a symbiotic relationship with white enterprise. Whipple, as a reformer, severely criticized the U.S. government's failure to respect its treaties with Indian nations, yet he served readily as a government spokesperson in negotiating the government's theft of the Black Hills from the Sioux peoples.

Reading the Source Material

As in any good scholarly monograph, I have tried to rely on the most vital primary sources. In this case, however, the available sources are still one or two steps away from the actual events that are to be interpreted. De Smet's letters, for instance, qualify at one level as primary sources for the nineteenth-century history of Jesuit missionary efforts among Indian peoples. Certainly, they are careful reflections of the most renowned missionary of the time. Yet, at another level, they are the reflections of only one of the parties involved in the process of Indian-missionary contact, and as such they remain De Smet's interpretation of his interaction with various Indian nations and individuals. The question remains whether, or to what degree, he himself understood the very events in which he participated. The other side of the conversation is wholly unrepresented in any extant sources, other than the oral traditions that may be preserved by the Indian nations involved.

In other words, De Smet's account of the mission events he reports is his interpretation of his own work. Missing is any contemporary Indian interpretation of De Smet. That can be reconstructed, however, speculatively but with some degree of probability, based on a careful interpretation of De Smet's interpretation, along with a variety of other documents that can fill in some of the gaps that become apparent when we read De Smet with a critical eye.

That De Smet's report is already interpretation becomes apparent in a simple illustration from the very beginning of his missionary endeavor, in fact, during the course of his travel from St. Louis to his first assignment among the Potawatomis who then were located at Council Bluffs, Iowa. Toward the end of that journey by steamboat up the Missouri River, late in May 1838, De Smet reports this encounter:

> One day when the boat had stopped and the crew landed to cut wood, I walked back from the river quite a distance. In my excursion I met an old man of ninety who halted as I drew near and looked at me with astonishment mingled with joy. He had judged from my garb that I was a priest, and when I had confirmed him in his idea, "Ah! my Father," he cried, "I am a Catholic, and it is many years since I have had the happiness of seeing a priest. I have so ardently desired to see one before I die! Help me therefore to be reconciled with God." I hastened eagerly

to comply with his request, and we both of us wept abundantly. Then he conducted me back to the boat and I parted from the good old man; but I cannot tell you the consolation that I tasted in this most fortunate meeting.[34]

To assess the plausibility of the scenario as De Smet recounts it, several points must be kept in mind. First, the Jesuit mission among the Potawatomis had not yet commenced. Indeed, De Smet, along with two lay brothers, was at that moment being sent to found the mission. Second, although several different groups of Indians lived along the Missouri between St. Louis and Council Bluffs in 1838, and some Protestant missionaries were active in the area, we know of no Catholic mission among these nations. This would indicate that the gentleman in question was not a part of this mission nor of any other Catholic mission in the region. De Smet does not tell us to which nation the man belongs. Third, if indeed this gentleman had been exposed to Catholicism and the role of the priest before, it must have been at some previous time, as De Smet indicates. Quite possibly, it would have occurred before his nation was either pressed (Sauks and Foxes) or removed (Potawatomis) across the Mississippi. The Sauks and Foxes were indeed exposed to Catholic missionaries from the time of Marquette's expedition, and the Potawatomis were surely exposed long before then during their residence in the vicinity of Michigan and Canada. In either case, the community to which the gentleman was attached, and he himself, might possibly have learned a little French or even some English.

Fourth, however one sorts out these issues, it seems quite unlikely that the conversation could have proceeded as De Smet has reported it. These nations were still rather remote geographically from the immigrant tide. Europeans had already crossed the Mississippi, but that far west the Euroamerican presence consisted almost entirely of traders in scattered outposts. It seems unlikely that the man's French or English could have been as proficient—as complex in both syntax and choice of vocabulary—as in De Smet's telling of the story. Second, it seems implausible that a man from an unmissionized nation, who had been exposed to Catholicism "many years" earlier, would have been so indoctrinated as to retain such a Catholic tone.

I would suggest that De Smet completely misinterpreted the import of this chance encounter for an elderly Indian man and, as a result, completely misinterpreted the conversation. What follows is my own speculative reconstruction of the encounter from a possible Indian perspective:

> The two men, a young Flemish priest and an old Indian man, meet by chance on a wooded path a short way from the river where De Smet's boat is docked. The old man is indeed surprised. Many years ago he remembers seeing similarly dressed whites, back in Illinois before the people crossed the big river. He remembers with a smile that these are the white people's medicine men, their spiritual leaders, and recalls that he too, like many of his relatives, had gone to the ceremonies these black robes put on for the people. And do not think that they are without power! Surely, they are as powerful as our own medicine people. With these thoughts, the Indian gentleman does what was expected in greeting a stranger, especially such a spiritual person. Drawing on what little French he can remember

from his youth and from his infrequent encounters with traders, the slightly more English he learned in his middle years, and some universal Indian sign language, he greets the young priest with genuine warmth, showing that he knows what the priest is and indicating his own deep respect for the priest's spiritual function. With smiles and a few words, repeatedly making the sign of the cross on his breast, the old man quite unintentionally convinces De Smet that he is a Catholic. When the priest insists on confessing him, the old man could not be more delighted and shows his joy. He has no idea what the ceremony is, but is simply glad that this white medicine man is summoning his power to bring the blessing of the spirits. Gratefully, the old man crosses himself at the appropriate times signaled by the priest's own actions. And all the more, the priest is convinced he has indeed found a wayward Catholic.

Farfetched? A story created practically out of whole cloth by De Smet? The episode is hardly farfetched and not wholly made up, but De Smet's telling is freely interpreted. In fact, it can be demonstrated again and again, choosing texts almost at random from his extensive writings, that De Smet's understanding of an encounter and the Indian perspective were in all probability very different, even at polar opposites. More than three years after his first immersion in Indian mission work, writing from his new assignment among the Flatheads in the Bitterroot Valley, De Smet recalls an incident that occurred on his return journey from his first visit with the Flathead nation. When an intimidating band of Sioux warriors discovers him hiding with his small party near a spring,[35] De Smet presents himself to their chief and, through an interpreter,[36] manages to win them over. Two things of note occur. First, the Sioux treat him with a great deal of deference, even carrying him in procession on a buffalo robe to their chief's lodge. Then De Smet uses the occasion to put on a liturgical demonstration, an act of prayer, to which the Sioux respond with a liturgical act of their own:

> I made the sign of the cross and said the prayer. All the time it lasted, all the savage company, following their chief's example, held their hands raised toward heaven; the moment it was ended, they lowered their right hands to the ground. I asked the chief for an explanation of this ceremony. "We raise our hands," he replied, "because we are wholly dependent on the Great Spirit; it is his liberal hand that supplies all our wants. We strike the ground afterward, because we are miserable beings, worms crawling before his face."[37]

"Miserable beings?" "Worms crawling before his face?" Either these Sioux have very quickly adopted Augustinian notions of human depravity, succumbing to Christian medieval gnostic tendencies against material existence in general and against the earth in particular,[38] or De Smet has fabricated what he would consider an appropriate response, given his own romantic fantasy. It can be demonstrated from the same text that he must indeed have fabricated the Indian response. Like every missionary of the time, De Smet was so culturally conditioned that in his interpretation of behavior patterns in another culture, he fit even the smallest cognate into his own frame of reference. The language he attributes to this Indian person is immediately suspect to an Indian reader. Moreover, even in a naive reading of the text, the quotation sounds far more European than Indian. As De Smet's letter continues, it becomes apparent that communication was strained at best, limited as it was on both sides by linguistic deficiencies. De Smet concludes his comments about the episode saying, "I desired to speak to these honest folk of the main points of Christianity; but the interpreter was not sufficiently skilled in the language to render my words into the Sioux."[39]

If the translation was only minimally competent—perhaps incompetent is a more apt description—then the entirely too European Christian sounding articulation ascribed to this chief becomes suspect. Indeed, a fundamental understanding of the Plains Indian worldview can point to an alternative understanding that is much more probable than this firsthand report of an actual participant contained in a "primary source." Surely, these Sioux people are respecting and even summoning, in their own prayer act, the spiritual power of the reciprocity of sky and earth, Grandfather and Grandmother, Tunkasila and Unci, spirit and matter, male and female. Recognizing and respecting the spiritual intent of De Smet's prayer, these people joined him in prayer in the way that they knew. And far from being a self-negating act, the touching of the earth was undoubtedly an act of piety calling on the power of Wakan Tanka (God?) as it is manifest in Earth.[40]

Cross-Cultural Miscommunication

If De Smet misinterpreted these encounters in some manner close to what I have suggested, his misunderstanding simply becomes one more example of classic cross-cultural miscommunication. For example, the first French missionary among Indian peoples seems, on paper, to have been wildly successful. Jesse Flesche, a secular cleric, came to Port Royal in 1610 and within a year had baptized well over one hundred Indians, including a powerful Sagamore and his family. In the spring of 1611, two Jesuits arrived to take over the missionary effort but were extremely critical of Flesche's work. Indeed, Pierre Biard argued that the baptized Micmacs had no understanding whatsoever of the traditional European Christian significance of the rite but had interpreted it quite differently and within their own cultural frame of reference. The "converts," he suggests, merely "accepted baptism as a sort of sacred pledge of friendship and alliance with the French."[41] Biard complains that some understood the word "baptized" but not the word "Christian." Again the issue here is translation and communication. Indian people, in characteristic fashion, demonstrated their willingness to form a bond of friendship by engaging in a ceremonial act—and would doubtless have wanted to reciprocate by including the French in some ceremonial rite of their own had the French been willing. Flesche, unexplainably, thinks he has effected conversion.

Implicitly, such acts of misinterpretation lay the foundation for cultural genocide. Once the missionaries have decided that conversion has been effected, they begin to feel a sense of proprietorship and a responsibility to hold the converts to their presumed commitment. When the cultural gap is wide, the commitment may mean very different things to the presumed converts. A non-missionary example from the earliest experiences of Indian people with the colony at Plymouth may be instructive here.

The people of the Plymouth colony entered their first treaty with native peoples in New England in the early spring of 1621, after a very rough first winter. They had lost half their number to starvation and disease and were in a position of pronounced weakness when the Pokanokets approached them entreating an alliance. Two aspects of the ensuing treaty are important to note here.[42] The first involves the differing interpretations of the treaty. Despite the abject weakness of the colony, the colonists chose to interpret the treaty as one in which the Pokanoket nation became subjugated to the superior English. That is, the colonists saw the generosity of the stronger Pokanokets as the rightful subordination of a lesser people. Second, the very nature of the international agreement was understood very differently by the two parties due to the disparateness of the two cultures. Namely, the Pokanokets seem to have viewed the treaty as having established something of a kinship relationship between the two peoples, bringing the English into their world of reciprocity. The Pilgrims, as strict separatists who had found neighborly relations with Dutch Calvinists too troublesome to endure, had no intention of conceding neighborly, let alone kinship, relations with these savage lesser beings. Given their assumptions about treaty making, the Pokanokets—all of them and not just the leaders—adopted a casual drop-in-and-visit attitude toward their new relatives and were demonstrably prepared to offer similar hospitality for food and overnight stays to the English when they traveled through Pokanoket territory. The separatists were aghast and hastened to explain the nature of European-style intergovernmental relation to their assumed new subjects. Only communication between respective leaders would be necessary or acceptable to maintain the treaty relationship.

Good Intentions, Naïveté, and Genocide

At one level at least, I have presumed a certain naïveté with respect to the complicity of the missionaries in acts of cultural genocide. They surely did not intend any harm to Indian people, yet their blindness to their own inculturation of European values and social structures meant that complicity was unavoidable. That is, even at this initial level of analysis, it is clear that the missionaries were myopic regarding their own cultural biases. They engaged in actions that were a genuinely naive imposition of their own cultural values and models of society on tribal peoples for whom the experience became dislocative and disruptive. The goals of the missionaries emerged out of a reservoir of what Wittgenstein called "common sense knowledge." They could reflect on that knowledge only within the limitations of their contemporary cultural self-awareness. The parameters of the world are defined by the subjective perception of the individual and the cultural community of individuals who tend to communicate easily with one another and agree generally about the interpretation of their experiences. The missionaries all came to Native American tribal communities with firmly established commitments to their own European or Euroamerican cultures with their social structures and institutions. As a result, they naturally assumed the superiority of the institutions and social structures of their own world and readily imposed them on Indian people. At the bottom line, then, this cultural myopia of the missionaries functioned to facilitate the exploitation of Indian people by both the government and the private sector or by the land-hungry immigrant farmers encroaching ever further onto the plains. Identifying their actions as well-intentioned but misguided certainly does not exonerate the missionaries. It merely serves to explain behavior that is finally inconsistent with the goal of salvation they proclaimed, and as responsible human beings they must be held accountable for the disastrous consequences of their actions.

At this level of analysis, the failure of the missionaries must be understood not just in individual terms but as systemic failure. The culpability of the individual missionaries for imposing their culture on Native Americans and perpetuating the lie of white superiority was in actuality prescribed from the outset by European and Euroamerican social structures. That is to say, it was impossible for any missionary to avoid complicity in the genocide of Native American peoples. Again in this case, recognizing the broader, structural impetus of Western social structures toward the assertion of white hegemony dare not become an excuse for exonerating the individual's participation in the dysfunctionality of the whole. Nevertheless, this recognition does push beyond the criticism of individual missionaries to an analysis of the systemic. This, in turn, raises two questions. First, what aspects of Western, Euroamerican culture have historically generated such myopic social and theological arrogance? Second, if the missionaries, with the best of intentions, perpetrated such havoc among Indian peoples, what does our own, modern myopia conceal from us, whatever our intentions to the contrary?

Finally, at a certain level of analysis, the presumed naïveté of the missionaries begins to fade as a justification for their behavior, and it becomes far more difficult to protect their memory even minimally by appealing to the spirit of the times or the pervasiveness of attitudes among Euroamerican peoples. How could these dedicated spiritual figures not see the role they inevitably played in the economic exploitation or the political manipulation of the tribal peoples of North America? More devastating to Indian communities than the imposition of new cultural standards was the missionaries' tendency to act consistently, sometimes self-consciously and sometimes implicitly, in the best interests of the economic and political structures of their Western cultural world. Thus, it was almost natural for the missionaries to participate in the political process of subjugation and to support the repressive efforts of their own government in whatever program had been devised at the time to serve that interest. It was just as natural for them to support the economic enterprises that manipulated and exploited Indian labor and resources. What finally must be realized is that the missionaries were deeply involved in symbiotic relationships with the very structures of power that crushed Indian resistance to the European invasion every step of the way, as Manifest Destiny moved "From California to the New York Island, from the redwood forest to the gulf stream waters. . . ."[43]

At some point we must conclude that good intentions did not simply fail but were suspect from the beginning. One could argue that naïveté dissolves when a mission institution accepts government monies (out of the so-called Civilization Fund, for example) in order to pursue its missionary outreach. At that point the church receiving the funds made the decision to serve the interests of the U.S. government. Even if the church had completely confused its own proclamation of the gospel with the interests of the government, the relationship between government and church predicates that the missionaries' activity with regard to native peoples was no longer simply an act of cultural unconsciousness. Eliot may have had good intentions or a self-image of good intentions toward Indian people in Massachusetts. Those intentions may be regarded somehow as naive because he failed to see the extent to which his proclamation of the gospel was intertwined with his own cultural values and social structures. The extent to which he functioned in concert with and as an extension of the General Court in Boston, however, was certainly not naive and was clearly intended to contain and pacify the Indian people in a buffer zone around white, English New England. Likewise, the Jesuits in Paraguay had a grand vision of bringing Indian people into a European model of the world. That much may be misguided simplemindedness, but the extent to which it became a grand vision of an emergent Jesuit political power was not innocent. As we shall see, the motivation for the Jesuit effort in Paraguay was to establish an idyllic society of Native American peoples on a European model, but firmly under the disciplined control of a Jesuit (European) governing hierarchy. The impetus to power and authority, the impetus to rule, is not naïveté. A similar breakdown of good intentions can be demonstrated for virtually every important missionary in the history of Native American missions in both hemispheres.

One aspect of this missionary complicity must remain somewhat enigmatic. While the missionaries clearly functioned to facilitate the exploitation of Indian people, they themselves usually did not benefit from those acts of exploitation.[44] De Smet derived immediate benefit from his relationship with the fur trading companies in that they helped to support his missionary enterprise with goods and services. He did not share, however, in the wealth they accumulated from their exploitation of Indian people, nor did he desire to do so. Serra was committed to living a relatively ascetic life, although the priests associated with his missions did not suffer the hardship of famine to the same extent as did the Indians in their missions. Eliot took on the added responsibility of preaching the gospel to Indian people for the paltry financial reward of twenty pounds a year. This hardly represents a share in the accumulation of wealth that his mission outreach helped to facilitate in the New England economy. Both De Smet and Whipple entered the service of the federal government in efforts to pacify Indian nations and win treaty concessions from them that would allow white settlements to expand onto Indian lands. De Smet explicitly turned down a government salary. Whipple, whose personal financial situation already provided a comfortable life, especially after his second marriage, served in a volunteer capacity. While the work of the missionaries helped to facilitate the political and economic exploitation of Indian people for the considerable benefit of the larger immigrant body politic, most had no interest in any significant personal profit. This might suggest naive innocence on their part. The direct support they provided to the white economic and political power structures would belie that assessment, however. At some level, they must have known what they were about.

EXCURSUS: THE REDUCCION

One major hurdle consistently confronted every European missionary endeavor. Namely, given the great disparity between European and Indian cultures and the thorough inculturation of the gospel to European culture in the minds of the missionaries, how were they to compete for the attention of Indian peoples, even after initial conversion? Usually, the missionaries sought some means of distancing Indian peoples from their cultural and social context. In the Catholic southern hemisphere, a paradigm emerged called the *reduccion*, a device whereby converts were physically and politically separated from their communities and families. The *reduccion* was an arrangement where the converts lived on the mission compound under the strict political governance (and spiritual guidance) of the missionaries. In the southern hemisphere, the political and disciplinary control of the missionaries was crucial, but it was quite often supported by a military presence at the mission or at a nearby presidio. Junípero Serra established *reduccion*-style missions from San Diego to San Francisco with great and explicit deliberateness. In the next century, Pierre-Jean De Smet functioned with the *reduccion* as his encompassing vision of mission outreach. Even the Protestant John Eliot functioned with a paradigm for Indian evangelization that reflects the *reduccion* development of the Catholics in the south.

The concept of *reduccion*, of course, came with Serra to California with a long history in the Americas that went back almost to the beginnings of the European invasion.[45] I would argue that the notion had already begun to emerge in the early thinking of Bartolomé de Las Casas, the great Spanish reformer. Las Casas devoted nearly fifty years of his life to a defense of Indian people against the brutality of his own countrymen. He wrote extensively, graphically describing the atrocities committed by the invaders against the native populations of the Americas.[46] Among the Europeans, the American natives had no more ardent and articulate supporter and the conquistadores no more virulent critic than Las Casas.

The beginnings of the *reduccion* system are rooted in Las Casas's attack on the *encomienda*, the pernicious system of reward instituted by Columbus shortly after 1495 that gave ownership of native peoples and the lands on which they lived to European settlers. Sanctioned by the crown in 1503, the *encomienda* quickly spread with the conquest to all the Caribbean, Mexico, South America, and Florida.[47] The result was an abject state of slavery marked by overwork and extremely high mortality as the European "owners" attempted to maximize profits from their *encomiendas* by exploiting the labor of the human beings whom they considered no more than property, and expendable at that.

Las Casas's solution to the deadly exploitation generated by the *encomienda* system was necessarily politically expedient. The *encomienda* not only provided the *encomendero* with an easy source of wealth, but it generated income for the royal treasury as well by way of tribute. Whatever he offered in its place had to project at least comparable royal income. The solution he offered was designed on the principle of the *encomienda* but replaced ownership by a private Spanish citizen with ecclesial hegemony and a set of rules intended to limit the exploitation of native labor. Both of these were to be more humane than the *encomienda*, but essentially, Las Casas's paradigm simply found a way to exploit Indian people more gently on behalf of the Spanish monarch and achieve the goal of conversion at the same time.[48] We must never forget that Las Casas, the hero of the 1992 Quincentenary, was just as committed to the conquest of Native Americans as were Cortés and Pizarro. He only hoped to do it less violently. He accomplished much of his goal by creating the *reduccion* missionary system, used so effectively—and destructively—by later generations of European Jesuits, Franciscans, and even Protestants in both the northern and southern hemispheres. Later in the sixteenth century, the *reduccion* system was further developed in the thinking and work of Franciscans like Toribio de Motolinía and Gerónimo Mendieta.[49] In the latter half of the century, the *reduccion* became institutionalized and a more developed ideology emerged.

The *reduccion* continued to exist as an institution under the authoritarian governance of the priests of various religious orders. In time, the rationale both for the *reduccion* as a mission strategy and for priestly governance developed more fully. First, it was justified by the need to keep convert communities separate from colonial communities and to provide an environment for cultural transformation. Exposure to European colonialists, it was argued, would be detrimental to Indian conversion since it would expose them to all the vices of European society.[50] Lest this appear to be overly contradictory, a second argument was advanced, one that begins to expose the early European attitude toward Indian peoples. This argument involves an unusual twist on the idea of the primitive. These early European mendicant priests saw Indian cultures in their pristine, first-contact condition as Edenic communities of untainted purity but primitive backwardness.[51] In particular, the Franciscans in Mexico believed native tribal communities had the potential for re-creating a new primitive apostolic church. The intrinsic character of those communities, before conversion, already reminded the missionaries of the ideal purity of the earliest church. Untainted by European excesses and vices, yet governed and disciplined by mendicant priests, who ironically came out of the tainted European culture, Indian convert communities were to replicate the apostolic communities as the missionaries understood them to have been. The incursion of European colonists or even the incursion of the regional European government was a constant threat to this vision of repristination. Equally threatening to this vision was the thought of native self-governance, which would put native governing structures into a compromising relationship as subjects with the regional colonial government, providing opportunity for infecting the convert community. Moreover, the very primitive character that generated a sense of the pristine also assured the missionaries that the Indian peoples were naive and unable to govern themselves. The greater wisdom of the missionaries—and thus the need for them to remain in authoritarian control of the community—was reaffirmed in their own minds.

The *reduccion* mission system was most keenly honed by the Jesuits during their hegemony in Paraguay from 1610 to 1757. During this time the Paraguayan missions maintained a more or less self-determining political status under priestly governance and remained quite separate from either Spanish or Portuguese rule. As in the other examples of the *reduccion*, the Jesuits attempted to reduce the native population to a settled, and thus controlled, existence and to develop ideal, self-sufficient communities of Indian converts. Isolated from other European influences and exposed only to the priests, these converts were shepherded into compounds projected as autonomous native towns with a semblance of self-governance but essentially under strict priestly rule. Held together in larger confederations, the *reducciones* in Paraguay held independent dominion status under the Spanish Crown until 1757. By then the Jesuit presence in Paraguay had become politically untenable in the face of a European power struggle for control of the territory, and they were expelled from Paraguay in that year and from all of Spanish America by 1767.

The chapters on John Eliot and Junípero Serra will examine how this paradigm worked itself out in both an early Protestant variation and a later Catholic version. Chapter 4 will give some indication of how the ideal continued to inspire the evangelistic fervor of Pierre-Jean De Smet. What becomes consistently apparent is that missionaries of all denominations could not trust American Indian converts with the gospel of Jesus Christ. Instead, fearing a reversion to old cultural habits, they constantly policed their converts, rooting out suspicious behaviors. Disciplinary control, the imposition of European culture, and even the imposition of European economic structures and technology actually became the gospel, even though it was necessarily a gospel of bondage rather than one of liberation.

John Eliot

Conversion, Colonialism, and the Oppression of Language

> . . . the most forlorn Ruines of Mankind, and very doleful objects.
>
> —Cotton Mather[1]

> As for these poore Indians, they have no principles of their own, nor yet wisdome of their own, (I mean as other Nations have).
>
> —John Eliot[2]

> From a cynical point of view, perhaps Eliot did nothing more than to ease the passing of a doomed race.
>
> —Samuel E. Morrison[3]

John Eliot, the highly publicized Puritan missionary to Indian peoples in Massachusetts and the most renowned of the early missionaries in what is today the United States—if not the most successful—comes out of a much discussed historical context. Indeed, so much has been written about Puritan America and about Eliot himself that some apology is due for including a separate chapter on him in this volume.[4] Yet the beginnings of the fundamental attitudinal structures that underlie Indian-white relationships in North America, even to the present day, can be traced to the first English colonies of which Eliot was a part. Moreover, the basic outlines of the Euroamerican missionary profile are already clearly evidenced in Eliot, and this combination of immigrant attitudes of superiority and missionary profile makes Eliot an interesting test case for my thesis. To wit, in Eliot we witness the intentional erosion of Indian culture along with its results, the unintentional devastation of those peoples, all accomplished by thorough confusion of gospel and culture.

This chapter will demonstrate Eliot's participation in the full range of what I have identified as cultural genocide in all its social, economic, political, and religious aspects. Although the categories somewhat overlap, each is readily apparent. Eliot's mission began largely as a political move with political motives, yet the political motivations also have economic undertones. Theological ideology characterizes the whole movement and laces it with overt elements of religious persecution and what I have called religious aspects of cultural genocide. Not infrequently, the political power of the Massachusetts General Court was summoned to facilitate the religious persecution of native peoples.

Social and cultural change was deemed a prerequisite to conversion and involved a wholesale restructuring of social institutions. Forced separation and alienation within families became an instrumental part of Eliot's strategy as he developed the notion of separate Indian mission communities called "praying towns." In turn, this strategy isolated the new converts both from their old communities and from the English, with whom they were not allowed to mingle. While the effort to "reduce" Indian people to "civilitie"—that is, to English cultural values and social structures—may not have been very successful, Eliot's mission endeavor did succeed in reducing native peoples to economic dependence on the English. In his mission work, Eliot was closely allied with and wholly committed to the ruling authorities of the Massachusetts General Council. Out of that political context came legislation from the beginning of Eliot's mission that outlawed the traditional Indian religious ceremonies and provided punishment for Indians who mocked or belittled any Christian preacher. All of these, combined with the particular style of Puritan theology, functioned to generate a psychological sense of low self-worth and finally facilitated the English subjugation of Indian peoples and Indian lands in New England. That Eliot's Indian missions were failures became apparent during his own lifetime with the dissolution of the praying towns during King Philip's War. The question to be asked then is not whether any positive results derived from Eliot's mission, but rather how significant was the damage caused by his well-intentioned efforts?

Puritans and Indians before 1646

Two separate motivations, one ideological and the other political, seem to have inspired Eliot's missionary work. Francis Jennings has argued most persuasively that the initial impetus was wholly one of political and economic necessity on the part of John Winthrop and the General Council of Massachusetts.[5] Moreover, Eliot clearly shared these political motivations until the very end of his career.[6] At the same time, Eliot was genuinely motivated by his own understanding of Puritan apocalyptic, which compelled his missionary activity as a prelude to the reign of Christ.[7] Whatever challenges scholars may register with respect to the ethics of his involvement,[8] Eliot surely did have a genuine concern for the conversion of Indian peoples to his understanding of Christianity and devoted considerable energies to that task. Nevertheless, his complicity in the political processes of the New England colony will forever taint his memory, as will the naïveté of his missionary message itself. Thus, Eliot's positive intentions were countered by both naïveté and ulterior motivation.

At least three other interrelated factors in the Puritan context contribute to the character of Eliot's seventeenth-century missions. When John Eliot finally "left his study" in 1646, much water was already under the bridge, as it were, in terms of Indian-white relationships in northeastern North America. First, Eliot and the Puritans came to the North American continent as participants in a European consciousness that already had over a century of experience with Indian peoples in the southern hemisphere. Moreover, the English had by then a nearly sixty-year history of direct experience with Indian people quite apart from the indirect reports from Spanish colonization in the south.[9] As a result, though the first New England colonists had never actually seen an Indian person before, they came with fully preconceived notions that functioned to dominate their own relationships with the indigenous peoples of New England.

Second, the native population already had a long history of trade with the Europeans, both the French and the English.[10] The native peoples had barely survived but still remembered the terrible "virgin soil" epidemic of 1616–1618 in which some 90 percent of the native population of New England died, even though they may not have linked the Europeans with the epidemic in their own minds.[11] More significantly, Indian people had had long and repeated experience with the peculiar viciousness of English power. Neal Salisbury describes the sources of early Indian frustration with the English on the eve of the establishment of the first colony in what was to be New England:

> The reciprocity that Indians sought to maintain in economic, political, and spiritual relationships was seriously undermined in southern New England by the sequence of English action and the plague epidemic. The propensities of English visitors . . . toward violence and kidnapping, and their refusal to enter into and maintain reciprocal relationships, finally succeeded in arousing the hostility of most coastal Indians from the Penobscot to Cape Cod.[12]

As the first English colonists made their way toward Plymouth, they established their formative relationship with Indians in a stopover on Cape Cod. Without having seen their first Indian or ascertaining whether the native peoples were friendly or peaceful, the colonists proceeded to raid Indian stores of corn, hauling the stolen booty off as "God's good providence."[13] With the establishment of the colony, the kidnapping and adventurer violence of earlier English explorers in the northeast gave way to the development of more permanent relationships with the Indian population, relationships invariably based on English need for control and eventually expansion. Yet these needs implicated a strategy of continued violence as a means of intimidation. Only two years after receiving Indian generosity in a time of crisis, Miles Standish could threaten to destroy an entire band over the theft of beads and trifles.[14] During the same winter of 1623, Standish led a small force in a preemptive assassination attack against a number of Massachuset leaders while they were invited guests in the English town of Wessagusset.[15] To complete the reign of terror, the head of one sachem was impaled on a post outside the fortification at Plymouth as a warning to other Indians.[16]

Third, the psychology of Puritan theology also came into play with its separatist/theocratic proclivities—even in the case of the so-called nonseparatists. The Plymouth colony struggled for survival through its first winter, losing half its original number to hunger and disease.[17] The Pokanokets, noticing the severity of the Pilgrim plight, attempted to enter into an alliance with the Pilgrims—for their own benefit, no doubt, but also to alleviate some of the English suffering.[18] For their part, when the treaty had been negotiated, the severely weakened English chose to interpret Pokanoket generosity and the treaty itself as initiating a relationship not of alliance between equals but as the only appropriate submission of the Pokanokets to Plymouth hegemony.[19] This aspect of the treaty negotiation and the resulting relationship highlight clearly the technically racist attitudes of the English from the outset of their encounter with Indian people in New England. Although they negotiated out of weakness and need and had been forced to accept the generosity of the Pokanokets, the English sense of their own moral and cultural superiority was so deeply rooted that they interpreted the treaty as an Indian acknowledgment of English hegemony. Eventually, the balance of power between English and Indian was definitively tipped in the English direction, and a relationship of Indian subjugation became entrenched. Yet even at these initial stages, at a time of English weakness, the English perceived themselves as the stronger and the Indians as the weaker.

Furthermore, the cross-cultural misunderstandings of the implications of the treaty are classic in proportions. The Pokanokets understood the treaty to signify a definite expansion of their reciprocal network of friendships, which would be further cemented by rituals of giving and receiving. With this understanding, they began to drop in on a more or less casual basis to visit their new friends. For the strictly separatist Pilgrims who had left Holland, their first place of refuge, over their needs for more discrete political and spiritual integrity, the assumption of such familiarity by the Pokanokets violated their vision of a spiritually pure community. They moved forthwith to clarify that the treaty was to be understood as an alliance between governments and not between peoples.[20] The treaty with the Pokanoket prefigures the Massachusetts development of "praying towns" under Eliot's leadership, in which missionized Indians were gathered to be civilized and converted and, in the process, were marginalized forever on the periphery of the Puritan social, political, economic, and ecclesial world.

The duplicity of the Plymouth colony in establishing treaty relationships was to be repeated habitually by Massachusetts under the governorship of John Winthrop. The summary executions by the English, intended to teach a lesson, eventually gave way to more brutal attacks, and in 1637, a decade before Eliot began his mission, the Massachusetts government instigated the "Pequot War." The war, which Jennings called "one long atrocity,"[21] featured as its major action Captain John Mason's very intentional massacre of an unarmed village of some three to seven hundred "women, children, and feeble old men."[22] Genocide, the military execution of Indian tribes, was clearly an open possibility for the Puritan colonies.

Even the reputation of Roger Williams is sullied by this blatant perpetration of military genocide. North American mythology remembers Williams as a friend of Indian peoples, who had a more accepting attitude toward native peoples than others. In actuality, Williams was convinced that the cultural differences were such that one could do nothing with Indians and that any attempt to convert them was destined to fail.[23] On the other hand, though he did develop more of a relationship with Indian peoples than other Puritans did, Williams did not hesitate to use that relationship to the political advantage of the Puritans with devastating consequences for the Indians of southern New England. Even after he had moved south to establish a new colony after being banned from Massachusetts by John Winthrop, Williams continued to maintain a relationship of collusion with Winthrop to ensure political support for his own Rhode Island colony. [24] He agreed in 1637 to intercede with the Narragansett Indians on behalf of Massachusetts to forestall an alliance then forming between the Narragansetts and the Pequots. Williams was singularly successful in destroying this alliance, which would have severely limited the expansionist designs of Massachusetts for decades. [25] He convinced the Narragansetts to support Massachusetts during the Pequot War, leaving the Pequots to fight the English alone. After the atrocity of the Mystic Massacre and the destruction of the Pequots as a people, the Narragansetts themselves were left unprotected from the long-term expansionist designs of Massachusetts. Thus, Williams's friendship with Indian peoples resulted in the immediate and clear genocide of one tribe and the less immediate but just as decisive genocide of another. Indeed, Jennings argues that Williams's intervention "guaranteed the isolation and ultimate destruction of the Pequots far more effectively than any troops fielded by General Endecott."[26]

For reasons of public relations in England, however, the more subtle and devious methods of cultural genocide were eventually preferred. Consciously or not, John Eliot became a key player in the process, and the Bay Colony's propaganda machinery was so successful that he is remembered today as the "apostle to the Indians," the earliest Indian mission hero in U.S. history, if one overlooks Eusebio Kino and Thomas Mayhew, Jr. An analysis of Eliot's work among Indians in Massachusetts forcefully demonstrates the important role of missionary outreach in the European colonization of America and the subjugation of its native peoples.

Whether missionary or military, the Puritan attitude toward the native peoples of New England is exposed in the words of Rich Mather, a mission associate of Eliot. In his preface to a tractate written by Eliot, Mather calls the native people "a poor people, forlorn kind of Creatures in times past . . . , that they have been little better than the Beasts that perish."[27] To those who expect too much, too soon, from the missionizing process, Mather adjures patience and understanding that the advanced state of English society is a result of "more time and means," to say nothing of "better help and breeding than they have had." Further on in his text, he refers to Indians as "rubbish," arguing again for patience in bringing the Indians to church estate. It takes time to form a true "Church out of such rubbish as amongst Indians."

Eliot and Missionary Conquest: The Social Aspects of Genocide

These Indians (the better and wiser sort of them) have for some years inquired after Church-Estate, Baptism, and the rest of the Ordinances of God, in the observation whereof they see the Godly English to walk. I have from time to time, delayed them upon this point, That until they were come up unto Civil cohabitation, Government, and Labor, which a fixed condition of life will put them upon, they were not so capable to be trusted with that Treasure of Christ. . . .[28]

From the outset of his mission work, Eliot was convinced that civilizing had to precede conversion proper, a perspective that was widely held in New England and by other Europeans in the Americas.[29] As a result, Eliot's mission efforts forced drastic changes in the culture and social structures of native peoples. He understood the task of civilizing in its broadest context and believed it extended from personal patterns of behavior to the larger structures of social organization, from the macro level of village/town structure to the micro levels of family life and personal appearance. The suppression of traditional religious forms became a key part of the process. Moreover, Eliot did not hesitate to use the political power of the Massachusetts Bay Colony to impose his will on Indian people or to create economic devices to ensure a dependency on the part of Indians that inhibited any possibility of reversion. Though all of these aspects of mission conquest were interrelated and overlapped considerably, the social aspects became symbolic of the others. Indeed, many of the transformations of personal values that fall into the category of social aspects of genocide appear relatively minor by comparison with the political and economic aspects. Yet even these seemingly minimal changes did damage to Indian people. The first sign of a man's conversion in New England was the cutting of his hair.[30] For both men and women, a transition to English-style clothing was likewise an initial signifier of new religious commitments.[31] Minor though they seem, these changes had two immediate effects. The first was to change the self-identity and especially the self-esteem of the converts. More importantly, these minor changes were a foundational preparation for the more substantial impositions that followed.

The more significant social changes imposed by Eliot on his converts were deeply destructive and genocidal in that they affected the general cohesion and social organization of Indian peoples. Changes such as European-style agriculture, fencing, and English-style buildings eroded Indian social cohesion more subtly, but they nevertheless contributed to the transformation of the peoples from self-sufficiency to dependency. The imposition of new language structures, especially in the recitation of a new theological discourse, also had its effect, as I shall detail later in the chapter. More immediate in its effect was the breakup of Indian families that resulted from Eliot's condemnation of Algonquian polygamous marriage practice.[32] As was true across the continent and through the centuries of missionary outreach, converts living in multiple marriage contexts were required to withdraw from a husband or from one or more wives so as to mimic the European-style nuclear family. Few historians have questioned what became of the countless women, with their children, who had lived in marriages of long standing but were now suddenly excluded from any marriage relationship and had few prospects.[33] It is surely not a coincidence that this proscription by the missionaries is consistently reported as the most difficult tenet of the new faith for Indian converts.[34]

In the creation of the praying towns, the imposition of a new social structure takes on economic and political aspects. Yet the praying towns had their discrete social implications as well. In designing these mission compounds, either Eliot was influenced by the Spanish and French Catholic attempts to implement the reduction model of mission outreach, or he stumbled onto it coincidentally.[35] In either case, two distinct functions are apparent in retrospect. Eliot was sure that the praying towns would inculcate enough English culture that the Indians might finally be civilized.[36] Of course, this was possible only insofar as Eliot could enforce the rejection of the traditional native ways, which in turn meant the rejection of the convert's relatives back in the home village, including parents, siblings, children, and other relatives. Thus, alienation and separation within native families were imposed by the missionary process.

The second major function of the praying towns, whether Eliot consciously intended it initially or not, served a useful purpose for the English even as it was destructive for the Indians. Namely, since the towns were established apart from the English communities on the periphery of the settlements, they created a buffer zone of protection around the English colony,[37] separating the colonists from less friendly or even hostile Indian peoples. The native converts were not only denied free social and economic intercourse with the English communities, but they were also alienated from their home communities.[38] By separating and isolating Indian residents from the unconverted portion of their families, the praying towns further destroyed families and communal structures even as they attempted to institute some notion of the nuclear family. The extended kinship structures that gave Indian communities their internal stability and created cohesion among different bands related by marriage were destroyed overnight, only to be replaced by a relationship of subjugation and domination. In the final analysis, praying towns meant isolation and alienation from both the Indian world and the English world. Whether the motivation of Eliot and the English was conscious or subliminal, isolation became a fairly explicit mission strategy.

Political Aspects of Genocide

Eliot's mission endeavor has two discrete political aspects. The first involves the initial impetus for the outreach effort and the extent to which it was dictated by consideration of internal political expediency on the part of the Winthrop government. The other is the extent to which Eliot, as a missionary, was merely a government functionary using religion as a device to subjugate Indian peoples, as well as the extent to which he freely used the political muscle of the Bay Colony to achieve his desired mission ends. In either case, Eliot's firm connection with the Puritan body politic underscores his complicity in the cultural genocide of the people to whom he reached out with the gospel of Jesus Christ.

Jennings has clearly described the politics that surrounded the beginnings of the Bay Colony's mission effort, raising serious question as to the sincerity of the Puritan commitment.[39] He goes so far as to suggest that Eliot's motives for his mission to the Indians owed far more to economics and politics than to

Christian virtue. Jennings is surely right that political expediency had much to do with the inception of the mission and perhaps even with Eliot's initial movement. In England, persons outside the embrace of the Massachusetts Bay Company attacked the Massachusetts Puritans for failing to undertake missions to the Indians. "Of all that ever crossed the America seas," proclaimed one Presbyterian opponent in England, "they were the most neglectful of the work of conversion."[40]

The mission to native peoples was a fundamental part of the Massachusetts royal patent granted before the first group began their immigration. "The principall Ende of this Plantacion," according to the patent, was "to Wynn and incite the natives of [the] country, to the Knowledg and Obedience of the onlie true God and Savior of Mankinde, and the Christian Fayth."[41] Yet twelve years into colonization, Thomas Lechford complained that nothing in regard to this "principall Ende" had been accomplished. His critique of Massachusetts, written for an English audience, argued that no attempt toward Indian mission had even been made and that the colonists had preferred to attend to economic concerns instead: "They have nothing to excuse themselves in this point of not labouring with the Indians to instruct them, but their want of a staple trade, and other business taking them up."[42]

It is crucial to note that the mission endeavor finally began in Massachusetts as the result of a political decision made to improve the colony's public image in England, especially with Parliament. Winthrop and his magistrates in Massachusetts were politically astute. They fully realized the ramifications for their colony if Parliament and the Church of England believed the attacks levied against the Massachusetts Puritans.[43] Their Puritan empire was unraveling even as it continued to expand. It was political pressure exerted in England by the Bay Colony's Puritan and dissident opponents in Connecticut and Rhode Island that suddenly warmed the hearts of those in Boston toward their native neighbors. Jennings, even without summoning all the evidence for the case, has demonstrated the great probability that John Winthrop falsified the date of Eliot's first engagement in preaching the gospel to Indian peoples. Winthrop moved the date up by several months so that the mission would appear to have predated an event that was politically unsettling to Winthrop and his governing leadership, an event that demonstrated the erosion of Parliament's support for the hegemony of the Massachusetts government.[44] It now appears, from the evidence Jennings has summoned, that the official Puritan mission to Indian peoples began immediately following the appearance in Boston Harbor of a Connecticut rival who had been condemned to death as a heretic should he ever return to Massachusetts. That the man returned, and rather triumphantly, with a letter of protection from the English Parliament was a direct and startling challenge to the authority of the Puritan government in Boston. If Jennings is correct and the actual date of the start-up was altered by John Winthrop, then the mission was clearly an attempt at political cover-up, engaged in to reestablish support in Parliament and to ward off the economic and political threat of the Puritans in Connecticut.[45]

The other aspect of political genocide involves Eliot's connection with the governing authorities in Massachusetts and the part his mission effort played in the attempt to bring these praying Indians under the political umbrella of Massachusetts, that is, to subject them to Puritan rule and intentionally deprive them of their independence. There can be little doubt that Eliot was sincere at some level, though Jennings has also suggested that the prospect of winning a twenty-pound annuity to supplement his income was an incentive for his mission commitment.[46] In any case Eliot began his study of a Massachuset dialect in 1643, the year before Lady Armine's annuity became available, but did not begin his mission outreach until 1646. Nevertheless, implicitly and explicitly, Eliot participated in his missionary endeavor with a prior commitment to the body politic, that is, to the Massachusetts Bay Colony and its political/theological goals. While he would not have conceded that a conflict of interest clouded his proclamation of the gospel, it becomes clear with modern hindsight that he did intend a subjugation of Indian peoples under Puritan political control. It should be said that Eliot probably never realized the extent to which the intentional conflict of interest between his missionary outreach and his commitment to the Puritan political experiment contributed to the devastation of Indian people in New England.

Whether Eliot's first attempt occurred in July or in September, Jennings convincingly argues that at minimum political realities overshadowed Eliot's altruistic missionary zeal and provided the impetus for his initial movement to proclaim the gospel among Indian people. The collusion between missionary and government can be quickly surmised from the General Court legislation that followed his first attempt. All accounts agree that Eliot's first venture into mission evangelism at Dorchester Mill was an embarrassing failure, marked most pronouncedly by the open resistance of the local sachem or Indian leader. Although Cutshumoquin had been one of the five Massachuset sachems who had signed a statement of submission to the English in 1644,[47] Eliot was badly heckled by the Indian people under his leadership.[48] The Puritan body politic responded by passing legislation to ensure a gentler, more submissive response to Eliot's preaching. On November 4, the General Court passed legislation making blasphemy ("whether Christian or pagan") a capital crime within the jurisdiction of the Bay Colony.[49] Besides being an antiblasphemy ordinance, the legislation outlawed any practice of traditional Indian religion (". . . that no Indian shall at any time powwow, or perform outward worship to their false gods . . .").[50] With the signing of the treaty of submission two years earlier by five sachems, the court's jurisdiction encompassed a number of Indian communities, including that of Cutshumoquin. Finally, the legislation committed the entire colony, rather than individual churches, to the missionary effort. After ignoring the missionary impetus of their charter for the first sixteen years of the colony's existence, the colonists produced a flurry of activity in 1646 that resulted in Eliot becoming a missionary and the state facilitating the endeavor by supporting and protecting him. The religion he proclaimed to Indian peoples immediately became more palatable to the hearers when their own traditional ceremonial forms were made illegal.

Eliot's intentions with regard to the subjugation of Indian peoples under English hegemony became more apparent in the gerrymandering of the internal native political structures. Almost immediately upon his second venture into missionary outreach, Eliot and the Puritan government began to identify new possibilities for Indian leadership. Embarrassed by Cutshumoquin's resistance, Eliot chose to elevate others to leadership positions rather than focusing on the existing leaders; this decision marked the beginning of an intentional undermining of the authority of the traditional tribal leadership. In his mission foray to Nonantum on October 28, 1646, his second missionary attempt, Eliot chose to bypass Cutshumoquin and the other four sachems who were signatories to the 1644 treaty of submission in favor of the village of a man named Waban. Though Winthrop referred to Waban as a "new" sachem, Eliot acknowledged that he was "no sachem" but "the chief minister of justice."[51] Jennings, noting that the latter was clearly an English title and not a Massachuset tribal traditional category, has convincingly argued that Waban held no authority in his tribal political structure but was a comprador under political appointment of the colonial government.[52] Though this innovation certainly assured a warmer reception for Eliot's preaching, it represented an intentional undermining of native self-governance. Moreover, it represents the first movement on the part of Eliot and the Puritan government toward the establishment of the praying towns and the subjugation, dependence, and isolation that they represented.

The imposition of new models of government in the praying towns then followed, based on a combination of English political structures and Eliot's romantic appropriation of the Israelite model in Exodus. Though the praying towns were not so much a political as a cultural and social imposition, they began as an act of clear political collusion between Eliot and the Massachusetts General Court. It is difficult to ascertain what role, if any, Eliot had in the origin of the concept of the praying town. What is clear is that a formal statement of policy emerged from the General Court and not from Eliot or his Roxbury congregation. In November 1646, immediately after Eliot's first attempts at Indian evangelizing, Eliot and two other ministers were included on a court committee that was assigned the task of purchasing the first tract of land "for the incuragement of the Indians to live in an orderly way amongst us."[53] In other words, the establishment of the praying towns, as segregated Indian communities for converts, was an act of government, a political act in which Eliot, as missionary, participated explicitly as a political functionary, an agent of government serving the political aims of that government. To argue that New England was a theocracy where little distinction was made between government and religion and that Eliot, as a person of his times, could not have done otherwise in no way softens or reduces the historical fact of the devastation, oppression, and destruction of the native peoples of New England. The structural evils that we create and participate in cannot be excused by virtue of good intentions.

The establishment of these segregated Indian communities was intended to bring praying Indians more firmly under the control of Eliot and the Puritans, so that they might more readily abandon their pagan way of life and learn English "civilized" behavior. As such, the impetus behind the creation of the praying towns was precisely to destroy old social and political structures and replace them with new structures, imposing new economic structures, predicated on dependency, in the process.

Perhaps the clearest demonstration of Eliot's continuing collusion with the Puritan body politic is his close working relationship with Daniel Gookin, which spanned several decades. In 1656 the General Court appointed Gookin "superintendent of the Indians of Massachusetts," a position that he held until his death in 1687.[54] Eliot, as missionary, and Gookin, as a civil servant, traveled together a great deal through Massachusetts Indian country. Hand and hand they worked together to establish the correlative structural powers of church and state, establishing the political and economic authority of English civilization and the civilizing authority of Christianity as the Puritans conceived it. As Gookin reports:

> In July, 1673, Mr. Eliot and myself made a journey to visit some of them, and to encourage and exhort them to proceed in the ways of God. This year again, on the 14th of September last, 1674, we both took another journey. Our design was to tyravel further among them, and to confirm their souls in the christian religion, and to settle teachers in every town, and to extablish civil government among them, as in other praying towns.[55]

Eliot and Gookin clearly functioned as a team and fell into a pattern that can be described as a modus operandi. Their visit to a praying town began with Eliot holding a church meeting, preaching the gospel, and teaching catechumens. Gookin's civil function then followed. Building on the foundation laid by the missionary, Gookin held court, dealt with the more serious breaches of discipline, and approved or made civil government appointments. That the two were thoroughly intertwined is apparent in the subtle confusion of the two functions. Eliot's preaching and teaching never failed, we presume, to touch on "matters of religion and civil order."[56] Gookin, for his part, exhorted the native converts to obey both civil and religious authority and "to yield obedience to the gospel of Christ and to those set in order there."[57]

Here again one could argue that Eliot, as a missionary of the gospel, or even Gookin, as a committed Christian who also happened to be a Puritan civil servant doing his job, were well intentioned. Yet both functioned primarily as part of the Puritan political machinery, which was dedicated to the pacification of any hostile resistance to the progressive encroachment of Puritan economic exploitation of Indian land and Indian peoples. Both Eliot and Gookin were self-consciously a part of that process. Good intentions cannot make up for the resulting destruction of Indian families, Indian self-sufficient economies, Indian cultures, and Indian peoples themselves.

Economic Aspects of Genocide

The praying towns created a situation in which the Indian people of the towns were crucially dependent on the white economy of the Bay Colony. Indian persons living in the praying towns were immediately separated from their old economic resources and networks of community support. They were isolated on small, controlled pieces of land, serving the imposed need to prove their compatibility with white society. Cut off from their relatives and other Indian people remaining in traditional communities, praying town Indians were equally excluded from free intercourse with white society. The praying Indians had no choice but to be swept into the vortex of dependence on the economic structures of the colony, which had in mind only economic exploitation of native resources.

The model for the praying towns was already in existence from more than a century of Catholic evangelization in the south and half a century of work in New France. Though neither Eliot nor the General Court acknowledged the "reduction" or "reserve" paradigm, we do know that Spanish texts, including Las Casas, were read in England. In New England, as in Spanish America (the Caribbean, Paraguay, Mexico, Guatemala, and elsewhere) and New France, the praying town/reduction/reserve served primarily to increase the authoritarian control and domination of European colonial power. Of course, religious motives were cited, but the political motives were often just as easily, if naively, named. The isolation of Indian converts from their communities of origin, their families, their politically cohesive structures, and their aboriginal economic bases permitted the missionaries to work more or less uninterruptedly on the conversion of Indian people to European culture and values, which eventually paved the way for their conversion to the gospel.

Even the early Puritan historian Cotton Mather had to acknowledge with some hindsight that the attempt to develop an English-style economic base in the praying towns was merely a ruse. The Puritans never intended to empower the Indian towns but meant to maintain their status as client dependents. In the effort to create industry and agriculture in the praying towns, the English had only "contrived Indirect Ways to keep them under."[58] The praying Indians were implicitly forced to compete, but at the same time were restricted in how significantly and intimately they could compete in the Puritan economy. There was a strict, if implicit, segregation. Given their own communities and eventually their own churches, Indians were not allowed to join a white church or move into white communities. At the same time, both their churches and their communities were under the direct control of the governing authorities in Boston. In terms of technologies and marketable skills, Indian converts found themselves minimally abled and thoroughly marginalized. Their traditional tribal technologies and skills were quickly lost to an ever-increasing dependence on English trade goods. Axtell notes the devastating effectiveness of the Puritan strategy to introduce the Indians to an English-style economy, subverting "their traditional division of labor by imbuing them with an Anglo-Protestant work ethic and offering them a place in a radically different economy." He continues:

> One of the main goals of the New England praying towns was to provide "incouragements for the industrious" and "meanes of instructing them in Letters,

Trades and Labours, [such] as building, fishing, Flax and Hemp dressing, planting Orchards, &c." On paper, "Letters, Trades, and Labours" seemed to promise the Indians a full share in the complex market economy of the North Atlantic community. But in reality the missionaries could never muster the cultural vision or the social resources to enable their converts to become anything more dignified than tawny husbandmen who scraped a bare existence from the grudging soil of their reservations.[59]

Essentially limited in their ability to compete, the praying towns became suppliers for the more substantial and stable Puritan economy.[60] Allowed to produce goods and services for Puritan trade, the praying towns became a dependent, client economy. The resulting economic co-dependency is a phenomenon that continues to this day. Indian tribes in the United States today function largely around a carefully conceived and federally controlled comprador system that rewards an educated class of tribal members for maintaining the well-behaved client status of their tribes.[61]

That the praying towns had not achieved economic independence became readily apparent during King Philip's War, when the Puritans simply abandoned the praying Indians. Essentially, the Puritans distrusted the praying Indians in the same way the American government distrusted the Japanese Americans during World War II when it interred over 110,000 of them. The Puritans withdrew their support, leaving the Indians unprotected against Metacom's confederacy. Even though their initial intent was to support the English, the Indians were ultimately left with little choice but to side with their relatives. The evidence shows clearly that they tried at first to persevere in their support of the English, but many finally reverted back to their tribal ways and did not return to their adopted homes in the praying towns after the war had ended. The statistics following the war testify that the missions failed in Eliot's own lifetime. Only four towns survived out of fourteen in existence before the war, and even these had to be reconstituted out of the remnant from the fourteen. Even then they were in terrible shape, economically distressed, demoralized, and significantly reduced in size. Perhaps Gookin hints at a significant economic reason for their failure in his comments about the praying town of Okommakamesit:

> . . . the Indians here do not much rejoice under the English men's shadow; who do so overtop them in their number of people, stocks of cattle, &c. that the Indians do not greatly flourish, or delight in their station at present.[62]

The Language of Oppression and Confessions of Faith

In the final analysis, Eliot's mission strategy developed a no-win situation for his Indian adherents. Apparently, the primary device for accomplishing their subjugation was, ironically, Eliot's naive imposition of the language of Puritan theology and ecclesiology. The praying towns did work for about thirty years. At least these mission compounds functioned at a surface level in ways that

Eliot had imagined. The internees were able to learn European-style agriculture and building construction; they adopted European value structures up to a point (that is, at a surface level) and European civil and ecclesial self-governance. It is clear, however, that both Puritan expectations and Indian performance were largely illusions: the former an illusion that subliminally or overtly served the purposes of conquest, and the latter an illusion that was an attempt to comply with what could finally not be complied with.

The following analysis depends largely on distinguishing what similar language, at the surface level, may have meant to Indian and English speakers. At the outset it should be apparent that Puritan expectations concerning conversion, baptism, and "church estate" were built upon a narrow language of orthodoxy. Coming to Christian faith became a matter of holding sound doctrine. Although the process included some more subjective aspects, such as the recitation of one's conversion experience and the confession of one's sinful past, all of these things had to be done in theologically appropriate language. Moreover, conversion by itself was only the beginning of a process and did not automatically result in church membership or even baptism. These came later after a period of education, training, and proving oneself. Starting a new congregation, or "church estate," required a gathering of members sufficient to support a congregational structure. In the case of new Indian converts gathered in separate Indian communities (praying towns), the granting of church estate by the English elders was even more complex, since the new congregation would be based entirely on new members, whose conversion involved a radical cultural transformation that would not be immediately perceived as trustworthy by the English Puritans. It was nearly ten years before Eliot would consider church estate for Natick, the first of the praying towns. Even then it was a significant occasion. The English appointed a large examining committee to hear the confessions of these first Indian converts. The language was to be Massachuset, with translation; the theology had to be Puritan.

In the confluence of two radically disparate cultures, as in New England, any new surface structure language or behavior must somehow find meaning in terms of the old deep structures.[63] In other words, language and behavior must be understood in terms of people's experiences of the world. Whereas new surface structures may be learned by rote, people are not able to transform so easily the deep structures that give meaning to language or behavior. The old deep structures of meaning and cognition must continue to inform the new surface structures and give way only slowly to innovative transformation. Moreover, even as the initial deep structures of the native peoples began to be transformed by the new missionary surface structure, no one should be so naive today as to assume that the transformation resulted so quickly in the adoption of Puritan English deep structure, either at a linguistic or psychological level.

The examination of Natick converts in preparation for receiving church estate raises yet another issue. The record reports that the Indians articulated largely satisfactory answers to questions by the examining committee. In retrospect it becomes important to ask to what extent the surface structure language of the

Indian converts was actually rooted in deep structure images that would have been as satisfying to the English examiners or even recognizable to them as akin to their own deep structure images for identical language. The point is that the imposition of confessional theology is de facto the imposition of culture and values, even when it is a generally unsuccessful imposition. Although this chapter is concerned with Puritan theology and the Puritan missionizing effort, the same point can eventually be made for all the missionaries, conceiving of confessional theology at its broadest to include Catholic dogma, the Westminster and the Lutheran confessions, the Anglican Prayer Book, Wesleyan thought, and so on. The image of a young Indian boy from a newly evangelized tribe singing a Latin chant in the movie *The Mission* illustrates the relative ease with which new cultural surface structures can be learned. Yet those structures cannot be so easily internalized. It can be argued that for many, if not most, Indian tribes the old cultural values continue to live and provide explanations of the world at the deep structure level for a long time, even generations, after the new surface structures have been learned.

As Axtell argues, there can be little doubt that in most cases the reported conversions of Indian people to Christianity were genuine on their part.[64] The conversions can be explained by analyzing the particularities of the oppression people experienced. To this extent, the function of the missionaries among Indian people became simply a part of the complex mix of European oppression of native people. In New England the devastation of Indian people due to disease and conquest prior to the beginning of the mission effort surely left them extremely vulnerable to missionary pressures. Experiencing a 90 percent decline in a community's population over some twenty years undoubtedly left people confused and demoralized.[65] The impotence of the community's traditional methods of healing and the potency of the invader left many Indian people with little choice but to capitulate to the presumed power of a new spiritual way. In this context, conversions were undoubtedly genuine. The question remains, how deeply did the conversions affect the structures of the people's existence? Many New England tribes, especially the most devastated, were ready for some change. The ravages of disease and conquest began to raise questions among Indian communities about the old ways of being. And indeed a great many structures did change: men cut their hair, and all learned to wear European-style clothing; they also adopted new methods of agriculture, along with fence building, and learned European-style home construction. Yet significant as these changes were, they were still surface structure changes that did not yet affect people's deep structure imaging.

Even more to the point for this general discussion of the mission process is some recognition of unplanned transformation at the deep structure level. Some aspects of transformation defied articulation on the part of the converts and remained unnoticed by those who so easily imposed the new on them. The proclamation of the gospel was accompanied by the imposition of the new cultural values and social structures. The transformation generated included aspects of unmentionable pain—namely, self-hatred, alienation, and rejection—that have never really received attention in historical analyses of the period or in discussions of the contemporary context of Indian people.

Indian Confessions at Natick

In 1655, nine years into his mission endeavor among Indian people, Eliot wrote that Indians were finally ready for full church membership. As early as the fourth year of his outreach, the Indians had expressed a desire for baptism. After reflecting on their desire, he arrived at this response:

> After I had spent my poor labours among the Indians for the space of neer four years, it pleased God to stir up in them a great desire of partaking in the Ordinance of Baptism, and other Ecclesiasticall Ordinances in way of Church Communion. But I declared unto them how necessary it was, that they should first be Civilized, by being brought from their scattered and wild course of life, unto civill Cohabitation and Government, before they could, according to the will of God revealed in the Scriptures, be fit to be betrusted with the sacred Ordinances of Jesus Christ, in Church Communion. And therefore I propounded unto them that they should look out some fit place to begin a Towne, unto which they might resort, and there dwell together, enjoy Government, and be made ready and prepared to be a People among whom the Lord might delight to dwell and Rule.[66]

Indeed, the demonstrated ability to construct homes and other buildings, especially a church, in the English style of architecture became prima facie evidence that one group of Indians was ready to become a recognized church and provided the impetus for beginning the confession and examination process that would lead to the granting of church estate:

> But now being come under Civil Order, and fixing themselves in Habitations, and bending themselves to labor, as doth appear by their works of Fencings, Buildings &c. and especially in building without any English Workmans help, or direction, a very sufficient Meeting-House, of fifty foot long, twenty five foot broad, neer twelve foot high betwixt the joynts, wel sawen, and framed (which is a specimen, not only of their singular ingenuity, and dexterity, but also of some industry) I say this being so, now my argument of delaying them from entering into Church-Estate, was taken away.[67]

Already in 1652, a number of converts had taken the crucial step in Puritan ecclesiology of making formal statements of public confession and beginning a process that finally resulted in the granting of church estate to Indian people, that is, the founding of an Indian church. The next step for Eliot and the praying town of Natick was to submit those residents who had proven themselves ready for church membership in Eliot's eyes to an examination. Thus, the prospective members of what would become the first Indian congregation in New England gathered in Roxbury on April 13, 1654, to face the inquisition of an English examining committee. Both the purported verbata of the confessional statements made in 1652 and the list of examination questions used two years later have been preserved, published by Eliot himself.[68] In particular, the verbata of confessional statements lend themselves to an analysis that can be fruitful for understanding something of the process and results of conversion for these peoples.

Of course, the statements present inherent problems. Most importantly, they have been preserved only in English. The native utterances of the speakers are lost and cannot be reclaimed even remotely. Second, Eliot was the only English translator present at the examination.[69] Not only does this mean that the speeches have been filtered through the understanding and talents of a single interpreter, but that interpreter—Eliot—had a vested interest in the success of his converts and thus was not an unbiased, objective hearer. Whatever response the convert articulated, translation could serve to make it sound more rather than less normatively Puritan. Mather addresses the concern some might raise that the complexity of translating might have made reliance on a single translator somewhat tenuous, at best:

> But how shall we know that the Confessions here related, being spoken in their Tongue, were indeed uttered by them in such words, as have the same signification and meaning with these that are here expressed, for we have only the testimony of one man to assure us of it?[70]

Of course, Mather goes on to assure the reader that Eliot is unassailable in his task and impeccable in his integrity. Nevertheless, the examining committee heard the Indian responses only in Eliot's translation.

In the final analysis, though the confessional statements reveal much about the situation, there is no way to ascertain exactly what the Indians said on this occasion. First, we have to suspect that Eliot's translation was a very self-serving one, aimed at winning support for the starting of a church and affirmation for his mission endeavor. Another translator, such as Mayhew, might have kept Eliot somewhat honest, at least with regard to the blatant self-serving aspects of the translation. Eliot himself admits to some interpretive reworking of native speech in his reporting. In recording an exhortation of Waban, whom he had appointed under Puritan auspices as "chief" or civil ruler of the first of the praying towns, Eliot allows that he had taken the liberty of having "cloathed it with our English idiom."[71]

Second, we have to wonder how good Eliot's own understanding of the Indian dialect was and how deep his understanding of Indian idioms and metaphors.[72] A crucial question is the degree to which he might have read a Puritan meaning into all those metaphors and idioms. Moreover, the actual mental and emotional imaging of those native participants, in their use of the word "God," for instance, is irrecoverable.

The content in these confessions is devoted as much to the confessing of sin as it is to the confessing of their faith. As a whole, the confessions are undoubtedly shaped by the teaching and preaching of Eliot, and as such they clearly reflect the concerns of Puritan theology and the patterns of Puritan spirituality. The confession of sin is an overwhelming concern, yet it is minimally specific throughout the document. The individuals speak in the broadest generalities of having committed "all manner of sins" and show a proclivity for confessing service to "many gods." Sometimes the latter is the only case of specification. Typical is the opening sentence of Totherswamp, the first confessor in the document: "I confess in the presence of the Lord, before I prayed, many were my sins, not one good word did I speak, not one good thought did I think, not one good action did I doe: I did act all sins, and full was my heart of evil thoughts. . . ." In those cases where the confessor chose to specify his sins, a rather short list emerges that underscores a Puritan concern for sins of pride and sexuality. One list includes "pauwauing, lust, gaming, and all my sins." Another specifies, "I followed many women." "I prayed to many gods, I was proud, full of lusts, adulteries, and all other sins." "I greatly sinned, I prayed to many gods, and used pauwauing, adultery, lust, lying, and al other sins."[73]

Cleary, these are part of a stock list of sins that reflect the Puritan critique of Indian society in general. That the confessors repeatedly couch their confessions in broad generalities or limit themselves to such a stock list of sins raises again the question of how deeply the Indian peoples understood the missionary teachings. In arguing that Indian people were in many contexts most genuine in their conversions, Axtell goes so far as to assert that they did indeed have a grasp of the new language that was thrust upon them and that they were able to internalize the new teachings.[74] Axtell's position confuses two different issues, however. Surely Indian conversions were genuine from an Indian point of view. The argument can be made that they had no real choice in the matter, but that cannot finally detract from their genuine intent. The other question—whether there could possibly have been a genuine understanding of Christian doctrine as the Puritans preached it—is quite another matter. At best, it seems, the most genuine conversion resulted in a native understanding of the new Puritan religion that was only modestly more sophisticated than Roger Williams's celebrated understanding of native religious traditions.

In spite of Axtell's judgment that the Natick Indians acquitted themselves quite well in their 1654 examination at Roxbury, it needs to be said that the exam and the answers were short and superficial in nature.[75] It was a simple catechetical exam requiring no more than short memorized responses that had already been eight years in the making. They certainly do not reveal any deep internalization of the theological modes of discourse with which Eliot and his Puritan peers would have been most comfortable. Rather, they reflect the level of discourse one might rightly expect of young adolescent catechists with a minimal grasp of any deeper complexities. To recognize this dynamic is important in terms of recognizing that the Indian converts were marginalized theologically and ecclesiastically as much as economically, socially, and politically.

The intersection of two radically different conceptual worlds in Puritan New England was profound. Yet the complexity of the intersection was largely overlooked by the English except insofar as they pronounced an ethnocentric negative judgment against Indian people as a discrete cultural "other." The difficulty with which Indian people began to learn and internalize the conceptual world of the conqueror is apparent in the confusion of one Natick confessor who in two separate statements of confession recites stock tenets, both of which have their origin in the English critique of the Indian world, which turns out in this case to be ironically antithetical. In his first confession, Poquanum clearly says twice, "I did not think there was a God." Yet in his second confession, he turns around and confesses that he has prayed in his former state to "many gods."[76] This confusion calls for a lengthier and more sustained analysis than limited space permits here. Suffice it to say, the categories of discourse simply do not translate from one language or culture to another as if they were mere codes for one another that need only be transcribed. Even the notion of "God," which is so fundamental for the Western intellectual tradition, was an unknown for native American peoples in their first contact with Europeans; it is a cipher that must be filled in with meaning. As the cipher takes on meaning, it cannot be informed only by the analytical discourse of the missionary, but must necessarily be informed by the conceptual world of the hearer. Poquanum's "no God" and "many gods" become symbolic of the struggle to understand. In this case the distinction is not just between performance and competence. Even where performance seems adequate, albeit at a sophomoric level, the dislocative intersection of conceptual worlds may point to clashing deep structures that remain antithetical in spite of apparent surface structure compatibility.

The Puritan missionary attempt to give meaning to their English concept of God in the context of an Indian worldview, then, was problematic. It was not just problematic because Indian people structured reality in ways that made it difficult for them to grasp a new reality as it was imposed upon them by the English. More to the point, it was problematic because the English structured reality in ways that made it difficult for the missionaries to have any clarity at all about the Indian conceptual world and finally made it difficult for them to communicate genuinely across cultural barriers so severe. One can only wonder what must have gone through the minds of Eliot's early converts when they confessed that their traditional native ways of praying were actually worship of the devil. This question must be raised even in light of such a seemingly clear statement of "confession" as that made by this convert: "Before I prayed to God, I committed all sins; and serving many gods. I much despised praying unto God, for I beleeved the Devil. . . ."[77] Indeed, the very connection between devil and Colluchio, the name of one personified aspect of Algonquin deity, is an identity imposed on people of these tribes by the English missionaries and is in no way a natural identity.

When a person speaks from a position of power and leverage, however, something does get communicated. The hearer can hear the dictate of self-interest in responding to the more powerful, but what is heard and what is spoken may have only a superficial resemblance. In the case of the people of Natick, survival and self-interest dictated the adoption of European skills of farming, carpentry, and crafting and the learning by rote of answers to religious questions. No doubt, with time and the passing of generations, the old conceptual world begins to fade and the new begins to replace it. Yet nearly four centuries later, even having suffered the loss of language, east coast Algonquian peoples still see the world through Indian eyes and understand their Christianity in ways that make simple cross-cultural communication among Indian and non-Indian church people a relatively high-risk adventure.[78]

Axtell rightly argues that native peoples in the northeast came to the European encounter with no inborn or culturally taught sense of sin as an offense against an omnipotent God.[79] Of course, Axtell's statement itself consists of a string of at least three discrete European categories of knowledge, each lacking any immediate Indian analogy: sin, omnipotence, and God. "Raised in a cultural tradition that established community standards of right and wrong, but not sin against divine law," Axtell continues, "the Indians of southern New England had to be given a plausible set of new beliefs to replace them. Only then would they come to have a 'clear sight and sence' of 'gross and external' (or cultural) sins but also of spiritual sins of 'the Heart and Soul.' "[80] The question is not whether this accounts for Eliot's and others' mission strategies but to what extent the strategies were successful. Successes at the surface level are easy enough to tabulate, as Axtell readily does. Hiacoomes stands up to the power of the powwows on Martha's Vineyard with courage fueled by a genuine faith in the new set of beliefs gained from Mayhew's preaching.[81] So too, Eliot's missionaries sent out from Natick dressed in their austere English garb readily preached the new gospel to tribes ranging over much of southern New England.[82] In either case the question to be asked is not whether these converts genuinely believed in the power of their newfound belief system, but to what extent their deep structure appropriation of the new faith was substantially different from and structurally similar to what they had ostensibly abandoned. Although a definite linguistic shift occurred and modes of leadership certainly changed, the new must have nevertheless and necessarily functioned within the parameters of their existing (even if changing) worldview.

That Eliot's missionary endeavor ultimately failed at a political, social, and ecclesial level is a matter of historical record evidenced by the collapse of the praying towns during and after the Metacom uprising of 1675. The vast majority of converts, faced with rejection by their erstwhile English allies, returned to their traditional communities, joined the fight against the English, and finally rejected Christianity. Few of those who survived the war found their way back to one of the four remaining praying towns.

Yet the missionary effort was enormously successful as a tool of conquest and had a devastating and destructive impact on the aboriginal peoples of New England. In spite of his good intentions toward Indian peoples and his hopes for their conversion to Christianity, Eliot must be held historically accountable for the resulting cultural genocide of those peoples.

The imposition of Puritan theology and theological language across the cultural chasm that separated Indian and English certainly generated a sense of low self-worth on the part of Indian converts from which Indian people have not yet recovered. The missionary-mandated rejection of their culture and its values and structures of existence necessarily resulted in the denial of self and the inculcation of self-hatred. The Puritan theology of sin combined with missionary imperialism to erode what must have been an already endangered self-esteem. Moreover, native converts were allowed only a less sophisticated, second-class, Puritan theology, which meant that political and economic domination of Indian people by the English was paralleled and enhanced by ecclesial and theological domination. Those Indians who did choose to convert remained second-class church members, still not allowed to be a part of an English community or English congregation.

Indian people today still suffer a loss of self-esteem and a general level of self-deprecation that derive from the forced alienation of Indian people from their history, their culture, and their land. This contemporary alienation has its roots in the evangelistic impetus of missionaries like Eliot who from the beginning taught Indian people that Indian culture was largely inadequate and even evil. Yet to teach the rejection of one's culture, history, and structures of spirituality is to teach self-hatred.

CHAPTER 3

Junípero Serra

Spiritual Conquest and Famine in California

> On the 26th we [Serra and his expeditionary force] remained in this same stopping-place, because the excellence of it invited to the refreshment of the beasts, which in the last preceding journeys had been somewhat overworked. Two Gentiles [i.e., native Californians] were again visible on the same height, and our Indians, shrewder than yesterday, went to catch them with caution, that they should not escape them. And altho' one fled from between their hands, they caught the other. They tied him, and it was all necessary, for, even bound, he defended himself that they should not bring him, and flung himself on the ground with such violence that he scraped and bruised his thighs and knees. But at last they brought him. They set him before me, and setting him on his knees, I put my hands upon his head and recited the Gospel of St. John, made the sign of the Cross upon him, and untied him. He was most frightened and very disturbed. We took him to the tent of the Señor governor [Portola], trying to console him, that no harm would come to him.
>
> —Junípero Serra[1]

The California mission system (1769–1834) was and continues to be the legacy of Father Junípero Serra, OFM, the Spanish Franciscan "president" of the missions from their founding in 1769 until his death in 1782. The legacy includes forced conversions of native peoples to Christianity and the enforcement of those conversions by imprisonment; physical violence in the form of corporal punishment; the imposition of slave labor conditions on Indian converts for the support of the missions and the accompanying military presidios; a living environment that was akin to a concentration camp and cycles of famine and constant poor nourishment that were both unprecedented among these native peoples; an extraordinary death rate among converts;[2] and the devastation of many California native cultures. For these failures a great many would honor Serra with elevation to Roman Catholic sainthood.

That Serra was both pious and courageous cannot be doubted. His intentions in evangelizing American Indian peoples were, I believe, honest and genuine. He abandoned accomplished prominence as a theology professor to pursue a lingering medieval ideal of martyrdom as a "new world" missionary, committed to asceticism and mendicancy. When Serra left his Spanish homeland on the island of Mallorca for the mission fields of New Spain in 1749, he was accompanied by two of his former university students who were devoted disciples. One of these was Francisco Palóu,[3] who became wholly committed to Serra's canonization by the time of Serra's first expedition to California. After Serra's death in 1782, Palóu devoted several years to writing an extensive biography that was clearly intended to initiate canonization proceedings.[4]

Serra, with Palóu as a companion, spent nine years at Jalpan among the Pames in the Sierra Gorda in Mexico's interior, where Serra served as president of the Sierra Gorda Franciscan missions.[5] Despite being plagued with ill health, in 1769 Serra accepted the assignment for which he is most famous. With willing self-sacrifice, suffering a serious disability in his leg or foot, Serra became a key participant in the first full-scale Spanish invasion of California, founding the mission at San Diego in July of that year as a part of the Spanish occupation strategy. Palóu's biography makes repeated reference to this physical ailment that slowed Serra throughout his time in California. The descriptions always heighten the sense of the heroic. The dedicated friar was not to be stopped.

With the beatification of Serra on July 1, 1988, Palóu's efforts appear to be closer to achieving success. Yet Serra's canonization is not without controversy nor without modern political import. Serra's greatest fame, and in retrospect his greatest shame, is a result of his mission endeavor in California, where he began the establishing of twenty-one missions among the native inhabitants. For better or for worse, the descendants of those native inhabitants remain the most bitter opponents of Serra's canonization.[6]

The Politics of Evangelization and Conquest

> These missionaries became a veritable corps of Indian agents, serving both Church and state. . . . [T]he rulers of Spain . . . made use of the religious and humanitarian zeal of the missionaries, choosing them to be to the Indians not only preachers, but also teachers and disciplinarians.
>
> —Herbert E. Bolton[7]

Perhaps the most damaging critique of Serra and the Franciscans in California is the extent to which they functioned in complete symbiosis with the structures of Spanish civil government, and even as an extension of it.[8] The political aspects of cultural genocide are as explicit and transparent in Serra's case as was Eliot's symbiotic relationship with Winthrop and the Massachusetts General Court. While Serra and his missionaries belonged to the Franciscan order and thus owed allegiance to the president of the College of San Fernando in Mexico City, they owed an even greater allegiance in praxis to the civil government of New Spain. The missionaries were directly on the payroll of the viceroy and effectively functioned as a branch of the civil service in their mission endeavors.

Nearly two centuries earlier, in 1508 Pope Julian II's bull had provided for this relationship.[9] By the terms of this bull, church and state were bound together, a relationship maintained throughout the subsequent history of the Spanish conquest of the Americas. The state assumed responsibility for the conversion of the natives in return for papal support for the Crown's colonial expansion and concessions permitting royal intervention in ecclesial affairs of the colonies.

Spain's commitment to the conversion of native peoples entailed financial responsibility for mission expenses, including salaries and protection for the missionaries in these frontier posts.[10] The food rationing policy in Serra's day illustrates how well the state fulfilled its commitment. Under the standing government policy, the friars were to be given double rations while servants (i.e., natives) were to receive "ordinary rations."[11] Military officers received one and a half times the rations of a priest.[12]

While the missionaries, especially those associated with orders such as the Franciscans, Dominicans, and Jesuits, undoubtedly came to their task with pious intentions, the government in New Spain invariably saw their evangelistic outreach as serving the purposes of conquest in terms of pacification of the countryside.[13] In California as in other Spanish American contexts, the military was obligated to protect the missionaries from any hostile Indian resistance to evangelization, and the missions were to produce part of the sustenance for the regional military government. Thus, while the church defined its partnership with the Spanish state in the Americas in terms of the state's participation in evangelizing native peoples, in actuality the conversion of natives was of greater benefit to the state and its colonizing goal.

The development of the California mission system beginning in 1769 likewise was an integral part of Spain's strategy of colonialization and conquest. This much Serra himself understood clearly. In his *Diary* he readily acknowledges that the expedition was undertaken "by order of His Majesty, whom God guard, Don Carlos Third" and "for the greater honor and glory of God, and the conversion of the Ynfidels to our Holy Catholic Faith."[14] It cannot be overstated that the whole expedition, including the mission component, was a march of conquest. Serra's best intentions aside, the conversion of native peoples was merely a part of the larger strategy.[15] Whatever one's assessment of the failure of Serra's missions, the success of Spain's conquest of California and the missionaries' part in it cannot be denied.

Like so many missionaries before him, then, Serra conducted his evangelistic outreach to native peoples as part of the occupation force of a conquering army and as a part of a strategy of conquest. When Serra made his way north from Mexico through Baja California toward the site of his first California mission at what was to be San Diego, he and his fellow missionaries came with a military contingent that was the first Spanish expedition of colonial conquest into the region. It is crucial to note that the impetus for this movement into Alta California by Spain had nothing to do with converting the native population in the area and everything to do with the threat that Russian colonial expansion would move south down the coast of California and eventually threaten Spanish hegemony.[16] At the same time, the conversion of the native population was an integral part of the Spanish strategy to counter Russian expansionist designs with their own.

The account of Serra's missionary service some years earlier in the Sierra Gorda of central Mexico is instructive for understanding his later work in California. The picture begins to depict the possibilities and probabilities of violence as a mission strategy, as well as the collusion between missionary and colonial government. As would be the case in California, the mission enterprise in the Sierra Gorda was explicitly a part of the conquest strategy, insofar as the missions were undertaken by the Franciscans under direct order from the civil government of New Spain. Moreover, the missions were ordered explicitly as a pacification effort to ensure the government's control of central Mexico.[17] To the extent that the mission effort involved the explicit participation of the military in acts coercing native compliance, the outreach in the Sierra Gorda was overtly violent and dislocative. Palóu describes the process used to bring the Pame peoples into their mission:

> [T]he captain of the soldiers sent a sergeant with a detachment of troops to burn all the houses of the Indians that were scattered through these sierras, so that they would then live together in the new town. . . .[18]

That Serra's mission strategy already was predicated on coercion and strictly enforced discipline becomes apparent from the legalities that were imposed on all native peoples in the Sierra Gorda, converts and others. All Indian people were required by mandate of the local Spanish government to attend religious instruction and mass.[19] Recitation and teaching began at sunrise each day and constituted a command appearance for all adult Indians, for unconverted "pagans" as well as neophyte converts—"without any exception," Palóu writes. "One of the fathers is to recite with them the prayers and text of Christian doctrine and to explain to them in Spanish [sic] the principal mysteries of religion." Similar instruction was required twice a day for all children over five years of age, both converted and unconverted, as Palóu reports, "without allowing anyone to be absent from this holy exercise."[20] Attendance at mass was likewise obligatory for all, neophyte or pagan, and was checked by roll call:

> When Mass is over, one of the missionaries is to call each Indian by name out of the mission register, and each Indian is to approach the missionary to kiss his hand. By this means he can detect if anyone is missing.[21]

The requirement that unconverted Indians should attend mass and the instruction sessions provides prima facie evidence of the civil function of the missions, a function given over to the pacification of the countryside. Unlike Alta California, the Sierra Gorda was already surrounded by colonial occupation and had long experienced the presence of the Spanish. Hence, the imposing presence of the conqueror made it easier to require attendance at mass. Neither the missionaries nor the military suggested such a strategy for Alta California, since that territory was not nearly so ready for such a general pacification of the native population. To the contrary, the Spanish were only just beginning the European invasion of Alta California in 1769 and did not bring a military contingent large enough to enforce this sort of spiritual regimen upon the unconverted.

Serra seems to have been particularly clear about the relationship between himself as missionary and the structure of civil government. The initial success of his missions depended to a large extent on his own personal relationship with Bucareli, the viceregent of New Spain from 1771 to 1779. While Serra had a less than easy relationship with civil authorities in California from the beginning of the venture, as long as Bucareli was alive, Serra was able to appeal decisions directly to Mexico City. The collection of Serra's correspondence during his tenure in California contains several communications with Bucareli, and Serra traveled to Mexico City and stayed there for an extended period in 1773 to lobby the viceroy on political issues related to an ongoing dispute with the California governor.[22]

Serra was, in the final analysis, a mere religiopolitical agent for imperial Spain, helping Spain achieve its colonial goals in the late eighteenth century. Palóu's consistent definition of the missionaries' work as "spiritual conquest" is surely not entirely coincidental.

The Old and the New: Social Change as a Strategy for Control

> This which has been said about obliging the Indians to learn our language leads me to the conclusion that it would not be of less advantage if we should oblige them also to adjust themselves to Spanish usage in matters of dress and clothing and other customs. . . .
>
> —Juan de Solórzano Pereira, 1703[23]

> These Spanish missionaries, of whom Serra was one, believed that to be Christian one had to become Spanish. The native civilization and culture was not seen as an equal of Spanish civilization.
>
> —Father Michael Galvan (Ohlone), 1987[24]

Looking back on the history of missionary outreach among native American peoples, the social aspects of cultural genocide seem most obvious. In the case of Serra and the California mission system of the Franciscans, the social aspects of genocide are readily apparent in the broad structural changes, both social and cultural, that were part of the mission design. The most significant changes were the most immediately destructive, but the long-term devastation of Indian community and individual existence and self-identity became most visible at the time of the Franciscan withdrawal from California. In 1834, Indian converts were abandoned, after having been more or less successfully dispossessed from their own culture but before they were able to sustain themselves in their newly imposed European cultural milieu. On the other hand, the resistance of Indian peoples to the missions is evidenced in the primary sources from the beginning of Spanish occupation in California until their withdrawal and still continues at some level today as resistance to U.S. hegemony.

Many modifications of social structures, mores, and behavior patterns were imposed simply to satisfy European sensitivities and virtues. Surely, the style of one's dress—or even the lack of it—the length or shape of an Indian man's hair, the construction of one's home, or the state of a community's technology has little to do with whether one can believe in the gospel of Jesus Christ. The first

Spanish missionaries in California, like their predecessors in the Caribbean and the English on the north Atlantic coast, were surprised and appalled at the uninhibited and unembarrassed nudity of the native population,[25] and, of course, they found native marriage customs to be unacceptable and immoral. More to the point, the missionaries were convinced of the superiority of their own culture, social structures, and technologies. Hence, in their minds, conversion became explicitly linked to learning "masonry and carpentry, and to till the soil, etc., and that they must live together in a pueblo, which would have to be formed by the people, in order that they might live close together in their houses and not scattered out as now; and that they would have to make a house for the father and a church."[26] As Solórzano Pereira argued earlier in the century, more than just how and where the converts lived was involved. Ultimately, conversion became a matter of language and "Spanish usage in matters of dress and clothing and other customs. . . ."[27]

The Franciscans' intentions in pursuing this strategy were no doubt good insofar as they were marked by some genuine desire to help Indian people— whether those Indian peoples wanted said help or not. Serra and the missionaries who came with him were wholly devoted to their spiritual cause, to a life of a certain austerity (although, as we shall see, austerity had its limits, for instance, at times of famine), and to their goal of converting native peoples to Christianity. Nevertheless, their mission strategy was marked by a decisive intentionality where the destruction of native social structures was involved. Serra and his Franciscan cohorts were as convinced as Eliot and the New England Puritans that cultural conversion was a prerequisite to conversion to Christianity. Thus, with self-conscious determination, they went about the task of dismantling what they regarded as the backward traditional lifeways, social structures, mores, and values of Indian peoples.

Furthermore, these broad modifications of social structures served another explicit goal: to establish and maintain the political and disciplinary control over the Indian community that the missionaries believed was necessary to ensure appropriate and adequate attention to the details of conversion. It must be remembered that conversion for Serra meant more than conversion to a faith in the message of God's saving act in Jesus as the Christ. It inherently meant cultural conversion. In Serra's ongoing debate with the military governors of California, this need for control is constantly apparent, usually articulated in terms of its role in facilitating the conversion process and nurturing the budding Christian commitment of converts whose aboriginal culture was viewed as not only childish and retarded but aberrant and inimical to Christianity. Hence, all aspects of a neophyte's existence had to be carefully developed in a controlled community.

While Serra's strategy in California becomes apparent in practice, the primary sources do not explicitly spell out his underlying theory. Yet Palóu makes clear that the strategy agreed upon with the civil authority was essentially the same as that implemented in the Sierra Gorda. Joseph de Galvez, Mexico's visitor general and the government official responsible for initiating the California conquest by Portola and Serra, directed that the new missions be established "on the basis of the same mode of life and administrations as [Serra had established for] those of the Sierra Gorda."[28] Already in Galvan and Serra's preparations, the Sierra Gorda strategy of cultural replacement becomes apparent. While Serra collected the necessary items for conducting religious services, Galvan collected "what would be needed for dwelling places and agricultural use":

> . . . all kinds of articles for use in dwelling quarters and field, with necessary implements of iron for working the land and planting, and every type of seed for both Spain and New Spain. Nor did he forget even the smallest things, such as seeds for vegetables, flowers and flax, because as he saw it, that land should be fully fertile for it was in the same latitude as Spain.[29]

Thus, the replacement of native economies, especially in agriculture but also in construction and architecture, was fundamental to the perceived mission process.

These strategies would have proven futile without implementing that part of the Sierra Gorda strategy that would allow the easy imposition of these new "civilized" economies. An overall social structure that would allow for the immediate administration and governance by the missionaries over all aspects of native life had to be imposed. Although later civil authorities would demur, both Serra and Galvan believed it was imperative to separate the native converts from their old social structures, towns, families, and social relationships. Hence, they intended to implement the *reduccion* model of gathering Indian converts into closed mission social structures in some way analogous to the missions in the Sierra Gorda.[30]

Serra's primary mission strategy, then, was to isolate converts from their home communities and relatives. While this strategic initiative had political and economic as well as religious effects, its most devastating aspect was the imposition of a massive social modification. To implement this strategy, converts were collected into mission compounds somewhat similar to the praying towns of Eliot's New England missions a century earlier.

These "*reducciones*" already had a Spanish Catholic history of more than two centuries, going back to the early mission efforts in the Caribbean, Mexico, and South America. Under Serra's governance, as had been the case earlier, the *reduccion* system had several components. First, Indian converts were separated from their home community and relatives in new communal enclosures; that is, native persons were removed from their former mode of existence. If they were "hunter-gatherers" who wore little clothing, they were clothed and taught European agriculture. Second, once converted and relocated within the compound, the converts were permanently proscribed from rethinking their conversion and returning to their own homes. This was enforced by Spanish law and military discipline. In California as in the Sierra Gorda and other Spanish mission contexts, the missionaries had military assistance at hand to hunt down fugitives and return them to their missions for discipline.[31] Third, converts were committed to a rigorous regimen of work to support the mission, the missionaries, and their obligation to the military government. Fourth, converts gave up all aspects of self-governance to live under the strict and authoritarian governance of the missionary priests.[32] Finally, Serra's strategy included the inculcation of new value structures. Palóu describes teaching Indian converts a system of rewards that began with the distribution of sustenance only after the daily recitation of Christian doctrine. The missionaries controlled the mission's accumulation of agricultural produce, distributing the bare minimum as daily sustenance and storing the "surplus." Profit motives then were nurtured by teaching natives to sell surpluses, and by using profits to enhance the mission's capital by purchasing more livestock and tools from European markets. An appetite for luxury was also instilled with the purchase of blankets, cloth, and apparel from Mexico City. Moreover, these economic lessons were accompanied by the imposition of a new hierarchical valuing of labor that gave priority to certain kinds of work and taught specialization: the hierarchy was implicit in the superiority of the European priest, and was made explicit in the special gifts given, for instance, to those who did the more physical labor of tilling.[33]

Native forms of self-governance, of course, became an early and primary target for social change. The *reduccion* paradigm presupposed both the inability of native peoples to govern themselves as civilized peoples and the need for authoritarian governance by the missionary in each locale. Existing indigenous political leadership was recognized only to the extent that it could be exploited by either the colonial government or the missions themselves. Palóu reports that the governor of California appointed existing leaders to positions of leadership, but did so in ways that emphasized subordination:

> The governor told the one who was the chief that although until then he had possessed that title only by reason of the wish or the mandate of his people, from this day forward the governor appointed him as chief with the authority and in the name of the King our Sovereign.[34]

Curiously enough given modern democratic pretensions, native forms of self-governance were not recognized as legitimate and were assumed to be something less than civilized because they depended only on the will of the people for validation and accountability.

Replacement of the native language of communication was, of course, one of the most significant social changes imposed on native converts. By the mid-seventeenth century, the Spanish monarch had mandated the imposition of Spanish as the language of communication for Indian people.[35] Serra and his missionaries did attempt to learn the native languages, but found the task one of nearly insurmountable difficulty because of the great variety of languages spoken in California.[36] "[I]n almost each new area one finds a new language," reports Palóu, "and up to now there are no two missions where the same language is spoken."[37] Among the Indian tribes at the southern California missions, for instance, at least three distinctly different language groups—Salinan, Chumash, and Shoshonean—could be found, and each linguistic family might include several distinct dialects, making simple communication impossible. Moreover, the Franciscans had a proclivity for mixing language groups that had little prior contact by moving converts considerable distances away from their homes and into the missions.[38] Beyond the obvious practical difficulties posed by these language barriers, one can imagine the impossibility of conveying subtle meanings in matters of faith and spirituality.

In spite of the leanings of Gerónimo de Mendieta,[39] their Franciscan ancestor, Serra and the others quickly succumbed to the easy route of simply requiring their converts to learn Spanish. Since a great many of the initial converts were children, the imposition of Spanish served a secondary useful purpose for the missionaries by further isolating the young converts from their families and home communities and solidifying the political control of the missionaries over their convert communities. The importance of this tactic as a strategic maneuver must not be overlooked. It survived as fundamental educational policy in mission schools of all denominations in North America and in U.S. government boarding schools well into the 1960s; here Indian children continued to be separated from their families and punished when caught speaking their native language with a fellow tribesperson.[40]

Loss of language, loss of political self-governance, and changes in family structures, values, diet, modes of living, and architecture all portended a destruction of a people's culture and eventually the destruction of the people themselves. For the sake of Christianity and the proclamation of the gospel, Serra and his missionaries imposed social changes that resulted in "low-intensity" genocide over several generations.

Slavery and Famine: The Economics of Conversion

Serra became a near-absolute dictator, ruling Indian people as if they were mere slaves and forcing them to work to maintain an economic-military system whose sole purpose it was to control them, change their culture, and seize their land.

—Jack Forbes[41]

Despite the numerable lamentations, apologies and justifications, there can be no serious denial that the mission system in its economics was built on forced labor.

—Sherburne F. Cook[42]

The unhappy treatment which the Franciscans give the Indians renders the Indian condition worse than slaves. The fathers aim to be independent and sovereign over the Indians and their wealth.

—Felipe de Neve, governor of California, 1780[43]

The treatment shown to the Indians is the most cruel I have ever read in history. For the slightest things they receive heavy floggings, are shackled, and are put in the stocks, and treated with so much cruelty that they are kept whole days without a drink of water.

—Father Antonio de la Conception Horra, OFM, 1799[44]

The initial economic strategy implemented by Serra was to create a dependency on the part of native peoples for European trade goods. The first European trade goods the natives of California encountered consisted of colorful cloth, which immediately became much more than a novelty to a color-conscious culture. As with the introduction of metal tools and cooking utensils into nineteenth-century plains cultures, the incorporation of European trade goods into the everyday life of California natives ensured their entrapment into the foreign economic system brought by Serra's expeditions. To make sure that native peoples abandoned their historic self-sufficiency and became dependent on European trade goods, other social changes were introduced to reinforce the need. In this case the imposed necessity for clothing to cover native nudity ensured the need for a continual supply of cloth. This imposed need for cloth then played an important part in trapping the new native mission communities into an extensive and dependent trade economy with Europe. The situation of dependence that was thus generated first became definitive of the native-missionary relationship and then was expanded to form the long-term native/European relationship that largely endures to this day.

Concomitant with this new dependency, native peoples found themselves locked into a European culture and ethic of work that, in their case, was virtual slavery.[45] The slavelike context of California native converts has been carefully described by several authors[46] and was largely the result of the *reduccion* mission structure, modeled as it was implicitly on the old *encomienda*. Even Serra's most articulate apologist and co-religionist, Francis Guest, has been forced to acknowledge this reality and could only excuse it as a "legal" confinement of converts under both church and Spanish law.[47] Eighteenth-century Spain was still struggling to emerge from the medieval structures of feudalism, and it should not be surprising that Serra was only able to imagine his new mission in terms of the structures of feudal society. To recognize that Serra worked within the limitations of his own social inculturation may help to explain the historical reality, but it cannot change the experience of oppression and death suffered by tens of thousands of California Indians during the sixty-five-year tenure of the missions.

Certain facts of convert life in these mission compounds are incontrovertible. After conversion to neophyte status was completed with the sacramental act of baptism, formerly autonomous and free people were no longer allowed to leave the mission except for specific purposes with the express permission of the missionaries.[48] Here the distinction between a controlled society and incarceration is very narrow. A strict daily regimen of work was enforced, interspersed with regular periods of religious schooling and worship. Families were customarily broken up in ways unknown in the traditions of these indigenous people, with children removed from their parents and housed in dormitories separated by gender. Hence, not only was the extended family kinship system destroyed, but even the possibility of nuclear family was denied. The near-absolute political and disciplinary authority that Serra and his missionaries exercised over their converts extended to all levels of community decision making, from social to economic matters.

It was at the economic level, then, that new aspects of genocide were introduced, beginning with the planting of crops and the introduction of European-style agriculture. The overt intention of Serra's missions was to attain self-supporting status as quickly as possible. Yet the actual process is instructive. It should be noted from the outset that "self-supporting" did not refer to Indian self-support, which had succeeded for millennia, but to the status of the mission, maintained under firm priestly control. In other words, Serra had in mind the self-support of a more complex institutional structure, which suddenly included not only native producers but also the missionaries as nonproducing bureaucracy and the royal presidios as a nonproducing police institution. The missions were responsible for supplying food to the colonial government and its military detachments. [49]

European-style agriculture was first imposed on Indian people by Serra in the Sierra Gorda and then in California, so that "the Indians could maintain themselves living in community as was practiced in the beginning in the Church."[50] The announced goals of this shift in economy were "civilization" and the deliverance of Indian peoples from their perceived laziness. Palóu argues that Serra, in this way, "weaned them all from the idleness in which they had been raised and in which they had grown old. . . . The natives grew more civilized each day, becoming more inclined to sow their individual plantings of maize, chile, beans, pumpkins, etc."[51] Given the Spanish immigrants' general aversion to work[52] and their proclivity for exploiting the work of others, this is a curious reversal on the part of a priest—a psychological projection—except that the missions were ultimately just as exploitative of native labor as were other Spanish colonialists. Indians, he concludes, "who were barbarous and savage, became civilized and instructed."[53] It should not go unnoticed that civilization, in this context, meant not only European-style agricultural methods but the European style of individualization—imposed on peoples who were long accustomed to a communitarian life.

California Indian peoples at the time of contact lived in self-sufficient economies marked by consistent food surpluses. This makes the economic aspects of their genocide all the more pronounced. The missionaries came with rigidly preconceived ideas about economic production and work. Blind to the work performed in native communities and to native economic success, they categorized native peoples as lazy and proceeded to impose new categories of work and economy on them. The economic design these Franciscans brought to California Indians involved three aspects: agriculture, economic dependence, and work. Perhaps the most significant of these was the imposition of European-style agriculture. The other two aspects, especially the imposition of a European paradigm of work more aptly characterized as slavery, were thoroughly intertwined with the missionaries' notion of agriculture, so that the three seemed to work successfully together to form a dramatic whole. At another level, however, the failure of mission agriculture is astounding in itself as cycles of famine replaced the surfeit of native self-sufficiency.[54]

Despite the overwhelming ethnographic evidence for the success of pre-colonial Indian economies and technologies in California, some apologists for Serra continue to argue that Spanish technology and agricultural prowess attracted Indian converts. The increased stability provided by European agricultural production is supposed to have appealed to many native peoples in California.[55] Eco-historian Lester R. Rowntree argues contrary to these mission proponents that "mission conversion was least successful during drought episodes when aboriginal populations were better off pursuing traditional subsistence strategies."[56] For the California missions, the presumption of a new stability derived from the superiority of European agricultural technology is a myth fabricated by Serra's apologists that belies the facts. The mission records indicate very unstable production marked by mismanagement and incompetence that often resulted in food shortages even in years of normal or better rainfall.[57] Moreover, Sherburne Cook has argued that the mission diet of the Indians (but not that of the missionaries, who had access to imported foods) was nutritionally inadequate.[58] On the other hand, traditional native economies were far from "the bare edge of existence." Native adaptation had long resulted in technologies that ensured self-sufficient survival even in sequences of bad years.[59] Native acorn harvesting, for instance, often generated enough surplus for two years.[60] Furthermore, extensive indigenous trading was conducted throughout California, including trade based on surplus food production.[61]

In spite of his Eurocentric cultural narrowness, Serra himself recognized something of the self-sufficiency and well-being of the Indian peoples in California and the historical adaptation of aboriginal native economies. Toward the beginning of his initial expedition into California, Serra already acknowledged that the natives were well fed:

> Food they little care for, because they are stuffed, and accordingly are fat; the Señor Governor would like most of them for Grenadiers, on account of their lofty stature.[62]

During the expedition to San Francisco Bay for the founding of the San Francisco and Santa Clara missions, Palóu catalogs the great abundance of food resources enjoyed by the peoples of what is now the San Francisco Bay area. His keen recognition of the success of native economies there is so explicit and so paradoxically denied by his continued insistence on the superiority of European technology that he deserves to be cited at length:

> The pagans of this port maintained themselves on the seeds and grasses of the field, which it fell to the women to gather in season. The women grind these and make flour for their gruels. Among these seeds there is a black species, and from the flour of these they make a certain kind of tamale, ball-like, about the size of an orange. These are very tasty and juicy and have the flavor of roasted almonds. For food they add to these things fish of various species, which they catch along

the coasts of both seas, all of which are wholesome and tasty. They also eat
shellfish, of which there is never any lack, and various kinds of clams. They live
also from the hunting of deer, rabbits, wild geese, ducks, partridges and thrushes.
When a whale happens to be swept ashore, they seize the occasion to celebrate
a great feast, for they are very fond of its meat, which is pure blubber or fat. . . .
They do the same with seals, of which they are just as fond as of the whales,
because seal, too, is all fat.

They gather acorns, which they grind and use to make their gruel and ball-
shaped tamales. In the woods and valleys near-by, they obtain hazelnuts similar
to those of Spain. On the hills and along the sand dunes there is an abundance
of strawberries, which are very delicious and larger than those obtained in Spain,
and which ripen in the months of May and June. There also are blackberries.
Everywhere in the country and on the hills there is an abundance of soaproot,
which is the size of an onion, with a large and round head. These they bake in
batches in the earth, over which they keep a fire going for three or four days,
until they are sure they are well done. Then they take them out and eat them.
They taste as sweet and delicious as preserves.[63]

It is indeed curious that Palóu, after having described such native abundance
of food supplies, would still insist on the need for teaching European agriculture
as a superior means of subsistence and European culture as a "superior order":

> In order to encourage and stabilize this spiritual conquest, His Excellency the
> Viceroy charged the new governor, Don Felipe Neve, to make an attempt to settle
> the land with some towns of Spaniards, who were to be employed in agriculture
> and stock raising, and in this way aid in the development of these new establish-
> ments. Calling this superior order to mind. . . .[64]

Of course, one must wonder how Palóu, a "rational" person, a member of the
gente de razón, could see the plenty of the people and still have the arrogance
to impose his own superior economy on them.

Almost immediately on instituting the "superior order" of European agricultural technology, the missions were plunged into a cycle of famine, an experience
unprecedented in its severity for California Indian peoples.[65] The economic
effects of the reducciones become apparent in the descriptions of the famines.
Very early in the land expedition to San Diego, far to the south in Baja California,
Serra recounts in his Diary encountering missionized Indian peoples who were
suffering from what must have been the agricultural failure of the important
Mission Guadalupe. As he made his way north, Serra encountered some ten
families of Indian converts who curiously were some distance away from their
mission compound. Upon inquiry, Serra discovered that these families had been
sent out to forage for food due to famine at the mission. As Serra explains, the
missionary:

> . . . for want of provisions, had found himself obliged to send them out to the
> mountains to seek their food; and that as they were not accustomed to this, they
> were not handy at it; their hardship was much, particularly in seeing their babies
> suffer and hearing them cry.[66]

It should be noted that this was not a newly established mission, where the natives would have been in transition between their old economy and the establishment of European-style agriculture. Rather, it was an already established mission of some long standing. In other words, these hungry natives were far enough removed from their old methods of subsistence that they no longer remembered how to pursue them, having lost their original cultural affinity for self-subsistence apart from the mission. Unfortunately, Serra was not attentive to the crisis he encountered at Mission Guadalupe. Instead, he repeated the same mistakes at his own mission establishments in Alta California.

In Serra's California missions, failure was most immediately apparent in the economic failure, that is, in the famine that was quickly generated in the midst of this land of plenty. Before the missions, people had rarely traveled more than ten miles away from their village in a lifetime; the abundant food that surrounded them along the entire coast of California made longer trips unnecessary.[67] Serra himself observed that dialects changed about every ten miles, and at a distance of forty miles, people could understand one another's dialect only with difficulty because of the language shift. This extreme localism of language is also indicative of the hypersedentary nature of California coastal cultures. The marshlands, hills, and woodlands all provided a plentiful array of game and vegetation. Ranging from small animals and birds to larger animals such as deer, there was a surfeit of food for well-being.[68] Yet as soon as the missions were established, an unprecedented famine resulted almost immediately.

In late 1773, four years after the founding of San Diego mission, Palóu writes that self-supporting status had not yet been achieved. Moreover, the missions of San Diego and Monterey were so dependent on imported goods that the breakdown of shipping communications with San Blas generated a new siege of famine for all of Spanish California. When the frigate carrying supplies to California was disabled and returned to port, Palóu writes: "There it discharged its cargo of supplies, and since there were no ways or means to bring them up [to San Diego and Monterey], those lands suffered the greatest want yet experienced. For during the eight months this famine lasted, milk was the manna that fed all, beginning with the commandant and the priests down to the lowliest person."[69] Milk alone! Yet the mission had already had three full seasons to implement its European agricultural technology from planting to harvest. Again in 1776, San Diego experienced a severe famine. The failure of European technologies that led to both the San Diego famines was related to issues of political economy and not to unpredictable ecological events. For both dates, eco-historical research has demonstrated that plentiful water was available. Although 1777 was a year of severe drought for San Diego, Rowntree has shown that the five preceding years had enjoyed normal or above normal rainfall. Thus, these famines were due to production failures at the mission and its economic dependence on Mexico rather than to unfortunate weather conditions.[70]

Yet even in the midst of famine, Serra and his friars did not fare so poorly. While Serra is quick to point out that Captain Fernando "has not missed a single meal for a whole year," it should be noted that even in the midst of the most dreadful time of famine and starvation for the Indians of the mission, no priest died or even neared death by starvation. During the famine of 1776 at San Diego, Serra instituted a reform in which rations were distributed equally to priests and servants. Yet he baldly reports, "As for the Indians, the Fathers have nothing to give them. . . ."[71]

The cycle of famine that began with the missionary imposition of European-style agriculture is more than a little ironic in that these same missionaries unanimously described the abundant food available to the clearly self-sufficient native economies they found when they arrived in California. As I have shown, the evidence indicates that the native peoples of coastal California had had little experience with famine, at least the kind of famine introduced to them with the advent of missionary agricultural tutelage. The irony was compounded because, even in a time of famine, native converts were nutritionally restricted to the harvest of the missions' European-style agriculture and proscribed from their traditional agricultural economies. Before the missionaries undertook to instruct their neophytes in the virtues of "hard work," hard work was only occasionally necessary for the survival of indigenous communities. After the missions were established, hard work was not enough.

Punishing Neophytes: The Violence of Conversion

That the Franciscans and Serra used corporal punishment is hardly controvertible. A modern Franciscan apologist for Serra and the California missions admits as much and more. Francis Guest writes:

> Apparently, the missionaries had no qualms of conscience about putting an Indian in shackles for a while or giving him an eight-day term in the stocks. Spaniards spoke of themselves as *gente de razon*, people of reason, people who led a rational life. In their minds, the European way of life was immeasurably superior to the primitive existence of the Indian, which they conceived as haphazard, irresponsible, brutish, benighted, and barbaric. But the lash, the shackles, and the stocks were all a part of what the soldiers and missionaries had learned at home. These cruel forms of punishment were all a part of what it meant to be *gente de razon*, cultured and enlightened. Hence they became part of the western civilization with which the barbarous and uncultured Indian was "blessed. . . ." On the one hand, these methods of punishing recalcitrant Indians had been common throughout New Spain for over two hundred years. And the Franciscans of Spanish California, in employing these methods, were following a precedent sanctioned by long established custom and the example of thousands of missionaries. . . .[72]

It seems clear that the physical brutality that Serra reveals in his *Diary*[73] continued years later in the California mission. Serra does not question the use of punishment toward Indian people, just its degree. There can be no doubt, then, that corporal punishment, including flogging, was an ordinary part of the missionary-convert relationship—even though it was already controversial both among the Spanish authorities and naturally among the converts themselves.[74] Moreover, the saintly Fr. Serra came down decidedly on the side of violence as a necessary mission strategy, even when others were calling for gentler measures. To excuse violence and brutality as a European cultural affectation can never remove the stigma and pain from native recipients used to far gentler ways.

Already during Serra's administration of the missions, his superior, Fr. Francisco Pangua, was asking whether the discipline administered by the missionaries was unduly harsh. Thus, the punishment Serra meted out may have overstepped the limits of propriety, even in terms of his own acculturation and historical period:

> As to the question: do some ministers punish the Indian neophytes too severely? I copied out that part of Your Reverence's letter, and sent it to all the missions; and I added to it a few directions of my own. I feel confident that where there may have been too much severity, things will be put right. But, at the present time, I have no particular information in reference to this matter.[75]

Indeed, nowhere else does Serra entertain any thought as to whether punishments may have been too severe. In a letter to Governor Rivera only days earlier (October 1776), he had argued for leniency only to the extent of saying that punishment should be geared toward the conquest and assimilation of Indian people rather than toward revenge for their rebellion at San Diego. This, he argues, gives better promise for pacification of the countryside. On the other hand, Serra instructed Fr. Lasuén in 1778 that "punishment should be given to everyone who deserves it."[76] Lasuén was only too ready to agree. In the later years of his own presidency of the California missions, Lasuén made this pronouncement about those gentle natives of the region who had known so little violence and warfare before the arrival of the missionaries: "It is obvious that a barbarous, fierce, and ignorant country needs punishments and penalties that are different from one that is cultured and enlightened, and where the way of doing things is restrained and mild."[77]

Serra draws an explicit connection between the administration of corporal discipline to Indian converts by the priests and the protecting presence of the military in California.[78] He openly acknowledges that the presence of soldiers is crucial for the fathers' discipline of those natives deemed miscreants. This mission need for military support created a conflict between Serra and the governor over Serra's request for a larger contingent of soldiers to protect the priests at San Diego in the wake of the 1776 uprising there. In one exchange with the governor, Serra argues, "Everyone knows the character of these Indians," and the governor responds that the Indians should be flogged because of their character. Serra's retort is very revealing: "Troops are necessary even to carry out punishment of Indians so that there will not be reprisal." Though consistent with Serra's policy on punishment, this remark adds a further dimension to the need for safety in the administration of discipline. Moreover, in justifying a larger military contingent at the mission, Serra advocates a military presence and the use of punishment to keep the Indians under control. In a 1779 letter to Fr. Verger, Serra voices his objection to the establishment of self-government and the election of Indian alcaldes in the missions primarily because they would severely limit priestly control and discipline: "[J]ust because they carry staffs of office supplied by the King we no longer have the right to administer correction to them without consulting him [the alcalde]." This, he argues in a letter to Lasuén in August 1779, represents a "smashing up and breaking down" of the "uniform organization of all the missions."[79]

Guest argues that miscreant behavior with regard to corporal punishment by the Franciscan missionaries in California ought not to be judged too harshly in terms of modern, North American ethical standards, but should be considered in terms of eighteenth-century Spanish standards:

> Summing up, one concludes that whipping played a significant role in Spanish culture in the eighteenth and early nineteenth centuries. It was part of the domestic, social, and religious life of the people. Children were whipped at home and in the schools. Criminals were flogged in prisons. Servants were beaten by their masters. Indian house boys and ranch hands in Mexical California were whipped by their employers much as they had been by the padres at the missions. Among clergy, religious, and lay people self-flagellation was practiced by the devout for religious reasons.[80]

This sentiment misses the point. Of course, Serra and the others thought that they were acting appropriately in meting out discipline at the missions. The point is that what Europeans and the Spanish, in particular, thought appropriate was in fact brutal. Nor should the European behavior of the missionaries be excused on the ground that they lived in an age that was somehow lacking in a moral development available only to modern Europeans. California Indian tribes of the eighteenth century already possessed some such moral insight, as Guest himself allows: "It seems appropriate to recall, at this juncture, that, generally speaking, aborigines were unaccustomed to punish their children."[81] While it may be inappropriate to judge the brutality of Serra and his missionaries by late twentieth-century standards, surely it is appropriate to judge them by eighteenth-century Native American standards, since Native Americans were generally the recipients of Euroamerican violence.

It may be more to the point to press the analysis of eighteenth-century European standards. Criticizing Serra is too easy and would finally become a meaningless exercise. As Guest argues, Serra was, after all, a man of his own times, bound by those rather unsaintly limitations. Yet the legacy of the European society that produced a Serra is still a part of the American experience and demands our attention if we are to live better than those who stumbled before us. Milton Meltzer, in his analysis of Columbus, argues that the violence of the European conquest should not be surprising, given the European society of that time. He writes of a Europe that was numbed to the phenomenon of death, a society with a low life expectancy and a high infant mortality rate. Adults had a life expectancy of about thirty-five years while half of all children died before the age of one. One concomitant characteristic he describes is the prevalence of violence throughout European society: "Violence was a poison running through the bloodstream at all levels of [European] society. People were killed casually in quarrels. . . ." With a history of extensive warfare, inquisitions, crusades, and conquests, Europeans appear to have been quite comfortable with brutality, torture, cruelty, and organized violence on a massive scale by the church or regime.[82] Moreover, the pervasive history and thorough commitment of Europeans to violence as a mission strategy as well as a colonial strategy can be clearly articulated and identified.[83] The lesson to be learned from Serra's perpetuation of social structures of brutality has less to do with his saintliness or lack thereof than with our own participation in the modern social structures that are an ongoing legacy of Europe, the missionaries, and Serra's methods.

Native Responses to the Gospel: Uprisings and Desertions

One should not think that Indian people in California simply acquiesced to Spanish colonizing and missionizing efforts. To the contrary, overwhelming evidence indicates that native peoples resisted the Spanish intrusion from the beginning. The primary evidence, of course, comes invariably from colonial European personalities and not directly from Indian people. As an oral people, they lacked the resources to commit their experiences to writing. Nevertheless, they did pass down, from generation to generation, oral traditions concerning their mission experiences and resistance.[84] Even the European evidence, however, gives a relatively clear picture of native dissatisfaction and response, cataloging acts of resistance ranging from overt rebellion to less overt desertions. The problem of fugitive neophytes was so severe that the mission staffs constantly addressed it.

Armed resistance to the invasion began only a couple of months after the Portola-Serra expedition arrived at San Diego. The incident resulted in half a dozen deaths, mostly of native combatants, although one of Serra's priests was wounded.[85] The technological superiority of the Europeans with respect to warmaking overcame the immediacy of the resistance, but the Indian quest for freedom would create an ongoing problem for the mission. Violence erupted again in 1775 with a concerted attack on San Diego mission by several hundred Indians from some forty villages. While European armaments quelled the uprising, several people died, including a missionary priest, and the mission was virtually destroyed. Interestingly, although resistance came largely from the unconverted living in their home villages, the leadership appears to have been provided by two "converts" from the mission itself.[86] While the missionaries felt a sense of betrayal and accounted for it by deprecating native peoples, Fray Pedro Font, the Franciscan diarist accompanying the 1774–75 Anza expedition, hints at the reality. They were, he allows, "discontented with the subjection, as is usually the case with Indians. . . ." The European sources, both mission and military, are so implicitly committed to the naturalness of their own hegemony that none of them stops to consider the validity of native reasons for resistance. This failure to consider the native perspective, along with at least one cause for Indian resistance, is implicit in Font's naive report. Two mission converts ("apostates") who had joined the uprising were arrested and whipped by the military. The beatings were so severe that one of them died right away, Font tells us, and the other survived only in a very infirm condition:

> Father Fray Firmín undertook to cure this one, doing it with great charity and patience; but the Indian, little thankful and less attentive, finding himself now somewhat better, disappeared today, and they say that he went to his village. [87]

The most successful military resistance to Spanish occupation and spiritual conquest in California came in 1781 along the lower Colorado River. [88] The Anza expeditions in 1774 and 1775 had begun to open up an overland trail connecting the provinces of Sonora and Alta California. By 1780 the commandant general had ordered the founding of missions among Yuma peoples on the lower Colorado River to help secure the passage. Father Garces had been among the Yumas since the 1775 expedition, and when a military detachment under the leadership of Commander Fernando Rivera y Moncada arrived in June 1781, they found that two Franciscan missions had already been established. These missions, by order of the commandant general, had been established not as *reducciones* but under a new paradigm that involved mixing colonial settlers with Indian people and allowing the latter to maintain their existing villages. Palóu blames this new plan for the tragedy that befell the Europeans. Indians simply could not be trusted to a process of conversion that lacked some mode of coercion. Why, he says, left to their own devices they would not even trouble themselves to come to mass. [89]

Palóu, however, offers another, more persuasive clue as to why the Yuma peoples may have felt it necessary to protect their lands against European incursion. Namely, he acknowledges that the indigenous peoples of the area were less than happy that colonial livestock now grazed on the only fields that were fertile enough to support the seeds on which their daily sustenance depended. Then in June 1781, a month before the July 17 uprising, the Rivera expedition arrived with a sudden invasion of some thousand horses and mules. Settlers also took over, Palóu admits, the smaller, most fertile plots of land along the river valley where the native fields had been planted. In other words, Palóu describes very real reasons for decisive action on the part of the Yuma peoples. [90]

In any case, the Yuma uprising was highly successful. We are told that all four priests and nearly all the settlers, soldiers, and their families (including Rivera) were killed in the engagement. The missions and all the settlement structures were completely destroyed. Though the provincial government retaliated, Palóu tells us that "use of the pass was always barred." [91]

Less well known than these military engagements are the continuing problems that Indian discomfort with the missionary presence posed for San Diego and the other missions. Throughout the period of Serra's service and afterwards, a certain segment of the Indian population in the San Diego area remained quite recalcitrant in their opposition and resistance to the missionary pressure. Likewise, the Quechans, with considerably more success, held off Spanish incursions for a number of years. San Diego and the Colorado River missions were not alone in facing constant native discomfort with the Spanish presence, however. A close reading of the extant materials reveals that the missionaries continually feared rebellions against the missions and that they actually occurred with considerable frequency. At San Luis Obispo mission, for instance, at least three acts of arson occurred during the first ten years of the mission's existence. Palóu reports that the first of these happened in November 1776 when "a pagan set fire with a lighted fuse which he attached to an arrow and shot at the roof." Even four years after its founding, the mission's roof was still thatch, which burned readily, with "a considerable loss for the mission in housing and equipment." While Palóu is less clear that the other two fires constituted arson, such a conclusion seems warranted. One occurred during a Christmas mass, and the other, the most devastating of the three, at least aroused his suspicions, even though "no one was able to determine whether it was caused accidentally or maliciously."[92] Notable Indian resistance, in the form of military uprisings, occurred early in the mission history at San Francisco (1776 and 1793–94), Los Angeles (1785), and in the Salinas Valley (1804).[93]

Indian dissatisfaction with missionary or European hegemony had already become apparent during the initial Portola-Serra expedition to San Diego. The expedition began with a contingent of Indian converts from several Mexican missions. It is interesting to follow in Serra's *Diary* of the expedition the eventual desertion of nearly all his original Indian cohort:

> On the 18th we set out after eating, and at the time of starting two or three Indians ran away from us, that . . . remained to us from San Borja, without our knowing the reason. Thus, little by little, we go losing our companions, who are more necessary than some think, as only he who sees it from near could form a worthy conception of how they work, ill fed, and without salary.[94]

Like Serra, Fray Juan Crespi, in his diary of the continuation of the Portola expedition beyond San Diego in 1769, repeatedly catalogs Indian desertions,[95] and Font reports that the problem persisted during the second Anza expedition of 1775–76.[96] One should note the conditions of service for these Indian "companions." Serra had already discovered the benefits of slave labor. His attitude is apparent in an earlier account of a desertion involving nine Indians:

> After noon, all having eaten, nine Indians of those who accompanied us deserted us at one blow; six of them, from the Mission of San Borja, and three, from that of Santa Maria de Los Angeles. When, in the middle of the afternoon, they were missed, they were hunted for, but not even track of them could be found. . . .[97]

The problem Serra experienced with desertions during the expedition from Loreto to San Diego in 1769 also continued to surface among soldiers at the presidios.[98] Palóu reports that in 1772 many of the soldiers had a proclivity for desertion and would take up residence among the local Indian tribes "whose depraved habits they adopted." What he does not say but is implicitly the case is that the soldiers accompanying Spanish officers were invariably Indian converts or mestizos from Mexico who may have been missionized themselves at most only a generation before. When the situation in California entered crisis stages, not a few chose to desert, and most naturally chose to desert to local Indian communities.[99] Hence, both the natives of Alta California and the native converts who came north from Mexico to serve with the Spanish military regularly engaged in resistance against Spanish colonization by fleeing the missions or deserting from the military presidios.

Missions or Colonies? The New Mission Policy

In late 1772 Serra began to engage Pedro Fages, the presidio commandant at San Diego, in debate over the administration of the missions—a debate that resulted in Serra making the long trip back to Mexico City to protest Fages's administration of California and its impact on the mission endeavor. Serra had come to the abrupt realization that a shift in mission policy was in the process of taking place. Some people in the civil government wanted to move more quickly to secularize the missions, bringing them more directly under civil authority. Palóu notes that the emerging policy would not only hinder the founding of new missions but would threaten the continued prosperity of the existing missions.[100] Although this was the first major disagreement between the missionaries and the military government in California and became characteristic of that relationship, the dispute was actually part of a long-standing dispute in which Serra already participated in Mexico and even predated his arrival in the western hemisphere.[101]

The dispute can be seen as one of differing philosophies of conquest and colonization, but ultimately it was a struggle for hegemony. At the same time, the dispute itself is illustrative of the interdependent symbiosis of missionary and military, religion and politics. From the missionary perspective, the dispute involved both the missionary intent to civilize the native peoples and the question of discipline of converts. From the Spanish government's perspective, the issue was primarily economic. Namely, it concerned the potential revenue enhancement that would accrue to the royal treasury from the secularization of the missions. By closing the *reducciones* and intermingling the converts with new Spanish colonists or thoroughly hispanicized colonists from Mexico, production could be enhanced and the state treasury's revenues increased. The argument was regularly advanced that the Indians would also benefit from this arrangement because they would have Spanish role models who would facilitate the civilizing process. From the government's point of view, the sooner self-government could be reintroduced to Indian communities (albeit, self-government now with Spanish structures and institutions rather the traditional forms of Indian self-governance), the quicker new tributary communities would emerge.

For the missionaries, such an impending change meant much more than total loss of control over the mission communities. Secularization meant that a religious order, such as the Franciscans, would be replaced with "secular" diocesan clergy, and missionary hegemony would give way to the appointment of a diocesan bishop. Moreover, the closed community of Indian converts would be replaced by the much less controlled environment of a colonial settlement where Indian people would mix with colonial settlers.

Serra and other Franciscan missionaries in northern Mexico argued first that this plan would limit the civilizing process because it would expose converts to the worst vices and corrupting influences of Spanish society.[102] Moreover, they contended, strict discipline and missionary governance were necessary in teaching eventual European forms of self-governance. Against Serra and the religious orders, government personalities argued that the missionizing process would be enhanced by secularization. The establishment of Spanish-style pueblos would mix the native population with Spanish colonial settlers who would provide the natives with positive role models for civilized (i.e., European) existence. While economic motivations (reduced costs and increased revenue) were undoubtedly barely concealed in this argument, the needs of Serra and the other religious missionaries for authoritarian control were also patently obvious. For both sides, the bottom line was how most effectively to pacify the Indians. The immediate objective of civil government was conquest: political control and economic exploitation. Implicitly, this was also the missionaries' goal, although their explicit objection was the effective and efficient conversion of the native peoples to Christianity.

With the jurisdictional reassignment of California to Sonora under Commandant General Teodoro de Croix in 1778, and especially with the death of Viceroy Bucareli in 1779,[103] the threat of such a shift in mission policy became a looming reality for Serra and his missionaries. Almost immediately upon his appointment as commandant general of the interior provinces, Croix began to implement a change in the settlement strategy that called for colonization of California. Rather than concentrating on conversion and missionizing of the natives, the new plan hoped to bring settlers up from Mexico and to create towns (pueblos) where Spaniards, mestizos from Mexico, and indigenous California natives would mix. Serra responded by arguing for more time and more missionaries:

> Let these pueblos be established, well and good, if the authorities approve of the plan; and let the missions disappear. But I want it to be known that my final position is the same as I started with. . . .
>
> Missions, my Lord, missions—that is what this country needs. They will not only provide it with what is most important—the light of the Holy Gospel—but also will be the means of supplying foodstuffs for themselves and for the Royal Presidios. They will accomplish this far more efficiently than these pueblos without priests. . . .
>
> Later on, when the gentiles that are spread throughout all these lands have become Christian, and when they are settled in their various reservations or missions, in open territories or Crown lands—which will remain unsettled—and there will be much of it and of excellent quality—I assure you that then will be the proper time for introducing towns of Spaniards.[104]

Of course, Serra did not object in principle to European occupation of Indian land, in its proper time. His objection was to the disruption of his missions.

For Croix's new strategy to succeed, the autocratic control that the missionaries had exercised over their mission communities had to be broken. This attempt was bound to generate a vociferous objection from Serra and his missionaries, who saw their governance as indispensable to the success of the effort to civilize the natives. As a first step, in late 1778 the military government of California began to insist that Indians were capable of self-government and called for elections of an alcalde or mayor in each of the mission communities. Governor Felipe de Neve ordered Fr. Lasuén to prepare for an election at San Diego mission to name an alcalde. Serra, speaking for the missionaries, objected that the missions did not constitute a pueblo and that the Indians were not yet competent to govern themselves even minimally. Interestingly enough, Serra finally conceded but instructed Lasuén to appoint someone already placed in a position of some authority by the missionaries, rather than to allow an election:

> And so the program I have outlined is this: whatever the gentleman wishes to be done should be done, but in such wise that it should not cause the least change among the Indians or disturb the routine Your Reverences have established.
> Let Francisco, with the same staff of office he uses and his coat, be the first alcalde. All we have to do is to change the name.[105]

As this debate over the election of alcaldes demonstrates, Serra had only minimal respect for the intellectual abilities of native peoples.[106] In early 1780 in a letter to Neve filled with pathos and self-revelation, Serra articulated his objections to the new plan with full force. Again he argued that Indian people were not competent to manage their own affairs. He attributed this deficiency in part to the limitations of Indian intelligence and in part to their continuing cultural attachment to their old ways of life. His neophyte converts were described as "simple and ignorant people" who could not be trusted. Under the state's proposal for self-governing pueblos, the missionaries would be left with only spiritual duties. The Indian officials of the pueblos would be accountable not to the priests but to the regional state authorities. If the priests' authority to punish transgressors and even flog them when necessary were removed, argued Serra, the civilizing process would grind to a halt. Serra reminded Neve of the compromise established in the Sierra Gorda. There converts were allowed to elect their own governing officials, but, in turn, these officials were accountable to the priests of the mission:

> And in the matter of correcting the Indians, although we allowed them the distinction and title of being governors, alcaldes and fiscales, nevertheless, when it appeared to us that punishment was deserved, they were flogged, or put into the stocks, according to the gravity of their offense. In consequence, they took particular pains to carry out their respective duties.[107]

Canonization, Triumphalism, and the Strategies of Genocide

The building blocks for the Franciscan mission system in California included a variety of explicit and implicit principles that contributed to the missionaries' complicity in the cultural genocide of native peoples. The symbiotic relationship between the California mission system and Spanish political structures was fundamental to the strategy of both church and state for evangelization and conquest. In the abstract, this symbiotic relationship would benefit both sectors of Spain. The Spanish military intimidated California natives so that the missionaries could engage in their work with some security. At the same time, the missionary presence functioned to pacify native peoples, thus allowing more effective Spanish occupation and colonization of indigenous territory.

This strategy was not without its problems. The missionaries were direct employees of the Spanish government and, as such, were required to pay some homage to that political entity. On the other hand, the missionaries adeptly used their influence within state structures to secure their own political authority over and control of the mission and its converts. Franciscan control of the mission community could be ephemeral, however, given their dependence on the military for both security and mission discipline. Control remained an issue when the missionaries found themselves in controversy with one level of government or another, as Serra frequently did.

That Serra arrived in California as part of a military expedition and that soldiers were stationed near each of the missions are indications of the degree to which the missions depended on the military. In keeping with this dependence came the symbolic use of the military as a means of intimidation. Not only were weapons fired as part of the mass, but the military was employed in punishing, restraining, and incarcerating converts and especially in recapturing converts who had recanted their conversion and attempted to return to their native villages and families. Serra himself told a governor that without a nearby military presence punishing converts would become problematic for the missionaries.[108] This set of political and civil strategies culminated in the establishment of authoritarian rule by the friars themselves in each *reduccion*.

The symbiotic relationship between the Spanish military and the Franciscan missionaries was only one component of the overall strategy for evangelization and colonization. Economic strategies were also integral to the success of the Spanish effort. This economic offensive against Indian people began with the appropriation of native resources, in particular, the seizure of the best native farmlands and water sources for mission sites. Serra appropriated or considered appropriating sites with the best water supply and the richest natural resources with no regard to native occupation or farming. These become the sites for his missions and the locus of their objective to see the native "reduced to the bosom of the Church."[109] Economic aspects of cultural genocide became most pronounced in the explicit imposition of European economic modes of production, especially methods of agriculture, and the explicitly induced dependence on European trade goods and technology.[110]

Social strategies built firmly on the notion of civilizing (that is, Europeanizing or hispanicizing) savages. These strategies depended upon a social theory that stratified the world between superior Europeans and inferior Indian pagans. Thus, social strategies for the missions included the destruction of native culture, value systems, social and political structures, economic arrangements, divisions of labor, religious ceremonies, languages, marriage customs, child rearing methods, and family structures and relationships, indeed, the whole way of life of a people. As Robert Williams has so ably argued, the conquest, both religious and civil, had to be complete. To secure the conquest, all culturally divergent native peoples had to be either brought into compliance with Christian (that is, European) values or exterminated.[111]

The religious aspects of the cultural genocide perpetrated by Serra and the Spanish Franciscans in California were due more to lack of perception on their part than to an overt attempt to destroy Indian religious ceremonial existence.[112] From their first entry into California, the Franciscans apparently believed that the native peoples had little in the way of religious attachment at all. Already in Baja California, Serra met native peoples who attempted to greet him cordially and in a sacred way, but the deep spirituality of their greeting seems to have totally escaped him. He remarks frequently in his *Diary* on their use of the pipe and their gifts of food, but was apparently unaware that these were spiritual acts.[113]

It is at the social level, however, that Serra and the Franciscans were most complicit in acts that proved to be genocidal to Indian peoples. They came to California with nearly three hundred years of preconceived notions about the wrongness of Indian cultures and their social structures.[114] As a result, the Franciscans were most explicit and energetic in their attempts to change every aspect of tribal existence that they found wanting, in the smallness of their European minds, by comparison with the Christian culture and social structures of Spain. The gospel of God's liberating act in Christ Jesus came to California with its own price tag of vicious bondage. To paraphrase a strange scriptural reversal: Once they had been a people, but now they were to be a people no longer; they who had been free were now to live in captivity. Thus was born the mission system in California, a system of mission compounds that, in the final analysis, was a direct descendant of sixteenth-century Spanish mission strategies and bore a familial resemblance to the praying towns developed a century earlier by John Eliot in Protestant New England.

If I am right in my assessment of Serra, the intentions of the church in canonizing him are neither as honest nor as genuine as Serra himself, but are politically and theologically self-serving. His canonization would be first of all a glorification of Christian (in this case Roman Catholic) triumphalism, a celebration of dysfunctionality. As such, it represents a not too subtle attempt to exonerate the church's history of shame as a full partner in the conquest and destruction of the native inhabitants of the Americas. At another level, the canonization process also functions as a self-validation of Western culture and its political-economic structures of oppression, rooted in its history of colonialism and even genocide. That the social structures of the West still oppress countless peoples in the world today (politically, economically, and so forth) makes those who would canonize Serra fully complicit as modern partners in defending and extending the hegemony of the West. When political and economic truth claims wear thin, religious truth claims can be counted on to obfuscate historical realities and provide strength of conviction. Yet, finally, the canonization of Serra will become the canonization of genocide in California, of Europe's military victory in the Americas, and of the global conquest of capitalism.[115]

Much of the debate over the canonization has to do with ascertaining the extent of Serra's involvement in the corporal punishment of neophytes under his charge. The technical aspects of canonization are concerned less with Serra's missionary legacy or the "good" intentions we might freely ascribe to him than with an assessment of his saintly virtues and the extent to which they were evidenced in his life.[116] Maynard J. Geiger's commentary includes this explanation of saintly virtue:

> The virtues of a candidate for sainthood must be supernatural virtues, not merely natural ones. By supernatural virtues are meant those rooted in a supernatural principle and exercised for a supernatural motive. Thus, if Serra came to California to extend the kingdom of God, to save souls, to promote God's glory, and if in carrying out this activity he was motivated by this end, he was working on a supernatural plane. If he possessed sanctifying grace at the same time, his virtuous actions were rooted in a supernatural principle. If on the other hand, Serra came to California merely to extend the imperial sway of Spain, he would have been exercising a natural virtue of patriotism. If in his labors he exercised charitable acts towards the natives, fed and clothed them out of mere natural pity, or to satisfy his natural inclination to do good, to be philanthropic without reference to his own or the spiritual destiny of his beneficiaries, he would have been exercising merely natural virtue. . . . Catholic theology teaches that both the supernatural principle and the motive are necessary for the Christian to attain heaven. For a candidate for sainthood, they are necessary in an heroic degree.[117]

Obviously, extensive participation in corporal punishment would impede the counting of Serra's virtues. The debate continues because it cannot be shown that he actually administered such punishment, even though he clearly prescribed it and even defended it. As the opening quotation amply demonstrates, violence was a natural and significant part of Serra's mission strategy from the very beginning of his California venture. This question may not be the only or even the most significant issue in evaluating Serra's virtues and determining whether they achieved "heroic" stature, however. More important may be the acknowledgment that corporal punishment is finally a minimal issue compared to the larger systemic devastation suffered by Indian peoples as a result of Serra's own inculturation to the political and social structures of colonial Spain.

Whatever Serra's supernatural virtues of motivation and the evangelizing principles they may have been rooted in, it can be demonstrated that he and the others who built the California mission system participated explicitly in the political and economic conquest of native peoples in California and, as such, were complicit in the cultural genocide of those peoples. Indeed, Serra's failure to achieve the best of his intentions may be rooted not just in his individual lack of virtue, but in the sociopolitical structures of oppression in which he naively participated and which empowered his mission activity. In any case there appears to be sufficient lack of virtue all around to disqualify any heroizing of this missionary. Moreover, in the final analysis, the missions of California were failures at all levels except one—they succeeded only in helping to establish Euroamerican hegemony over the land and the peoples who inhabited it.

California Indian scholar Jack Norton (Hupa-Cherokee) sums up what is at stake in remembering the Serra legacy—without discounting the possibility of good intentions on the part of Serra or his colleagues:

> It is logical, then, that tribal peoples throughout the state of California are expressing outrage at the proposed canonization of Junípero Serra. He formulated and implemented a system that demeaned and lessened the human spirit. To make this man a saint would make the living complicit in his crimes against humanity.[118]

CHAPTER 4

Pierre-Jean De Smet
Manifest Destiny and Economic Exploitation

But what appeared to interest them more than aught else, was prayer (religion); to this subject they listened with the strictest, undivided attention. They told me that they had already heard of it, and they knew that this prayer made men good and wise on earth, and insured their happiness in the future life. They begged me to permit the whole camp to assemble, that they might hear for themselves the words of the Great Spirit, of whom they had been told such wonders. Immediately three United States flags were erected on the field, in the midst of camp, and three thousand savages, including the sick, who were carried in skins, gathered around me. I knelt beneath the banner of our country, my ten Flat Head neophytes by my side, and surrounded by this multitude, eager to hear the glad tidings of the gospel of peace. We began by intoning two canticles, after which I recited all the prayers, which we interpreted to them: then again we sang canticles, and I finished by explaining to them the Apostles' Creed and the Ten Commandments. They all appeared to be filled with joy, and declared it was the happiest day of their lives.

—Pierre-Jean De Smet[1]

The 1972 Ye Galleon Press reprint of Pierre-Jean De Smet's *Origin, Progress, and Prospects of the Catholic Mission to the Rocky Mountains* includes an afterword that calls the author "the most famous missionary to the western Indians."[2] The preface to the 1978 reprint of *Oregon Missions* only somewhat more modestly ranks De Smet as the equal of Junípero Serra, the Franciscan in California, and Eusebio Kino, the Jesuit in Arizona.[3] Whatever our final analysis here, biographies of De Smet clearly tend toward the hagiographic, from the pious romanticism of Helene Magaret[4] to the more scholarly treatment with lavish footnotes by fellow Jesuit E. Laveille.[5] Even the non-Catholics H. M. Chittenden and A. T. Richardson, in the 150-page introduction to their four-volume collection of De Smet's letters and writings, display a romantic attachment to their subject and his exploits.[6] Interestingly enough, the Jesuit historian of the American Jesuits, Gilbert J. Garraghan, SJ, has written the most critical interpretation of De Smet's work.[7]

Yet the De Smet story and his resulting fame are curiosities that call for considerable analysis beyond that provided in the standard hagiographies. First of all, the actual time he spent with Indian people in Indian country was extremely short. Second, the missions he was directly responsible for initiating were actually failures, collapsing within three and ten years of start-up, respectively. Any critical explanation of De Smet's enduring and endearing fame must somehow account for these anomalies, just as an analysis of Lt. Col. George A. Custer's fame must account for the embarrassment of his death—namely, his inexplicable stupidity in attacking a superior force at the Greasy Grass (Little Big Horn).

The words of De Smet quoted at the beginning of this chapter immediately raise two different issues about the historical interpretation of his work. First, the quotation either reveals a profound missionary naïveté that wholly misread the response of these Indian people, misinterpreting both their actions and their words, or it exposes a callous falsification of reality for the sake of missionary propaganda and fund-raising among supporters. Second, it immediately reveals this Flemish immigrant was a patriot who clearly identified his gospel message with his patriotism. It should come as no surprise that De Smet was an outspoken exponent of the doctrine of Manifest Destiny who devoted as much of his bountiful energies to realizing the American conquest of the West as to converting native peoples. It is often difficult to determine whether conquest or conversion provided him with the greater impetus for mission. Indeed, the latter goal appears to serve the former in ways that belie a distinction between them.

Flemish Immigrant

De Smet was undoubtedly a man of tremendous energies and sincere dedication. Furthermore, he was a man of no small intellectual ability. Though he was never a top student, he was more than capable academically and was instrumental in the founding of St. Louis University in 1827 (formally chartered in 1832).[8] His subsequent appointment as director of the departments of languages, history, and philosophy[9] is somewhat ironic in light of his difficulty in learning Indian languages, an accomplishment for which Jesuit missionaries are customarily still respected today.

De Smet was a prolific writer and published several books about Indian missions with which he was involved. For the most part, these books are collections of letters. Many of the letters are long, running to several printed pages of narrative, and many were actually written for publication as separate pieces in such contemporary periodicals as Home Journal and Précis Historiques. Even his personal letters were often meant for publication, however. He regularly made copies of his correspondence, retaining the copies for later editing and publishing.[10] Among his talents he was an amateur naturalist and collected samples of flora and minerals wherever he traveled. He sent these back to St. Louis University, to financial supporters in Europe, and to his family.

Born in 1801 into a well-to-do merchant family in Termonde, Belgium, he stole away from his family in 1821 and, along with five other young men, followed a Jesuit recruiter to the mission fields of North America. By 1823 these novices were sent west from the novitiate in Maryland to open a new Jesuit establishment, including a novitiate, in the growing frontier city of St. Louis. Interestingly, it was the U.S. secretary of war, John C. Calhoun, who was instrumental in facilitating the Jesuit expansion to St. Louis in 1823, arranging for a tract of land and an annual government subsidy of $800 to run an Indian school. Thus, the collusion between church and state to "establish" a religion among Indian peoples,[11] namely, Christianity, is apparent from the early beginnings of the history of the United States.[12]

Numbering six novices and two priests and lay brothers, the Jesuits literally built the mission from the ground up. With their energies focused on setting up the St. Louis establishment, they could give little attention to Indian missions except for a small Indian boarding school run on the premises under a contract with the federal government. Not until 1838 was De Smet able to engage in full-time Indian mission work. His assignment came after he had returned to Europe for several years for health reasons (1833–37). He made eight additional round trips to Europe, each time touring to secure support and resources for the university and especially for the missions under the direction of the St. Louis province. Each journey, of course, took a minimum of several months. Together, they eloquently attest to his energies and commitment.

Mission to the Potawatomis

De Smet's first assignment to direct Indian mission work came almost immediately upon his return from Belgium. Rome and the Catholic bishops of the United States had finally agreed that Indian missions in North America would be the responsibility of the Jesuits. De Smet and three others were to start a new mission among the Potawatomis, some five hundred miles up the Missouri River from St. Louis at what is today Council Bluffs, Iowa. At the age of thirty-seven, he was to get his first real immersion into the Indian world. Yet, less than eighteen months after his arrival, De Smet returned to St. Louis to ask for reassignment, volunteering for service to the Flathead Indians further west.[13] His stay among the Potawatomis had been a time of some frustration as the realities of Indian mission work became apparent.[14] Told that the Potawatomis were ready for their mission effort, De Smet and his missionary companions found themselves ignored by about two thousand Indians who had gathered to greet the steamboat.[15] As De Smet's written reflections on the occasion make clear, the Potawatomis, far from expecting the missionaries, had been awaiting the arrival of the traders and several dozen barrels of whiskey. Later De Smet recalled, ". . . for since the arrival of the steamboat, which brought a large quantity of liquor, they are quarreling and fighting from morning till night."[16] Not only did the missionaries have to deal with the incursion of Euroamerican vices into the depressed community of a conquered and displaced people,[17] but the Potawatomi life-style did not easily facilitate conversion. The various bands preferred to live apart from one another in smaller camps, which meant the mission staff had to spend a great deal of time on horseback. De Smet wrote at one point that the missionaries tried to visit all the camps within a twenty-five-mile radius each week.[18] Since De Smet was dependent on a translator, one can only wonder what level of communication took place during these visits.

Considered in retrospect, De Smet's departure from the Potawatomi mission in the fall of 1839 was preemptive.[19] Although he wrote positive letters, recounting accomplishments, conversions, baptisms, and the like, the mission clearly never really took among these people. In any event, the mission did not survive more than three years. De Smet himself found the mission in a troubled condition when he passed through in the fall of 1840, and in August 1841 the mission closed its doors.[20]

While Jesuit mission attitudes can surely be faulted for the failure at Council Bluffs, a number of other factors also played major roles. Most importantly, the Potawatomis had been in Council Bluffs only a year, having been relocated by the government from their original homelands in Michigan, Wisconsin, and Illinois.[21] Unable to provide for themselves during the move, impoverished as a result of the relocation, and intimidated by the other tribes who were the natural inhabitants of the new territory, the Potawatomis were in a desperate state of dislocation and demoralization when De Smet arrived. Given the state of their cultural dissolution, it should not be surprising that many Potawatomis turned to alcohol, or that they were more or less unresponsive to Jesuit ministrations. A relatively more successful Jesuit mission among the Potawatomis was begun anew in September 1848, after two bands of the tribe had been moved to a new reservation in Kansas; however, De Smet was not directly involved. Interestingly, the Council Bluffs band resisted evangelization by the later missionary outreach while the Osage River band succumbed to the Christianizing/ civilizing process with devastating effects.[22] By 1938 only the Council Bluffs band was still in existence. The Osage River band had given in to anglicizing pressures, including the allotment of their land to individual private ownership. From private ownership, their lands passed irrevocably into white hands, usually by unscrupulous means.[23] By 1877 even this mission was forced to close, and, as Garraghan reports, "the Jesuit attempt, lasting through four decades, to christianize and civilize the Potawatomi of Kansas passed into history."[24]

The Flathead Mission

The Jesuit mission to the Flatheads was in response to a direct request from the Indians, who had been influenced by Iroquois trappers who had been converted by French Catholic missionaries in the Northeast. Over a period of several years, four separate delegations had been sent to St. Louis. Thus, when De Smet descended into Pierre's Hole in mid-July 1840, his reception by some fifteen hundred people was far different from his reception among the Potawatomis two years earlier. Caught up in genuine religious fervor fueled by years of expectation, the Flatheads greeted De Smet most enthusiastically. It is crucial to note that their warm reception was not for De Smet *qua* De Smet but for De Smet as religious functionary. The assembled people were highly expectant and excited by the prospect of new spiritual teaching. If they were to learn to love and respect him as a person, that would have to come later. That De Smet, in turn, was excited by the prospect of a vital mission among the Flatheads, there can be no doubt. But I would argue that he completely misunderstood the religious fervor of these people. He and the Flathead people had quite different expectations of the missionizing process. This difference was to be the undoing of the mission ten years later.

The 1840 journey to the Flatheads was an exploratory one. De Smet spent only about ten weeks with them that summer before returning to St. Louis to report his success and the potential for the mission. His arrival at Fort Hall with a mission staff and the necessary supplies the following August (1841) marked the real beginning of the mission. On July 31 of the next year (1842), De Smet left again for St. Louis. His departure marks the end of his direct service to this mission. In the final analysis, De Smet actually spent less time in direct mission service with the Flatheads than with the Potawatomis. Counting most liberally, his pastorate among the Flatheads lasted a mere eleven and a half months (from his arrival at Fort Hall on August 16, 1841, to his departure for St. Louis on July 31, 1842). Even then, he spent six weeks on a journey to Fort Colville to fetch provisions for the mission.

De Smet returned to the Northwest for two years in 1844, but not as a direct service missionary. In between he engaged in fund-raising expeditions to New Orleans, the east, and Europe (1843). After an eight-month voyage, he arrived by ship at Fort Vancouver. By this time five missions had been established in the region, and De Smet fell into the task of administration, spending much of his two-year stay traveling among them. During these two years, some nine months were spent on pure exploration. Although this exploratory journey was undertaken under the guise of a mission to persuade the Blackfeet to make peace with the other mountain tribes, De Smet spent very little time in contact with any Indian people at all.[25] By his own count, he encountered only thirteen Blackfeet during this long and arduous winter trip.[26] Upon his return to the Columbia River, the mission ascertained that funds and supplies were dangerously low. De Smet was dispatched again to the east to engage in fund-raising and recruitment. At this time the Society relieved him of his position with the Northwest missions.[27]

De Smet visited the region again in 1858–59, but his 1846 departure effectively marked the end of his missionary career with Indian people. Later in his life, he was to make seven more excursions into the Indian country of the northern plains, either on behalf of the St. Louis province or as an emissary of the U.S. government. His total direct service as a missionary, however, amounted to less than thirty months, including travel time away from the mission station. And if his service as an administrator in the Northwest is factored in, a most liberal counting still gives less than five years among Indian peoples. This is precious little time to have become so famous a missionary.

Cultural Imposition and the Failure of the Flathead Mission

More significant than his all-too-brief immersion into specific Indian communities is the failure of the missions that De Smet himself initiated. Moreover, in terms of De Smet's own assessment of the potential, the failure of the Flathead mission is even more striking than that of the Potawatomis. The Flatheads had spent ten patient years trying to secure the services of a Catholic missionary and had greeted De Smet's arrival with an abundance of religious fervor. Yet less than ten years after De Smet's first contact with the tribe, the mission closed down for lack of Flathead participation,[28] or as Fr. Nicholas Congiato wrote to Father General Peter Beckx, "From lack of zeal and love of the Indians and of tact on the part of Ours resulted the fall of the famous mission of the Flatheads."[29] The historians and biographers generally blame the failures on resistance from within the Jesuit order itself; that is, from De Smet's superiors or perhaps his own colleagues in the field. Alternatively, they blame external circumstances beyond De Smet's control, not recognizing that he participated in the very structures of power that created those external circumstances.[30] De Smet likewise suffered from a tendency to blame external circumstances for any failure of the missionaries. Nowhere does he directly blame either the U.S. government or the trading companies for the missions' failure, although he does in a most general and sweeping way blame the immigrant incursion with "all the vices of the worst of European society."[31] To the contrary, as we shall see below, he quite handily absolves both the government[32] and the trading companies[33] from any responsibility for the devastation of Indian tribes. Even supposing that he might have been at least vaguely aware of his own complicity in conquering the west, De Smet never openly acknowledges it. Perhaps it would be more accurate to suggest that De Smet did not see the conquest of the west as wrong or as an injustice to Indian people. As a missionary, he devoted himself to bringing European culture and values to Indian people, certainly an aspect of conquering the west. The introduction of European vices was not part of the plan.

Laveille accounts for the failure of the mission by citing a sudden decline in morality among the Flatheads, which he attributes to the negative influence of an influx of new Euroamerican settlers. Hunters and trappers took to wintering near the Flatheads and finally led them astray by debaucherous example:

> From being docile and devoted to the Black Robes they gradually drew away from their benefactors, and forswore the promises made in baptism. Their passion for play was awakened, and whiskey brought by the white man began its ravages.[34]

He also notes, but brushes aside, the internal Jesuit criticism of De Smet for exaggerating the potential for the missions in order to recruit new staff and for having instilled too little discipline among the Flathead people. Perhaps even more to the point is Laveille's brief mention of a letter from the father general in Rome, who feared "that Father De Smet had been too optimistic and had entertained projects too vast."[35] There is some hint that De Smet's grandiose vision of a Paraguayan system of reductions in the American Northwest had become threatening to the Jesuit hierarchy and perhaps even threatening to the Roman Catholic presence in the United States.[36] The memory of the lack of political viability of Jesuit expansion only three-quarters of a century earlier must still have been very much alive.

All of these factors may account for the decision to close the mission, but they do not account for its failure. Indeed, the true reason for the mission's failure was surely unrecognized by De Smet, his superiors in St. Louis or Rome, or any of his missionary colleagues in the Northwest. More was involved in the failure of the Potawatomi and especially the Flathead missions than either the unending onslaught of the European immigrant invasion moving steadily westward from the east and now even inward from the west coast; or the Flatheads' exposure to the worst of Euroamerican vices, which are said to have contaminated them beyond redemption. Even these events are not entirely external when one evaluates the missionary's social and political participation in those processes. In retrospect it becomes evident that De Smet's commitment to Euroamerican culture and its economic and political structures doomed his mission to failure. He undoubtedly thought he was manipulating those power structures, with the help of divine guidance, to establish and strengthen the missions. But, quite contrary to his expectations and with his unwitting and unknowing complicity, those same structures became a major source of the missions' undoing. The failure was also due to another problem, however, one that De Smet's hagiographers have preferred to ignore and De Smet himself never even began to see. Namely, De Smet and his missionary companions simply did a terrible job. He was consistently and inevitably insensitive to Indian cultural realities, just as Eliot and Serra were before him.

Even while criticizing the Jesuit missionaries, one must acknowledge that they had little chance of doing a "good" job. De Smet certainly tried, and many have actually praised his sensitivity to his converts, but any Euroamerican's understanding of or appreciation for Indian cultures was subject to severe cultural limitations. Many of the inadequacies I will identify are of the kind that the missionaries could not and did not avoid. If anything, these inadequacies are especially glaring in De Smet's case, in part, because he wrote so extensively about his missionary career. Not only did the Europeans and then Euroamericans lack the analytical tools and skills to understand any culture that was radically different from their own, but their inherent sense of the natural superiority of their own culture functioned to preclude understanding of any other. In spite of De Smet's implicit claim to understanding, he consistently misunderstood and misinterpreted Indian culture and Indian responses. As I noted in chapter 1, De Smet actually seems to have invented Indian responses or at least invented an English translation of some Indian articulation.[37] An intimation of what was to come is already apparent in a report De Smet wrote to the father general only some seven weeks (July 20, 1838) after arriving among the Potawatomis. In his list of "great obstacles to be overcome in converting an Indian nation," he includes a critique of "their inclination to a wandering life." According to De Smet, this inclination was so strong that "they become melancholy and morose if they stay three months in the same place."[38] Despite this firm statement, De Smet's only experience of Indian people to this point was of a more sedentary, woodlands tribe, not a plains tribe on horseback. Moreover, the Potawatomis could not have been nomadic at this time even if they had wanted to be. The

U.S. government had moved them from their original homelands east of the Mississippi and settled them in the confined area of Council Bluffs.

In the final analysis, the extent to which De Smet did or did not understand Indian peoples does not matter, since he and his colleagues moved quickly and decisively in their missions to impose European cultural values, and did so in a rigid and legalistic way. Like generations of missionaries before him over 250 years, De Smet argued from the beginning of his missionary career that cultural change was the only appropriate way to ensure real conversion to the gospel of Jesus Christ. In other words, he saw the replacement of purported inadequacies of Indian traditional culture with the gospel-nurturing social structures and cultural values of European Christian civilization as the necessary prolegomena to faith in Jesus Christ. Cultural change as the foundation of De Smet's philosophy of mission is apparent in his reflection on the Flathead mission:

> It would be impossible to do any solid and permanent good among these poor people, if they continue to roam about from place to place, to seek their daily subsistence. They must be assembled in villages—must be taught the art of agriculture, consequently must be supplied with implements, with cattle, with seed.[39]

Clearly, for De Smet, to become Christian meant to adopt the Euroamerican way of life. He gave little consideration either to the disruptive effects of such a sudden cultural shift or to the alienation it would generate.[40]

For instance, the imposition of European marriage customs may have done the most to alienate the Flatheads, although they tried valiantly at first to comply with the new discipline imposed by the Jesuits.[41] Two things were clear to De Smet, the first of which had been equally clear to Serra. Both missionaries saw Indian polygamy as a signification of untoward evil, the dominance of sin in Indian societies.[42] De Smet went one step further in proclaiming by fiat— although it was theologically consistent with Catholic doctrine—that Indian marriages were not proper marriages to begin with. On the ground that they were no more than pagan couplings outside the church, he declared all Indian marriages among the Flathead invalid.[43] Serra had accorded at least some validity to native mating practices and had required that converted males maintain their first marriage and have them sanctified.[44] Flathead men in the Northwest and Osage men in Kansas and Oklahoma who had more than one wife were forced to choose among their wives, keeping one and sending one or more away.

This imposition of the cultural value of monogamy, a seemingly straightforward Christian value indoctrination, introduced severe cultural dislocation at a number of levels that De Smet, like Serra before him, could not have foreseen. Having little appreciation for native culture and values, he could not have seen that the integrity of the tribe's economic system was wholly dependent on the attachment of each person to a large, interconnected, integral interdependent family unit. Nor did he seem to notice that the women considerably outnumbered the men. Even as late as the turn of this century, tribal roles show that this was still the case among the Osages, for instance. The rigors of hunting, to say nothing of the devastation of the new style of warfare that came with the European invasion, certainly took their toll on the male population of every Indian nation. John D. Hunter, a white captive among the Osages in the 1700s, told of the severity of life for Osage men. He also noted that in times of scarcity the men would restrict their food consumption to ensure food would be available for the women and children.[45] Another less explicable factor was also at work among the Osages and perhaps among other tribes as well. From the early reservation period, Osage agency birth statistics reveal a consistent imbalance in the birth rates of males and females, with nearly twice as many females as males being born between 1847 and 1890.[46] Whatever the reason for the im-balance, polygamy in this context served a useful social function, one that De Smet never considered. In a culture where women outnumbered men and where a woman's livelihood depended on close interdependent participation in a family unit, polygamy became a way to ensure that everyone's needs were met. To break up these marriages in the interests of imposing European moral standards was to engage in another, more serious kind of immorality. Some women, indeed a significant number, were no longer cared for because they no longer had a husband on the hunt to provide dietary protein and skins, sinew, and bone, the raw materials for women's manufacturing. More significantly, they suffered the disgrace of being put out of their husband's lodge with no recourse except to return to their mother's lodge with few prospects for remarriage. Children likewise had fathers one day and became bastards the next. In societies that had never had any illegitimate children, suddenly this derogatory category was imposed on a tribe.[47]

The social and cultural dislocation introduced by this singular shift in moral values necessarily resulted in an overall shift in economic structures as well. The Jesuits imposed their marriage values on the Flatheads with little attention to the resulting impact on the infrastructure of Indian society.[48] The missionaries seem to have believed that a culture could be transformed by replacing some of the building blocks one at a time. Instead of transformation, the missionaries were most often faced with collapse, because they failed to realize that the block they had removed for exchange provided the foundation for much of a tribe's life. The collapse that invariably followed proved very frustrating and demor-alizing to the missionaries at times. The higher their expectations for a tribe, the harder it was to explain the failure. Since, in their view, the failure could always be attributed to Indian insufficiencies and inabilities, the missionaries never entertained the notion that the failures might indeed be their own.

In light of the failure of the Flathead mission, it is clear that De Smet misjudged the vitality of Indian cultures and the coherency and integrity of the whole of a culture's value system. As early as 1846, in the mission's fifth year, the Flatheads suddenly began to withdraw from the mission and abandon their new Christian commitment in favor of their traditional tribal values and economies. The missionaries evidently experienced a recovery of sorts in 1848 and 1849, but a further lapse by the Flatheads in 1850, accompanied by what the missionaries perceived as the threat of a Blackfeet attack on the now unprotected mission, finally resulted in the closing of the mission.

The sudden withdrawal of the Flatheads is explained in different ways even by those who were associated with the mission at the time.[49] Curiously, all of these explanations have some validity, although sometimes unintentionally, and must be considered in combination with another, more fundamental explanation. One explanation centered on De Smet—Fr. Ravalli's criticism of him was heard as far away as Rome. Ravalli initially suggested that De Smet had "promised" the tribe too much.[50] On further reflection Ravalli raised the possibility, voiced also by Palladino and Laveille,[51] that intruding white trappers had debauched the Flatheads and led them astray. Mengarini, on the other hand, suggested that the war casualties suffered by the Flatheads, including Christian Flatheads, had left them disillusioned with the power of Christianity.[52] De Smet himself suggested that the Blackfeet initially understood Christianity as a source of war medicine.[53] Although De Smet's interpretation of the Blackfeet response is clearly nuanced by his own Europeanness, his comments indicate that the Blackfeet's initial understanding of Christianity quite naturally put Christianity and its trappings into their own Blackfeet frame of reference. It is highly unlikely that the Flatheads would have been unsusceptible to this sort of interpretation.[54]

Claude Schaeffer, in a most insightful early essay that shows a quite profound understanding of Flathead people in particular and Indian people in general, has argued that cross-cultural miscommunication rooted in a decisive difference in expectations finally led to the Flathead disenchantment.[55] The Jesuit imposition of cultural transformation, on marriage and family customs, for example, led to a "thin veneer of white culture,"[56] which the Jesuits read at the surface level as a positive success, but which in the final analysis was easily and suddenly shattered when Flathead expectations were not met. Schaeffer's analysis depends on recognizing the proclivity of Northwest, primarily Salishan, Indian communities for movements of prophetic religious fervor during the early to mid-nineteenth century.[57] This correlation has the advantage of explaining why the Flatheads persevered for ten years to secure a Jesuit missionary effort and why De Smet received such a fervent welcome from the tribe during his exploratory visit in 1840. Moreover, it goes a long way toward explaining why members of the tribe were seemingly so malleable in allowing their social structures to be transformed along European lines—for example, the ease with which families agreed to break up and the large numbers of monogamous marriage rehabilitation ceremonies that De Smet performed. At the same time, it also explains the utter fragility of the conversions, both religious and cultural, which the missionaries never suspected. The missionaries, under the leadership of De Smet, simply mistook the Flathead fervor for religious renewal and misinterpreted it too easily in terms of cultural transformation. Even if they had understood the real nature of the Flathead expectations, it is highly doubtful that Catholicism or any other form of Christian proclamation could have satisfied the Indian need. The miscommunication, the clash of expectations, and the conflict of

cultures were inevitable and unavoidable, given the level of cultural self-awareness that was possible for either nineteenth-century Europeans or Indian tribal
peoples. In retrospect, we can see that the failure of the mission was equally
inevitable. Though De Smet never gave up on his ideal of conversion as both
cultural and spiritual, to his credit he did come to a deeper understanding of
the complexities of the task. By 1867 he recognized the difficulty of achieving
his ends, noting, "It is not possible to change the nature of any race of men in
a moment. . . . It will take patience to transform them into cultivators; the
thing will necessarily require some years."[58]

Thus, I must conclude that, in spite of good intentions rooted in his understanding of the gospel of Jesus Christ and its evangelical imperative, De Smet
was complicit in an act of cultural genocide. The imposition of new social
structures and values on Flatheads and other native peoples of the Northwest
involved what I have categorized as the social aspect of cultural genocide.
Moreover, at this point I have demonstrated that cultural imposition and the
missionaries' rigid application of that principle not only contributed to the
destruction of the Flathead as a people, but also helped to account more ana-
lytically for the real sources of failure that doomed the Flathead mission and
the initial relationship between those Indian peoples and the missionaries who
came to them with such high expectations of developing an ideal Christian
community.

De Smet's complicity in the cultural genocide of American Indians was by
no means limited to these overt attempts to impose new social structures. More
serious was his complicity in what I have called the economic and political
factors of cultural genocide. That Chittenden and Richardson discuss the failure
of both the Potawatomi and Flathead missions, at least in passing, is testimony
that their real interest was not in De Smet's missionary activity per se, but a
more secular and political interest in the role he played in the pacification of
the western tribes, thus helping to facilitate a new nation's manifest destiny.
Moreover, it is here that De Smet's real fame lies as well as the seeds for the
myth of the "super missionary." After all, his great success and reputation came
as a government functionary, not as a priest—although the latter made the
former possible. Accordingly, it is to these economic and political aspects of
cultural genocide that we now turn.

Economics and Mission Outreach: De Smet and the Ideal World of Paraguay

> It seems that the idea of renewing the miracles of Paraguay amid those mountains
> was a Utopia. In the first place, we could not hope for the means which our
> Fathers received from the Crowns of Spain and Portugal. Then, it was impossible
> to keep the whites at a distance; then, too, the nature of the land is quite
> different and one cannot hope to wean the bulk of the savages from their
> nomadic life during a great part of the year when they are on the hunt and
> scattered and disbanded, some to the right and some to the left. Impossible for
> the missionary to follow them—their savagery is renewed,—perpetuated, with

great danger of profanation of baptism and the other sacraments. I declare, my dear Father, I don't see how one can have any success at all.

—Father Roothaan[59]

To this point, we have seen that the cultural genocide of American Indian peoples included an economic element and that economic genocide was carried out with the complicity of the missionaries John Eliot in New England (chapter 2) and Junípero Serra in California (chapter 3). Under Eliot's leadership, the missionized Indians of New England were herded into isolated native townships, intentionally separated from the villages of their birth, their families, and their traditional economies. Part of the conversion process involved the imposition of economic transformation to English-style agriculture and business. As a result and by intention, these once independent people were reduced to total dependence on the Puritan economic structures of the Massachusetts Bay Company. At the same time they were locked into the Puritan economic network, they were implicitly excluded from any significant benefit from their participation, having been explicitly denied any free intercourse in the Puritan world by having been segregated in their townships on the periphery of the Puritan colony. In Serra's California, where no large-scale European colony existed as yet, economic genocide functioned somewhat differently, but with the same disastrous consequences for the native peoples. In his attempt to re-create the reduction experiment first designed by Las Casas in the early 1500s and pursued on a broad scale for over a century in Paraguay by the Jesuits (until 1750), Serra also tried to separate his converts from their former residences and familial associations. Like Eliot, he herded converts together into new living arrangements based on a European pattern—this time Spanish-style peasant villages—and imposed a wholly new economic system on the assemblage. Serra's system differed from Eliot's in the immediate ruling presence of the missionaries and the more complete isolation of the converts from European communities as well as from native villages. Hence, the particulars of the resulting devastation to Indian tribes were somewhat different if no less destructive. The new dependence on European economic structures—namely, European-style agriculture, a new culture of work, and an unprecedented hierarchical approach to authority—resulted in an extraordinary death rate as well as the terrible cultural dislocation of coastal California tribal peoples from 1767 into the 1830s. The terrible irony that the mission's imposition of European-style agriculture and work ethic resulted in horrible famine and starvation in what had been a land of plenty is a matter of record.

Some three-quarters of a century after Serra, De Smet also had designs on the reduction paradigm of his Jesuit predecessors. His letters make repeated and explicit reference to his Jesuit forebears in Paraguay, and he makes their experiment the goal of Jesuit missions in the Northwest, even calling Muratori "our Vade Mecum."[60] The Flathead Indians seemed to De Smet to be ideally suited to the reduction model in ways that the Potawatomis had not. In 1841 when the mission to the Flathead began, the tribe was still substantially isolated from the European tide of invasion in the east,[61] still relatively pristine and open to the good influence of a superior religious force. At least, this appears to have been De Smet's thinking. The "elect of God," he called them, ". . . the seed of 200,000 Christians, who would be as fervent as were the converted Indians of Paraguay."[62] For De Smet the implementation of the Paraguay paradigm was first of all a means of achieving the necessary life-style transformation that would result in the Indian tribes adopting Euroamerican social structures and values. Yet the model also had explicit implications for the economic well-being of those tribes and resulted invariably in the abrupt end of their economic (and hence, cultural) independence. That the experiment failed in his own missions is undoubtedly due as much to the different historical circumstances of the mid-nineteenth century as it is to his own inadequacies. From the start of the Flathead mission, as we have seen, De Smet was clear that any real missionizing attempt had to be coupled with cultural and economic change. Following his "congregation" around the plains on the buffalo hunt not only was wearing for the missionaries, but it also made the process of cultural transformation, of teaching and churching, far more difficult and uncertain.[63]

Economics and Mission Outreach: Fur Traders and Power Brokers

> On the 29th of April [1839] I went on board the American Company's steamboat, which makes every year the voyage from St. Louis to the Yellowstone river to furnish the Indians of those countries with whatever they need and bring down their furs in return.
>
> —Pierre-Jean De Smet[64]

> [De Smet is] a good simple minded old man but completely under the Company's control.
>
> —Mahlon Wilkinson[65]

The intentional imposition of a new economy along with a new culture was not a significant element in De Smet's complicity in the cultural genocide of Indian people. His complicity, however, was limited not by intention, but by his inability to achieve his goal, which was to replicate the Paraguayan reduction along with its cultural and economic conversion. The failure of the mission at least limited the short-term disruption to the Flatheads, although the long-term effects, combined with the full complexity of the immigrant invasion, proved to be finally unmanageable within the traditional social structures of the tribe. De Smet, however, managed to engage in another category of activity that makes his collusion perhaps more nefarious, if more naive. This complicity is more directly related to the economic exploitation of Indian people across the northern plains and west to the Oregon Territory. Namely, De Smet received material and financial favors in support of his mission work from the large fur trading companies that had moved very early onto the plains to exploit Indian labor. De Smet was certainly not an uneducated man and expended great energies in endless travels across the continent. Nevertheless, Mahlon Wilkinson's assessment appears to have been close to the mark, "a good simple minded old man but completely under the Company's control."

The Company was the American Fur Company, one of the largest corporate enterprises in the United States during the first half of the nineteenth century. John Jacob Astor, its owner prior to 1834, was the richest man in the country,[66] and the company itself reportedly generated profits of up to one million dollars a year during the 1820s and 1830s.[67] The fur companies, the American Fur Company and the Hudson Bay Company (HBC) in particular, were the fore-runners of the modern corporation. They were already experts at developing ever more efficient and systematic means of generating wealth, especially by manipulating and exploiting labor. Their employees in the field were selected with great care given to standardization of size and strength. Employees were not to differ greatly in size so that four could easily and quickly portage a canoe together, nor were they to be too tall so that maximum space in the canoe could be reserved for the cargo of pelts. Though immortalized as rugged individualist frontiersmen, even the pace at which they paddled a canoe was regulated by the companies. Far from independent, these "voyageurs" or "engagés" were actually a form of de facto indentured servants.[68]

The exploitation of Indian labor by the fur companies, and the resulting erosion of the Indians' economic independence and cultural vitality, is only now coming under the scrutiny of historical analysis,[69] although the devastation of Indian tribes caused by the alcohol trade has long been understood and was even freely acknowledged at the time by major participants such as George Simpson, governor of the HBC, John McLoughlin, the HBC chief factor in the Northwest,[70] and Pierre Chouteau of the American Fur Company.[71] The mis-sionaries' interest in replacing the "nomadic" life-style of the hunt with European-style agriculture based on a sedentary life, private ownership of property, and a money/trade economy intensified changes initiated by the earlier traders. Before the missionaries came into Indian country, the traders had already introduced European trade goods, creating some desire for them among the tribes. Although various tribes responded differently to these new symbols of wealth, any desire to possess them imposed a new economic reality on the tribe and triggered the beginnings of a social transformation that immediately affected the value struc-tures of their society and initiated the erosion of their cultural integrity. For instance, hunting economies, where hunting was conducted to meet the basic needs of a people, gave way to hunting and trapping as business ventures. Where hunting had been part of an independent wholly internal economy, now the tribe had suddenly entered a dependent relationship in which they engaged in hunting as part of a trade economy in order to accumulate goods from an external source.

The inherent exploitation in the new dependent relationship should be readily apparent in that the new economic structures were not at all new to the traders or the large companies that had sent them. The latter already knew the rules of commerce, indeed had created those rules. On the other hand, the cultural values of generosity, sharing, community welfare, and the like that characterized virtually all Indian tribes did not die immediately. Indeed, these values functioned to further ensure the political and economic dominance of the more powerful trading partners, people who were thoroughly inculturated in a value system that emphasized competition, individual achievement, aggressiveness, and the accumulation of individual wealth. Moreover, the perseverance of Indian cultural values of community well-being actually enhanced the Europeans' sense of cultural and economic superiority. From their perspective with its emphasis on individual achievement and the accumulation of wealth, the Europeans found it easy to pass self-righteous judgment on the inability of those who did not share those values to attain the same rewards.

My point is that De Smet's function as missionary was enhanced—for good or bad—by his relationship with the two most powerful economic powers in the west, and he in turn functioned to enhance those economic powers and to facilitate their exploitation of the very people to whom he hoped to bring salvation. The symbiotic relationship had already been spelled out in 1824–25 by George Simpson, the head of the HBC. His journal of his travels across Canada that year contains extensive remarks on the potential for starting Indian missions in the Northwest. An astute businessman with administrative and management skills, Simpson carefully set out a proposal for realizing that potential, in which Indian missions would function in close relationships with the HBC factors in those locales. It should be emphasized that Simpson evidently had a genuine interest in the welfare of the Indian tribes of the Northwest, although whether his interest in establishing missions was motivated more by the presumed benefit to Indians or the obvious benefit he saw for his company is unclear:

> There may be a difference of opinion as to the effect the conversion of the Indians might have on the trade; I cannot however foresee that it could be at all injurious, on the contrary I believe it would be highly beneficial thereto as they would in time imbibe our manners and customs and imitate us in Dress; our Supplies would thus become necessary to them which would increase the consumption of European produce & manufactures and in like measure increase & benefit our trade as they would find it requisite to become more industrious and to turn their attention more seriously to the Chase in order to be enabled to provide themselves with such supplies; we should moreover be enabled to pass through their Lands in greater safety which would lighten the expense of transport, and supplies of Provisions would be found at every Village and among every tribe; they might likewise be employed on extraordinary occasions as runners Boatsmen &c and their Services in other respects turned to profitable account. [72]

Simpson's commentary is self-revealing. Ever searching for more effective ways to exploit Indian people, he realized that the gospel offered him a tool of great potential. Even if Simpson's concern for Indian well-being was genuine to some degree, one should note that he saw the missions' potential, as did the missionaries, in terms of the necessary cultural transformation of Indian peoples. Moreover, he argues that any missions in the Northwest should not only be established in cooperation with the HBC, but should be under company supervision:

> The Society [London Missionary Society] should place the Clergyman in a certain degree under the protection of the Coy's [Company's] representative (say the Chief Facter in charge of the District) and direct him to look up to that Gentleman for support and assistance in almost every thing as a superior.[73]

Simpson clearly believed that the proposed missionary enterprise would ultimately benefit the company, even as it reduced Indian tribes to the peaceful poverty of economic dependence on the European presence with its new but soon to be essential trade goods. Simpson makes explicit what is otherwise implicit in the whole history of Christian missions among American Indians. The missionaries were to be the agents of pacification, which would facilitate the economic exploitation of Indian peoples by white business interests. While a philosophy that argues impoverishment as a way to peace may seem obviously inadequate, it does offer significant benefit to the nonpoor. In this case, Simpson knew well that his business depended on a pacification of Indian peoples that would not destroy their usefulness as an efficient source of fur pelts. Military force could be used to subjugate them but would also destroy the will to work. Pacification by the missionaries, however, enabled the effective exploitation of Indians necessary to the HBC's success.

John McLoughlin, Simpson's chief factor in the Northwest, was to implement this plan as consistently as possible over the next twenty years, offering company hospitality to each and every missionary who entered the territory, from Protestants like Jason Lee and Markus Whitman to the Catholics under De Smet. Although the HBC never formally supervised the missionaries, a clear relationship of collusion and interdependence emerged immediately.[74] McLoughlin's letter of welcome to De Smet on his arrival in the Northwest in 1841 already begins to build that relationship:

> I am extremely happy to find that you and your worthy associates are to be residents in this part of the world and intend to devote yourselves to the laudable object of teaching the doctrine of the Christian religion to these poor deluded savages . . . I presume it is unnecessary for me to assure you it will be my great happiness to have an opportunity of affording you the least assistance in furthering your pious object. . . .[75]

In De Smet's case, the relationship between trading company and missionary was established at the beginning of his career and maintained to its end. His relationship with the Protestant-owned HBC and John McLoughlin was no less firm than with the Catholic-owned American Fur Company. He readily accepted free travel, free lodging, and free and greatly reduced merchandise from representatives of both companies, always with gracious appreciation. During an 1863 voyage up the Missouri to the Northwest, De Smet reports the generosity of the American Fur Company in these words:

> My little cargo amounted in all to nearly 1,500 pounds. The worthy captain of the steamboat, Mr. Charles Chouteau [son of Pierre, Jr.], was so exceedingly

obliging and charitable as to give me a free passage, together with the two brothers, as well as transportation for our baggage and all the things destined for the missions—a charity on his part, which would otherwise have cost us upward of $1,000. We shall pray, and venture to hope, that heaven will reward him, with all his respectable family, for his great goodness and charity to the missionaries and their missions. This good work he repeats every spring and at each departure for the mountains.[76]

Likewise, in 1841 De Smet had reported the exceeding generosity of the HBC:

. . . I feel bound . . . to pay Mr. Ermatinger, the captain of Fort Hall, the tribute of gratitude which we owe him.

Although a Protestant by birth, this noble Englishman gave us a most friendly reception. Not only did he repeatedly invite us to his table, and sell us, at first cost, or at one-third of its value, in a country so remote, whatever we required; but he also added, as pure gifts, many articles which he believed would be particularly acceptable. He did more: he promised to recommend us to the good will of the Governor of the honorable English Hudson's Bay Company, who was already prepossessed in our favor; and, what is still more deserving of praise, he assured us that he would second our ministry among the populous nation of the Snakes, with whom he has frequent intercourse.[77]

What was the price for accepting the charity of these trading companies? What was in it for the companies? One must keep in mind that the trading companies were enormous operations, the epitome of nineteenth-century free enterprise capitalism. They were part of the birthing of the modern Euroamerican economic system or what Wallerstein calls the "modern world-system."[78] Several other points further illustrate the symbiotic relationship between De Smet and these companies. One is the effusive praise that De Smet consistently voices in all of his writings for the support these companies provided for his mission enterprise. His appreciation is directed to all levels of the company, from the highest ranking administrators to individual factors in charge of the widely dispersed company outposts. At the implicit level of his support for these companies, De Smet's comments sometimes seem to be a naive misinterpretation of the relationship between the traders and Indian peoples. To wit, the quotation at the beginning of this section from a De Smet letter implies or even asserts that the primary purpose of the traders and their expensive steamboats was to serve the needs of the Indians: ". . . to furnish the Indians of those countries with whatever they need." Even the secondary purpose he mentions is ambiguous and, in context, implies that the traders were doing the Indians a favor by bringing "down their furs in return." De Smet's naïveté dissolves, however, in the light of his symbiotic relationship with these companies. Far from being naive, De Smet's comment intentionally misleads the reader. It perpetuates a lie, a particular occasion of "the LIE," in order to enhance the business potential of these important benefactors of De Smet's missionary enterprise. By giving the distinct impression that the traders acted in the best interests of the Indians, De Smet conceals the traders' role in the genocide of Indian people.

Although he graciously accepted the gifts of the companies, from $1,000 steamboat excursions to extravagant luxuries like sweetmeats and chocolate in the wilderness of Indian country, De Smet never stops to confront, indeed has no comment on, the participation of these same companies in the deadly practice of trading liquor among the tribes. Perhaps the exploitation inherent in the relationship between the fur traders and the Indian tribes is most apparent in the widespread use of alcoholic beverages as a trade item.[79] De Smet was, in fact, a great critic of the alcohol trade with Indian tribes and, while he was among the Potawatomis, wrote one of the most depressing descriptions of the liquor trade and its effects on Indian people.[80] Although he knew firsthand the ravages this trade perpetrated on a tribe and spoke out against it early in his missionary career,[81] he later avoided any intimation of impropriety in this regard on the part of the trading companies. Yet De Smet was sufficiently sophisticated that he must have known the source of the liquor. Nevertheless, having written once on the subject, he falls strangely mute on the issue throughout the rest of his career—offering only an occasional comment, but no more severe homilies.[82] Moreover, his one critical letter, written early in a career that was filled with publishing letters, was not published during his lifetime.[83] Most particularly, De Smet does not offer any overt criticism of the trading companies, yet it was precisely their outposts that engaged in the practice, and they did so simply to further exploit the Indians and enhance their profits. In 1833, one AFC trader on the upper Missouri even managed to set up a still.[84] For the most part, however, the liquor was shipped in barrels, usually in high-proof concentrations that were diluted on site.[85] This illegal trade involved far more than a stray company factor or agent acting on his own. After all, the companies themselves shipped all of those barrels of whiskey. They owned the boats and controlled the shipping.[86]

It is apparent that De Smet sold himself in return for support for the missions and the comfort of the missionaries. This is not to argue that he fully understood the compromise he had made or its consequences for Indian people, even though he was acutely aware of the ravages of Indian people and clearly identified them in other contexts. A more likely explanation is that this son of a Flemish merchant found himself completely at home with other merchants, considered their quest for profits useful and honorable with no tint of injustice, and within the context of his own inculturation naturally enjoyed their hospitality and sang their praises. He became the epitome of what George Simpson had described as a useful missionary presence among Indians doing business with the company. As for the trading companies, supporting the missionaries was good business and also a good public relations ploy.[87]

De Smet as Patriot and Government Functionary

A colony established in such a neighborhood, and against the will of the numerous warlike tribes in the vicinity of those mountains, would run great dangers and meet heavy obstacles. The influence of religion alone can prepare these parts for such a transformation. The threats and promises of colonists, their guns and sabres, would never effect what can be accomplished by the peaceful word of the Blackgown and the sight of the humanizing sign of the cross.

—Pierre-Jean De Smet[88]

I have said in Europe, and I repeat it, there is no country in the world that has greater resources than this; none that is making such progress; where everything is developing in so wonderful a manner as to draw the admiration of the civilized world. Providence has laid out this country on a gigantic scale; its destiny is to march onward, and no power on earth can stop it. It is a mighty country, young and vigorous, and possesses a vast space which time will fill with millions of men.

—Pierre-Jean De Smet[89]

As I have already intimated, De Smet's most enduring fame appears to rest not on his service as a missionary but on his service as a functionary of the U.S. government in its dealings with Indian tribes from about 1850 to 1868.[90] The missionaries, of all denominations, often worked with the strong support of both governmental authorities and the military. Unknown to the missionaries, however, these very allies doomed to failure nearly every missionary enterprise. Perhaps Bishop Whipple of Minnesota understood this a generation later, especially after the 1862 Little Crow uprising in Minnesota, but it did not stop him from working closely with the U.S. government during the 1870s and 1880s. Likewise De Smet had some understanding, even as he gave much of his enormous energies during the last twenty years of his life to the direct service of the U.S. government in its dealings with Indian peoples.[91] His service was certainly not rendered for personal financial gain, although he was susceptible to the desire for personal prestige. Moreover, to borrow a metaphor from mental health discourse, there was some of the same co-dependency at stake that we saw in his relationship with the economic powers of the west.[92] That is, De Smet served the interests of the government, the agency of power, in order to facilitate its dominance of Indian tribes on the plains. As a result, the government and De Smet functioned as enablers of one another, each enabling the dysfunctionality, the addictive behavior, of the other. For De Smet, this was the payoff for taking federal help in the first place: by continuing to participate in the government's program, De Smet held out hope for further assistance and support for the Jesuit missionary presence, and perhaps even for the Catholic presence in the United States. His commitment to the United States had already been in the making from the time of his first arrival in the country. As we have already noted, the Jesuit province in St. Louis began with federal dollars and a land grant. Similarly, the Potawatomi mission began with the help of Col. Stephen W. Kearny, the U.S. army commander at Council Bluffs, who turned over an old army fort to the missionaries to use as their initial facility.

By 1833 De Smet had become a naturalized citizen, a step he took just prior to his departure for Belgium for health reasons to ensure his return and eventual participation in missionary service. The nature of his commitment quickly became clear. His concern for Indian people was subservient to his concern for this new developing nation. Like Las Casas before him and Whipple afterwards, De Smet had a keen awareness of the long history of military genocide and its continuation in his own day.[93] Yet, in spite of this he remained an immigrant patriot who defended and excused the atrocities. Chittenden and Richardson, after several paragraphs that detail De Smet's sensitivity to Indian suffering, note that he goes on to absolve the government in a way that elicits this remark from them: "[His] exoneration of the Government from complicity in the wrongs practiced upon the Indians is an example of broad-mindedness which one does not often meet with among the so-called 'friends' of the redmen."[94]

Perhaps the significant measure of De Smet's patriotism is his continual articulation of the national vision of Manifest Destiny. Although he never uses the explicit language of Manifest Destiny, the vision is there in all of its awful glory. It was the will of God that this young and vigorous country should settle the entire continent.[95] Already in 1845, he was advocating U.S. possession of the Oregon Territory and expressed fears that Canada might annex the territory before the United States made its move. Where Indian peoples saw homelands, De Smet saw only "desert" and the potential for settlement that would bring the desert to life.[96] As he crossed the plains in the 1850s, he sang the praises of settler communities that had sprung into existence since his first passage through the territory in 1840.[97] Yet all this is in curious contradiction to the discouragement he felt during his time with the Potawatomis over the effect that the vices of the colonists would have on those Indian people. Again, his plans for the Flathead mission, building on the Jesuit experience in Paraguay, had envisioned a relative isolation where Flathead Christianity might grow in some freedom from "the worst vices" of the immigrant peoples.[98] Perhaps De Smet had been converted to a new perspective by the advice of John McLoughlin that Indian civilization and conversion might best be effected by exposure to proximate immigrant communities.[99] Yet, in the end, De Smet even reversed this image and began to admit that missionary outreach actually served the goal of immigrant colonization by pacifying otherwise hostile tribes.

Political Function on Behalf of the U.S. Government

In 1851, only five years after his removal from the Jesuit missionary efforts in the Northwest, De Smet was back in the northern plains, in Wyoming territory, for the first Fort Laramie Peace Council. De Smet had no major negotiating role at this council, and spent his days simply circulating among the camps of various tribes and bands that had gathered for the event. Indeed, this appears to have been his function as a participant. Namely, the government negotiators used his presence to build up the confidence level of the Indian participants. As such, De Smet's task was to help pacify Indians who had been adversaries of the U.S. government and encourage them either implicitly or explicitly to sign the treaty. Even at this juncture, however, De Smet knew quite clearly that he was participating in the government's strategy and that the council had not been held in order to negotiate a treaty. Rather, the treaty had already been carefully worked out to the best advantage of the immigrants, and the council was simply the place to negotiate the Indian agreement. In letters that record his participation in the council, De Smet notes, "that the object of the assembly was the acceptation by them of the treaty, such as it had been prepared beforehand, with the consent of the President of the United States."[100] In spite of his friendship with so many Indian people and the missionary impetus that commanded so much of his energy, De Smet's loyalty was, in the final analysis, given over completely to his adopted country and not to Indian people. In later engagements as a government functionary, he took on increasing responsibility and stature, but this sentiment continued to dominate his service and commitment.

In 1858 De Smet was appointed U.S. Army chaplain to accompany General William S. Harney and his troops to quell the Mormon Rebellion (1857–58). Although the hostilities were over by the time they arrived, De Smet continued his service with Harney and went with the army to the Northwest to interdict Indian troubles there.[101] Initially, he had tendered his resignation at the completion of the Mormon Rebellion action, but it was turned down because of an Indian uprising in Oregon Territory (the Yakima War). He accepted the continued appointment in the hope that he could be helpful "to the Indian tribes of the mountains . . . [and] be in touch with my missionary brethren in the difficulties which the war would doubtless bring upon them." Yet his function was to pacify the Indians, to facilitate their continued subjection by the invading immigrant power. Upon his arrival in the Northwest, De Smet found the hostilities already settled, but commented, "The task, however, remained of removing the prejudices of the Indians, soothing their inquietude and alarm, and correcting, or rather refuting, the false rumors that are generally spread about after a war, and which otherwise might be the cause of its renewal."[102] Indeed, the events that followed and De Smet's primary participation in them are indicative of his civil function on behalf of the invading force, no doubt with considerable genuine concern on his part to make the invasion as gentle and painless as possible for the indigenous inhabitants of that land.

Under orders from Harney, De Smet brought the leaders of several of the mountain tribes with him to Fort Vancouver for a conference with government officials and then a guided tour of the white occupation of the Northwest, as Chittenden and Richardson note, "in the hope that an acquaintance with the number and power of the whites would be a wholesome restraint upon further outbreaks."[103] Clearly, De Smet's assignment was one of pacification, to facilitate conquest, and in the latter case he achieved that pacification by what was intended to be an intimidating exposure to white power. Captain A. Pleasonton, Harney's assistant adjutant general, clearly articulated Harney's hope for De Smet's service in a letter of instruction to De Smet:

> While informing the Indians that the Government is always generous to a fallen foe, state to them that it is, at the same time, determined to protect its citizens

in every part of its territory; and that they can only expect to exist by implicitly obeying the commands they receive.

In a later letter Pleasonton praised De Smet's successes, announcing, "The victory is yours, and the general will take great pleasure in recording your services at the War Department." The real consequences of De Smet's service to the military are apparent in Harney's own letter of praise, in which he underscored the importance of De Smet's presence for achieving military goals:

> From what I have observed of the Indian affairs of this department, the missionaries among them [among the Indians] possess a power of the greatest consequence in their proper government, and one which cannot be acquired by any other influence. They control the Indian by training his superstitions and fears to revere the religion they possess, by associating the benefits they confer with the guardianship and protection of the Great Spirit of the whites. The history of the Indian race on this continent has shown that the missionary succeeded where the soldier and civilian have failed. . . .[104]

And if De Smet succeeded in a demonstrable manner in this campaign, just as Roger Williams and John Eliot succeeded in New England and Junípero Serra in California, his service on behalf of the U.S. government would be all the more prominent in the following decade.

De Smet's writings contain considerable evidence that he was acutely aware that accepting an assignment from the U.S. government could put him in a compromising position. When he was approached by the commissioner of "the Indian Department at Washington" to pursue directly a peacemaking mission among the Sioux in 1864 on behalf of the federal government, De Smet expressed concern that government service might cause him to "lose all caste among the Indians." He finally agreed to the mission, but insisted that he conduct it by himself and not as part of a larger government party: "I have written to the Commissioner, that if I can go [health permitting], I will go on my own hook, without pay or remuneration. . . ."[105] Thus, he clearly was concerned for his role as a peacemaker between Indian and white. Eventually, however, his own bias becomes apparent in an 1864 comment on the Sioux: "It is going to be very difficult to obtain peace with those terrible savages." In the final analysis, his commitment and loyalty to the white, Euroamerican country of the United States become clear in a comment written in preparation for an 1863 trip through the northern plains. The trip was intended as a combination peacemaking and missionary journey to "promote . . . religion and friendly dispositions toward the Government and its white travelers. . . ." In that context he says,

> My adopted country, for these forty years I have lived in it, has been always truly dear to me. Its welfare has been the constant and uppermost wish of my heart and the end of my poor prayers. I have sworn obedience to it and from this sacred duty I have never and shall never swerve.[106]

Needless to say, he never understood that his role as "peacemaker" was both compromised by his primary commitment to the nation and complicit in the very genocide he condemned.

Again in 1867 he was recruited by the secretary of the interior to travel across the northern plains negotiating a peaceful solution to the Powder River War. As in 1864, De Smet traveled alone and sought private dialogues with Indian people, not wanting his efforts to be unduly compromised by the presence of other government functionaries or soldiers. His attitude changed in June, however, when he crossed paths with Generals Alfred Sully and Ely S. Parker, who were on a similar mission.[107] Not only did De Smet agree to travel with them and participate in their negotiating strategy, but he also accepted a nomination to the Peace Commission several months later for service the following year. It was as a member of that commission that De Smet achieved his greatest fame. Working together with William T. Sherman, Harney, Alfred H. Terry, John B. Sanborn, and Philip Sheridan, De Smet performed the formidable task of delivering a delegation from the hostile bands to the Peace Council at Fort Laramie. Parting company with the other commissioners in Cheyenne, De Smet traveled through the hostile territory, made contact with the hostiles, and delivered a delegation to the Peace Council. While this achievement ought not to be devalued, it does need to be put into context.

De Smet clearly understood the causes of Indian dissatisfaction that led to various wars and acts of violence. Even as he calls the Sioux "terrible savages," his comments on the Powder River War in particular and Indian wars in general repeatedly point out white American "incessant provocations and injustice" perpetrated against Indian peoples: "It is always true that if the savages sin against the whites it is because the whites have greatly sinned against them." And, "I repeat it, if our Indians become enraged against the whites, it is because the whites have made them suffer for a long time."[108] Yet, at the same time, De Smet announces his intentions for his government peacemaking role in terms that elevate the importance of white lives and thrust Indian people into a subservient relationship. He describes his 1867 mission as intended "to bring them [hostile Indian tribes] back to peace and submission and to prevent as much as possible the destruction of property and murder of the whites." While protecting himself against obvious compromise by refusing to accept remuneration for his service to the government, he also claimed that that service involved "nothing contrary to my duties as a missionary."[109]

"Black Robe" and De Smet's Identity among Indian Peoples

While the hagiographies make much of De Smet's personal appeal to Indians, and certainly on occasion friendship was involved, it is quite likely that Indian people more often than not, especially at first, responded not to De Smet as a person but to his black robe of office. They recognized him as one of the spiritual leaders of the Europeans, a "medicine man" or the European counterpart of a tribal medicine person. This may indeed be the significance of the title "Black Robe" that many Indian people used to refer to De Smet and his Jesuit colleagues, as well as to other Catholic and occasionally Episcopal priests. General David S. Stanley implies as much in his letter to Archbishop Percell praising De Smet's participation in the work of the 1864 Peace Commission: "The Reverend Father is known among the Indians by the name of 'Black-robe' and 'Big Medicine Man.' When he is among them he always wears the cassock and crucifix."[110]

As the title "Big Medicine Man" implies, De Smet's "presence" among Indian peoples depended to some extent on pretense—and I think he was fully conscious of the fact and modeled his own presence on that of the first Jesuits to work among North American Indians, especially Pierre Biard. Biard was not above using his scientific medical knowledge to compete with traditional healers in Indian communities and using his successes to pass himself off as the spiritually superior.[111] De Smet could perform the same sort of mixture of pretend magic and European medicine as Biard and even used his reputation as a healer to gain access to small children whom, by his own account, he proceeded to baptize surreptitiously.[112]

De Smet took his "medicine man" act further than Biard, as his first encounter with a Dakota leader named Red Fish illustrates. Red Fish credited De Smet's prayers with facilitating the return of his daughter who had been captured by enemies.[113] De Smet allowed this deception (the end justifies the means) for the sake of winning converts, and, indeed, a long friendship with Red Fish ensued.[114]

Applying the word *deception* to these encounters might not be appropriate, if De Smet himself were not so clear on the issue. Joseph La Barge, a riverboat captain for the American Fur Company and later a small competitor of the company, told of seeing De Smet function as a rainmaker for an Arikara village.[115] During the spring of 1851, the rains were slow to arrive on the northern plains. White Shield, the Arikara leader and an acquaintance of De Smet's, took advantage of the boat's presence to approach De Smet and ask him to "send" rain for their corn. After De Smet put on what seems to have been a considerable show in the Arikara village, in the presence of La Barge and several co-passengers, it did indeed rain, "as good fortune would have it," says Chittenden. De Smet reportedly laughed and said: "They will think I did it. They will give me all the credit for it." Proven correct, De Smet responded with another laugh saying, "Did I not tell you they would say I did it?"[116] That he had lived a lie or toyed with someone else's reality seems not to have concerned the ever-pragmatic De Smet. In fact, his actions here belied his preaching. He had implicitly used the religious convictions of the other (i.e., Indian peoples) not to advance his own religious convictions but simply to enhance his personal reputation. De Smet called the religious beliefs of western tribal peoples pagan "superstitions." De Smet's trifling caricaturization of an Indian culture and beliefs in this way would seem to belie the assumed superiority of rational Catholic theology. Indeed, it would seem that he has merely twisted what he saw as Indian superstition into a superstitious affirmation of himself and of the Catholic church.[117]

This part of De Smet's profile is revealing in yet another way. It is only his attitude toward tribal peoples that allowed him to engage in this sort of deceptive practice. It bears repeating here that De Smet himself undoubtedly never self-consciously thought through these actions. Rather he fell into a pattern of behavior that was defined first of all by the historical relationship between Europeans and Indians, and then by his own inculturation in the Euroamerican world. Surely, he never considered his actions to be the conscious deception I have described, and he would not have recognized it as such had someone had the insight to articulate it. Nevertheless, it would be relatively inconceivable to think of De Smet or any other Christian missionary, Catholic or mainline Protestant, pretending to be a Jewish rabbi in order to make converts of "poor, deluded Jews." It is not merely a matter of cultural affectation or what we today would call cross-cultural insensitivity. For better or worse, and no doubt with the best of intentions on De Smet's part, this is deception deeply rooted in racist notions of white superiority, deception that moves in many instances towards outright mockery.

De Smet's mockery of Indian culture and religious traditions occurred concomitantly with his genuine concern for and appreciation of Indian peoples. Perhaps both were generated by the same implicit internalization of cultural superiority. More to the point is the conclusion that despite his genuine concern there can be no doubt that De Smet's primary commitment was not to Indian people or to the evangelization process but to the Euroamerican process of conquest, accomplished through the social, political, and economic structures with which De Smet had a symbiotic relationship from the time of his birth.

The internalization of white superiority in post-Columbian American history began with religion and served as the foundation in white/Indian relationships in the missionary efforts of all our churches.[118] De Smet brought with him to Indian country a firm sense of moral superiority. And perhaps moral superiority is even too mild a term. Rather, he came with a sense of moral Catholicism versus amoral Indian savagery. Like Whipple and many others, he asserted the superiority of his own culture and social structures by identifying them with his own religious commitment to the gospel, speaking about the influences of a "Christian civilization" on Indian peoples. From such a vantage point, it was just a small leap to universalizing a dichotomy between white and Indian culture, where white culture is all good and Indian culture is all bad.[119] Occasionally, De Smet found aspects of an Indian culture that quite impressed him. He even became so carried away in his praise of the Flatheads that he was driven to ask, "Who are the civilized?"[120] Yet his actions belied these words. The sentiment of white superiority was too deeply culturally ingrained in De Smet. Perhaps we should not expect otherwise, but certainly we must be cautious in bestowing our praise. It should be stressed that De Smet's sense of moral superiority became not just a seed, but a plant that took root in the Indian subconscious, as Indian people began to internalize the attitudes of white oppression. Finally, the values De Smet evangelized among Indian people pertained not just to religion and morality, but to culture itself. The message was—and is—that white, Euroamerican culture and its values are good, while Indian culture and values are inferior and outright bad. The white world has lived out this lie consistently and has even believed it. The tragedy is that Indian people have also believed and lived out of the lie, reaping not benefits but the implicit consequences of self-destruction.

Henry Benjamin Whipple
The Politics of Indian Assimilation

Toward the end of his life, Bishop Henry Benjamin Whipple reflected with great optimism on his long episcopacy in its context of Indian mission work:

> Never in the world's history has there been such enthusiasm in all humanitarian work as now. It is not a mere pity for suffering, it is a hopeful, helpful, personal work, that human touch which makes the world akin. Not even in the Primitive Church have greater victories been won in leading heathen folk to Christian civilization.[1]

Yet Whipple would likely be sorely disappointed to see the results of his missionary zeal nearly a century after his death. He would find the continuing economic impoverishment and social dysfunctionality that characterize Indian tribes today as appalling as the scandals that plagued the federal conduct of Indian affairs, which he so eloquently criticized during the 1860s. Perhaps he would also be open enough to see the modern Indian situation as an indictment of his own best intentions.

The story of Henry Benjamin Whipple and Indian people is an example of cultural genocide with clear political and religious aspects. Again, we are dealing with a man of the highest moral character who had only the best of intentions. Not one of his contemporaries, Indian or white, friend or critic, nor anyone since has questioned his commitment to the gospel of his ordination, his love for Indian people, his sincerity in arguing for reforms in federal Indian policy, or his courage and long dedication. Yet I will argue here that modern Indian oppression and dysfunctionality are as much the heritage of Whipple's involvement in the Indian context as of the U.S. cavalry or the federal policies he worked so hard to reform.

Outline of Whipple's Episcopacy

Whipple was elected bishop of Minnesota in 1859, at the age of thirty-seven. Unlike Pierre-Jean De Smet, Whipple never served directly in an Indian mission.

Minnesota was already experiencing the rising tide of the immigrant invasion, and Whipple's diocese included the budding cities of Minneapolis and St. Paul as well as numerous other towns and white settlements.[2] It also, however, included Indian people from three different tribes, largely unmissionized and unconverted. Whipple took immediate and rather intense interest in Minnesota Indians as soon as he set foot in his diocese and bore his responsibility seriously over Indian missions and the Native American converts. In 1859, only forty-five days after his consecration, he made his first venture into the Indian country of his diocese and was thereafter a frequent visitor to native congregations and native communities.[3]

Whipple was a genuine friend of Indian people and often spoke out on their behalf throughout his career. With his accession to the episcopacy and his first visit to his native constituency, he began to demand reform in the conduct of federal Indian affairs. Only months after his election as bishop, Whipple wrote to President James Buchanan (April 9, 1860) outlining his proposals for such a reform. In other words, on the basis of just one visit to Indian country in late 1859 shortly after his arrival in Minnesota, Whipple was already proposing solutions to what he perceived as the problems characterizing Indian-white relations. By late 1862, he had an audience with President Abraham Lincoln to press the same issues, this time in the context of reporting to Lincoln on the Little Crow War.[4] These events mark the beginning of extensive correspondence and communication with government officials at all levels, including several presidents, and with key personalities in the reform movement.[5] They also mark the beginning of the reform movement itself. Although few commentators on the movement have acknowledged the reality, Whipple provided one of the initial sparks that ignited the fires for reform of Indian affairs and clearly artic-ulated the platform that would characterize the reform movement for the rest of the century.[6] That the "reforms" were solutions summarily imposed on Indians and that they finally worked much destruction among Indian people should not conceal from our modern eyes that Whipple was genuinely committed to the well-being of Indian people and intended his reform ideas as positive contri-butions to their survival. His commitment to reform consumed the rest of his life and indelibly marked his episcopacy. For his honesty and outspokenness, Indians gave Whipple the name "Straight Tongue," and indeed few white people as influential and as politically well connected ever earned the level of trust and respect of Indians as did he among the Indians of Minnesota.

On the other hand, Whipple irritated a great many white settlers in the territory, who identified him as an Indian sympathizer.[7] His reputation among Minnesota whites, for example, took a decisive dip around issues related to the Little Crow uprising of 1862, as local newspaper letters and editorials clearly show.[8] At that time, and consistently throughout his career, Whipple chose to articulate the injustices perpetrated by the immigrants and their federal gov-ernment and to identify those injustices as the ultimate cause of Indian retali-ations and uprisings. In the case of the Little Crow War, Whipple acknowledged publicly that the federal government's failure to live up to its treaty obligation was the primary cause for the eruption of violence.

Lest we overly romanticize his support for Indian peoples in the face of immigrant injustices, it should be noted that Whipple suffered a tendency to heroize any white who died in an Indian-white dispute and always villainize the Indian as the "savage." In his autobiographical *Lights and Shadows*, he refers to the "massacre of the *gallant* Custer and his heroic soldiers" and in another place gives Custer the commonplace promotion to general that American mythology generally gives him even though his active duty rank was merely lieutenant colonel.[9] In a piece written two years after the Little Crow War, he reminisces that "eight hundred of the most generous people on the earth perished by savage violence."[10] He goes on in this context to say, "A great crime has been committed." Yet he fails to include the overly quick trials and hanging of presumed Indian perpetrators as part of the "great crime."[11] Quite to the contrary, Whipple wrote an article for the Minnesota press shortly after the outbreak of hostilities in the Little Crow War in which he called for the execution of the "guilty"— even though he clearly understood and argued at great risk to himself that the war itself was the fault of the U.S. government's blatant violation of its treaty with the Sioux in Minnesota.[12] Already, we begin to see that Whipple was a captive of his own culture and its implicit set of values, especially where the priority of white, Euroamerican citizens was at stake. Whipple was simply an influential representative of a system that constructed a double standard of justice whereby the "guilty" must be punished, even when it is evident to participants in the system that these "guilty" are in fact victims. Such was the case with the Sioux.

Political Pressures of Fellow Immigrants

Some understanding of frontier issues will provide the larger context to which Whipple's ministry belongs. In the aftermath of the Little Crow War, the cry to exterminate all Indians in Minnesota grew to a furor. Already, for some years insightful people, Pierre-Jean De Smet among them, had begun to doubt that Indian people could survive in the face of the ever-advancing invasion of white immigrants.[13] In 1840 the only whites between St. Louis and the Sierras in California or the Rockies in the Oregon Territory were largely traders, a few missionaries, and government Indian agents and army units. That is what makes De Smet's travels in the early 1840s so spectacular. By 1850, however, the immigrant invasion was rolling unabated over the plains to both Oregon and California. What had been inviolable Indian country suddenly became American. In 1843 the invaders set their sights on the farming lands of the Willamette Valley, and the first onslaught across the plains and mountains into Oregon began. By 1848 some fourteen thousand immigrants had marched across countless Indian lands on what had become known as the Oregon Trail. In that same year, the discovery of gold in the Sierras set off massive new migrations, this time into California. Highways filled with wagon trains suddenly divided what had been undisputed tribal lands. Game began to disappear; Indian hunting patterns and lifeways were thoroughly disrupted; the ecological balance tipped heavily to the side; and Indian claims to their own lands were suddenly confronted with the nationalistic impulses of the "Manifest Destiny" of white America.

This opening of the Oregon Territory and California to immigrant settlement began to expose the interior tribes of the west to the European incursion. Thus, by the time Whipple came to Minnesota, the western tribes were already experiencing constant immigrant pressure. Already by 1856, the Commissioner of Indian Affairs, George W. Manypenny, anticipated the blossoming of new cities and agricultural communities across the prairies and the effects these developments would have on the native populations:

> When that time arrives, and it is at our very doors, ten years, if our country is favored with peace and prosperity, will witness the most of it; where will be the habitation and what the condition of the rapidly wasting Indian tribes of the plains, the prairies, and of our new States and Territories?
>
> As sure as these great physical changes are impending, so sure will these poor denizens of the forest [sic] be blotted out of existence, and their dust be trampled under the foot of rapidly advancing civilization, unless our great nation shall generously determine that the necessary provision shall at once be made, and appropriate steps be taken to designate suitable tracts or reservations of land, in proper localities for permanent homes for, and provide the means to colonize, them thereon.[14]

Extinction of the Indians loomed as a real possibility in the minds of many. Yet a more radical notion in the white mind-set confronted Whipple in Minnesota, a notion that indeed was present across the west, even if in less virulent forms than in Minnesota after 1862. The notion that the Indians should be exterminated lived not only in the popular mind of white immigrants living in the west, but also in military figures such as Gen. Philip Sheridan and Lt. Col. [a.k.a. Gen.] George Armstrong Custer, some of whom even attempted to implement it. It fueled politicians in Colorado in the 1860s and even captured the hearts of some missionaries. So the massacre of Black Kettle's peaceful, treaty-signing encampment at Sand Creek (November 29, 1864) was engineered by the Rev. John Chivington, former missionary to the Wyandot Indians in Kansas. A Methodist minister on leave from his conference where he had served as district superintendent, Chivington became the erstwhile commandant of a ragtag territorial militia assigned the task of ridding the territory of "the Indian infestation." Extermination was a real, if horrible, option, the only option for satisfying the blood thirst of many frontier whites.

The expression of these sentiments energized Whipple's reform commitments all the more. As he went about the task of arguing for Indian justice and the righting of past wrongs, he was in continual correspondence both with political leaders, including several presidents, and with other influential people involved in the reform movement. "My correspondence in this cause," he claims, "with the Presidents of the United States, public men, and the press of the country would fill volumes."[15] He spoke powerfully about the need for reform at church conferences and meetings, wrote on these issues for the public press, held political appointments, and was a popular participant in the Lake Mohonk Conferences of Friends of the Indian.[16]

The Beginnings of Cultural Genocide

Nevertheless, Whipple was a man of his own times and especially of his own cultural heritage. As a result, he came to Indian country with a particular frame of reference for understanding the Indian context, from which he formed notions for the solution of Indian problems. He did not hesitate to impose these on Indian people. To begin with, Whipple was heir to over three-and-a-half centuries of European thinking and debate about native peoples of the Americas. That meant that he had inherited a particular self-image of European peoples as well as a set of images of Indian people and their place in the world.

Race or Culture: An Appropriate Taxonomy?

By the 1860s and beyond, two disparate but correlative developments had begun to emerge with respect to the earlier Euroamerican notions of superiority. On the one hand, notions of genetic superiority had been given added weight by so-called scientific investigation. In the 1830s, the American School of Ethnology, under the leadership of Samuel Morton, began to argue a qualitative distinction between races on the basis of such scientific criteria as cranial measurements.[17] As an academic movement, Morton's premise became possible in no small part because of the tenor of a major segment of public opinion, implicit as well as explicit. As the discussion of Eliot in New England has already demonstrated, the ideology of white superiority was internalized very early, even before the first settlers established their colonies. The ideology thrived in a people's subconscious, finding frequent enough opportunity for conscious articulation. Moreover, Charles Darwin's writings on his theory of evolution certainly give notions of genetic differentiation among human beings a dose of implicit credibility.

On the other hand, the widespread commitment to a biblical notion of monogenesis pressed another significant segment of white America to embrace Indian peoples as sisters and brothers since they held to the unity of all humankind.[18] To say sisters and brothers may go a bit too far, however, since the ideology of white superiority does not leave any group of white Americans unaffected. The result in this case was a firm sense of responsibility for younger siblings or even children. Thus, while Darwinian theories of evolution seemed to underwrite one trajectory, theories of cultural evolution became popular in circles that proclaimed the unity of all humankind but continued to affirm their own image of self-superiority. Genetic superiority gave way then in people like Henry Whipple to cultural superiority. The significant question here is whether the deeper, psychological levels of internalization do not make the genetic-cultural distinction moot.

Prucha would challenge historians who have concluded that notions of racial distinction taught by the American School of Ethnology played a significant role in federal Indian policies.[19] Those involved in creating and implementing these policies, he argues, were largely untouched by the efforts of Morton and the American School of Ethnology to differentiate races.[20] Yet, Prucha cites some of the plentiful proof explicitly to the contrary, quoting from the commissioners of Indian affairs and others in government service. In 1851, for example, the commissioner, Luke Lea, stated in his annual report that:

> The history of the Indian furnishes abundant proof that he possesses all the elements essential to his elevation; all the powers, instinct, and sympathies which appertain to his white brother; and which only need the proper development and direction to enable him to tread with equal step and dignity the walks of civilized life. . . . That his inferiority is a necessity of his nature is neither taught by philosophy, nor attested by experience.[21]

Four years later, Manypenny similarly argued "that the Indian may be domesticated, improved, made a useful element of our population."[22] In the next decade Whipple himself uttered a similar but more renowned dictum in an extensive letter to Lincoln in 1862:

> The first question is, can these red men become civilized? I say, unhesitatingly, yes. The Indian is almost the only heathen man on earth who is not an idolater. In his wild state he is braver, more honest, and virtuous than most heathen races. He has warm home affections and strong love of kindred and country. The Government of England has, among Indians speaking the same language with our own, some marked instances of their capability of civilization. In Canada you will find there are hundreds of civilized and Christian Indians, while on this side of the line there is only degradation.[23]

Even as Whipple seems to extend the hand of human unity, the explicit sense of Euroamerican superiority, expressed here as cultural superiority, is quite transparent. Whipple, like every other good churchman of the era, was thoroughly convinced of it and, in fact, never gave any indication that he had considered otherwise. Obviously, the missionaries were in the business of convincing Indian people of the superiority of their religious convictions and perforce opposed at every juncture all forms of native spirituality. But they did not stop there. In Whipple's mission churches, the first signification of an Indian man's conversion to Christ was to give up his braids for a short Euroamerican-style haircut and the sporting of Euroamerican clothing in lieu of breech clout and buckskins.[24] This mission policy had been established nearly eight years prior to Whipple's arrival. In 1852, at the very outset of the Ojibway mission, James Lloyd Breck wrote to his supporters in the east asking for clothing:

> The work that I now propose to the ladies is to assist in the preparation of clothing for youth, male and female, of the ages above mentioned. The children come to us, of course, from the *blanket* [emphasis added], and must be provided for entire.[25]

The following summer Breck reported back to the Seabury Society on how their gifts were being used. His account is also useful in demonstrating the depth of cross-cultural misunderstanding. Breck referred to the first recipient as an orphan who "was living with his uncle." The comment, of course, totally misses the import of the extended family that functions in the tribal context, where there are, strictly speaking, no orphans. In any event, proper dress and a haircut came next:

> We soon furnished him with jacket and trowsers, which delighted him much, and he threw away his old blanket most gladly. Upon this change he soon wished his long flowing hair to be cut off, but he could not prevail upon any of my brethren to act as barber, for they feared it might displease some of the Indians. But after some days he came to us, evidently much pleased about something—what it was we could not tell, until he turned to us the back of his head, when, lo! his native beauty was shorn! He had persuaded an Indian to perform the deed. He was now, indeed, the white child, being about twelve years of age. [26]

Of course, even becoming civilized had its cross-cultural entrapments. Reporting the conversion of Nebuneshkung, one of Hole in the Day's headmen, Enmegahbowh, attributes this appeal to the convert:

> If the Great Spirit has so big a love for poor Indian, surely Indian ought and must give back big love. . . . Now, dear Brother . . . to be true to return my big love to the GREAT SPIRIT, I brought this scissors, to have you cut my hair locks which I shall throw away for ever. [27]

The language here indicates that Nebuneshkung's understanding of the act was quite different from that expected by the missionaries. The latter saw the haircut as an outward sign of cultural conversion. Nebuneshkung appears to have viewed it as a spiritual act of self-sacrifice or offering so characteristic of many Native American cultures. If clothing makes the man, two can play the game, of course. When a convert thinks twice of his commitment and chooses to revert, then a symbolic change in clothing also follows. Enmegahbowh expressed his discouragement when one of his converts, Manitowaub, became caught up in the resistance movement of Little Crow and Hole in the Day and took off his "civilize[d] dress and put on a piece of cloth between his legs." [28]

Throughout Whipple's episcopacy, the Indian missions in Minnesota among the Ojibway were engaged in an ongoing struggle against the influence of all forms of Indian spirituality, from daily face painting to the powerful ceremonies of the Grand Medicine Lodge and the Medewin. Indeed, the full sentiment of Whipple's missionaries can be sensed in Breck's comment on his first visit to Hole in the Day's camp. In a letter to an eastern supporter, Breck refers to the Ojibway as "poor people, who know not how to call upon His Name." In the same context he reports being awakened the next morning at daybreak "by one of the Indians singing their wild chant." [29] Not even the slightest consideration is given to the possibility that this "wild chant" is indeed calling upon "His Name," probably as both Grandfather and Grandmother with a balance and perspicuity more evident than in Breck's own observance of Matins that same morning. Breck is so infused with the unthinking superiority of his own culture that he even finds the names (untranslated) of Indian people to be crude.[30]

Eventually it becomes clear that civilizing—that is, europeanizing—Indian people evidently took precedence over conversion, or was the proof of conversion. Indeed, the two discrete acts seem to have been thoroughly intermingled in the minds of the missionaries, evidenced by Whipple's repeated invocation of "Christian civilization."[31] His clear sense of white superiority becomes most transparent at this point. He functioned out of a philosophical base that argued, "There is a deeply rooted antipathy between the habits, religion, and customs of a savage race, and the pursuits and teachings of civilization."[32] Indeed, throughout the 1860s one of his consistent criticisms of the federal government's handling of Indian affairs and the history of government-Indian relations to that time was that "no mark of disapprobation is placed upon the savage and pagan customs of the Indians."[33] And again, he criticized "the glaring defects in our Indian system" in part because it "placed no seal of condemnation on savage life."[34]

As Whipple and his missionaries engaged the battle they were clear that civilizing the Ojibway meant weaning all converts away from the community relationships that defined that culture and replacing them with new bonds. The result of mission pressure, then, was ultimately to divide the community and finally to break up tribal allegiances. This meant, among other things, separating children from parents, even from Christian parents, in order to remove the more promising children from the tribal environment entirely. To this end Whipple established schools immediately upon his arrival in Minnesota in 1860. His commitment to restricting what he called the nomadic tendencies of Indian peoples was paired with his antidote, namely, the introduction of private ownership of property. Here again the solution backfired in ways that exacerbated the problem. In attempting to teach—that is, impose—their own model of civilization on Indian people, the missionaries generated a disintegration of the societal structures of Indian civilization. European-style agriculture with its farms spaced at a distance from each other contributed to the breakdown of Indian communities just as readily as did the removal of children from the community. The attempt highlights Whipple's goal of detribalization and assimilation, but it just as readily highlights the devastation he brought to Indian people, which resulted in such cultural dislocation and disintegration.

With more than a century of hindsight, we can now look back on the resulting cultural and community breakdown, which affected whole Indian communities and not just Episcopal converts. Indeed, much of the community dysfunctionality so apparent in all of Indian country today is a direct result of the "faithful" and well-intentioned work of dedicated missions like Whipple's Minnesota diocese. But the story does not end here. Whipple, like so many others committed to Indian missions, found himself in a position to shape public policy along the lines of his own vision of Indian well-being. As a participant in the political process at both the state and national levels, he was able to pursue his misguided notion of civilization for Indian people and to press for detribalization and assimilation. If the immediate missionary presence among the Sioux and Ojibway in Minnesota functioned to erode the culture and community cohesion and strength of those peoples, Whipple's political involvement nationally pressed those concerns even farther.

Genocide and the Politics of Assimilation

When Whipple intervened in a dispute between the Red Lake Ojibways and a trader, he met with some initial resistance. "We know you speak for the Great Father," the people supposedly retorted in frustration. Whipple's response went a long way toward winning them over: "No," he reportedly answered, "I speak for the Great Spirit." Conveniently enough for Whipple, the two did not significantly differ in his mind, especially after the initiation of Grant's Peace Policy in 1869, despite Whipple's ongoing critique of that policy.[35]

As we have seen, Whipple's commentary on Indian affairs beginning with his accession to the Minnesota episcopacy marks the start of a long, sustained movement for reform of Indian affairs that came to substantial maturity after the end of the Civil War. The reform movement, which he helped to precipitate already in the early 1860s, was a solid political phenomenon by the late 1860s. It had links to the pre–Civil War antislavery movement and was championed in the U.S. Senate and in the executive branch by liberal Lincoln Republicans.

Already in 1862 Whipple and a few others were able to raise some consciousness that the Little Crow uprising had less to do with Indian savagery and much more to do with the consistent failures of the U.S. government's Indian policy. The massacre at Sand Creek in late 1864 fueled the fires for reform and generated enough interest that Whipple and a few others were no longer individual voices crying out. Many of the ideas espoused by the reformers seem to have been in the air, as it were, and erupted in the general consciousness of the movement all at once without being ascribed to any one person or group. Yet the underlying assumptions were all clearly articulated by Whipple (along with John Beeson, in some cases) in advance of the movement's birth. Its basic presuppositions held that survival of Indian peoples depended on their civilization and assimilation into American society; that dismantling of tribal structures was therefore a necessity; that learning agricultural pursuits and the value of private land tenure was fundamental to the process, and a prerequisite to granting Indian citizenship; that education and Christianization were also necessary components.[36]

Whipple was well connected politically even before his episcopal consecration. He had been born into an old colonial family and had given up a political career to enter the ministry. Nevertheless, he retained contacts and skills that he quickly put to use in the cause of Indian affairs reform. His involvement began with his letter to President Buchanan in 1860 and his audience with Lincoln in 1862 after the Little Crow War. He then continued to serve in a

variety of ways with the commissioner of Indian affairs and on several com-
missions. His participation in the Lake Mohonk Conferences is a sign of his
continuing influence after 1883.

1876 Sioux Commission and Federal Accession to the Black Hills

Perhaps the lasting effect of Whipple's political involvement can be most quickly
noted by documenting his service on a federal commission in 1876 only weeks
after the spectacular defeat of Custer at Greasy Grass.[37] In August 1876, the
annual Indian service appropriations bill included a rider creating a new Sioux
peace commission. The president appointed Whipple and seven other illustrious
citizens long familiar with Indian people and the Sioux in particular to negotiate
with the Sioux. Briefly stated, the facts are as follows:

1. The Sioux War had been caused by gross white American violations of the
1868 Fort Laramie Treaty. The violations became the rule after gold was discovered in the Black Hills. The army not only was unable to prevent these
violations but actually supported them.[38]

2. The commission itself openly acknowledged that the treaty and those before
it had been broken in every case by the United States and its citizens. In their
report to the president and the Congress, the commissioners recounted the
frustrations voiced by Sioux spokespeople and their own discomfort in recognizing
the injustices committed by the government.

> While the Indians received us as friends, and listened with kind attention to our
> propositions, we were painfully impressed with their lack of confidence in the
> pledges of the Government. At times they told their story of wrongs with such
> impassioned earnestness that our cheeks crimsoned with shame. In their speeches,
> the recital of the wrongs which their people had suffered at the hands of the
> whites, the arraignment of the Government from gross acts of injustice and fraud,
> the description of treaties made only to be broken, the doubts and distrusts of
> present professions of friendship and goodwill were portrayed in colors so vivid
> and language so terse, that admiration and surprise would have kept us silent had
> not shame and humiliation done so. That which made this arraignment more
> telling was that it often came from the lips of men who were our friends, and who
> have hoped against hope that the day might come when their wrongs would be
> redressed.[39]

3. Yet the Sioux Peace Commission carried out its responsibilities exactly as the
Congress and the commissioner of Indian affairs had instructed. The subtitle of
the Senate document receiving the commission's report is telling enough: "The
Report and Journal of Proceedings of the Commission Appointed to Obtain
Certain Concessions from the Sioux Indians." Most significantly, the commission
was to request huge new land cessions from the Sioux, including the Black Hills
and a similarly large piece of farming land, and to gain the right to build up to

three roads through Sioux territory. Whipple served as primary spokesperson for the commission in explaining the government's position to the Sioux.

There is great irony involved in the service of this commission. All of the members qualified as "friends of the Indian" and were articulate participants in the reform movement.[40] Others besides Whipple had a knack for winning the confidence of Indian adversaries. These men heard the Sioux frustration with government promises and treaties. They recognized the injustices that had been perpetuated and duly reported them back to the president and Congress. Yet they themselves proceeded, apparently in all good conscience, to perpetrate the next injustice by carrying out Congress's instructions to secure new land cessions.

Whipple clearly understood the injustices perpetrated against Indian people in prior U.S. history, just as he understood the task of the commission. He was well aware of the Indian Peace Commission that had been established by act of Congress in 1867 and its reports back to the Congress. Indeed, Whipple mentions this commission and its illustrious makeup at least four times in *Lights and Shadows*, even reprinting several pages from one of its reports in an appendix.[41] Furthermore, the report of the Sioux commission on which he served in 1876 also quoted extensively from the Indian Peace Commission. The immediate cause for establishing the Peace Commission had been a report of a Joint Special Committee of Congress that concluded that "most Indian wars could be traced to the aggressions of lawless Whites."[42] The Peace Commission's members consisted of a balance of four civilians and four military officers, including Generals William T. Sherman, Alfred G. Terry, William S. Harney, and Christopher C. Augur. In their first report (January 1868), the commissioners tried to understand events on the frontier from more of an Indian perspective. They concluded that wars between Indian people and the United States had inevitably been the fault of the United States:

> Among civilized men war usually springs from a sense of injustice. The best possible way then to avoid war is to do no act of injustice. When we learn that the same rule holds good with Indians, the chief difficulty is removed. But it is said our wars with them have been almost constant. Have we been uniformly unjust? We answer unhesitatingly, yes.[43]

The sense of U.S. injustice toward Indian people is overwhelming and convincing. The reports of this commission and those that follow are clear on this point. Nevertheless, the commission found a solution to the "Indian problem" in the perpetration of further injustices. Echoing themes sounded half a decade earlier by Whipple, the January report went on to call for the imposition and enforcement of white civilization on Indian tribes. Part of the proposal explicitly advocated detribalization:

> The object of greatest solicitude should be to break down the prejudices of tribe among the Indians; to blot out the boundary lines which divide them into distinct nations, and fuse them into one homogeneous mass. Uniformity of language will

do this—nothing else will. As this work advances each head of a family should be encouraged to select and improve a homestead. Let the women be taught to weave, to sew, and to knit. Let polygamy be punished. Encourage the building of dwellings and the gathering there of those comforts which endear the home.[44]

Lydia Maria Child, an eastern social critic and social reformer of the day, was a lone voice speaking out against the commission's argument for "blotting out" native languages in favor of English and for outlawing Indian polygamy.[45] The contemporary notions of "English Only" she calls "our haughty Anglo-Saxon ideas of force."

Prucha argues that the 1868 report was a "jeremiad, a denunciatory tirade against the evils in the Indian system."[46] Yet the makeup of the commission lends definitive authority to the report. Prucha cites a letter from Sherman in which he claims that the military commissioners were not in favor of the conclusions but were outvoted and had to sign the report.[47] Nevertheless, Sherman's own comments, recorded in the report, about the Chivington (Sand Creek) Massacre are very much in keeping with the general tone of the whole:

> The scenes which took place that day would have disgraced any tribe in the interior of Africa. This Indian problem, and a good many other problems, can be solved by one sentence in an old Book, 'Do unto others as ye would have them do unto you.'[48]

Indeed, the differences of opinion could not have been too great. The officers did sign the document after all, and they participated in a second report the same year that was equally critical of the U.S. government's lack of good faith toward the Indians. To the contrary, it was even more specific in its condemnations. This second report argued that all Indian wars had been caused by the misdeeds of white U.S. citizens; that treaties had too often involved fraud on the part of the whites; that once made the treaties and their obligations were often ignored or that treaty annuities and other appropriations fell into the hands of white traders before they reached the tribes; and that Indians had been murdered and their lands occupied illegally by settlers. The commissioners concluded that:

> When the true history of the Indian wrongs is laid before our countrymen, their united voice will demand that the honor and the interests of the nation shall no longer be sacrificed to the insatiable lust and avarice of unscrupulous men.[49]

The commissioners negotiating with the Sioux in 1876 were very much aware that they were functioning in the tradition of the Indian Peace Commission nearly ten years earlier and even quoted extensively from its words of national confession: ". . . we are alone responsible. . . . The treaty was broken, but not by the savage. . . . Wrongs are borne by him in silence that never fail to drive civilized men to deeds of violence."[50] Whipple, especially, was aware of the U.S. track record of broken treaties. He mentioned the fact often and straightforwardly wrote in his 1881 preface to Helen Hunt Jackson's famous *A Century of Dishonor*[51] that there was not one treaty that the government had not broken. Yet herein lies the greatest irony of the work of the Sioux Peace Commission: Namely, to accomplish the commission's assigned task, Whipple and the other commissioners blatantly violated the treaty that defined Lakota-U.S. relationships.

After reciting the litany of wrongs perpetrated against the Indians, the commission report goes on to document the negotiations with the Sioux, recording all the speeches made by both commissioners and Indian participants. In reality, these were not negotiations but merely a heavy-handed laying down of the law. Of the seven commissioners able to participate,[52] Whipple was by far the most outspoken, accounting for nearly half of the commission's entire speaking time apart from the actual reading of the government's provisions. At each Sioux agency, his main speech had two general purposes. The first was to assure the Sioux that the proposal was fixed in stone and could not be changed. They could either accept it or reject it, and Whipple made clear that rejection meant self-destruction for the Sioux. The following is the opening of Whipple's first speech at the Red Cloud agency (September 7). He spoke immediately after the introductory remarks by the chairman.

> I am very glad to meet you to-day, for my heart has for many years been very warm toward the red man. We came here to bring a message to you from your Great Father, and there are certain things we have given to you in his exact words; we cannot alter them, even to the scratch of a pen. . . . We are simply the messengers. It is exactly what the Great Father and Congress have made as strong as they could make when they put it in our hands.[53]

Whipple repeated this theme at other agencies as the commission made its rounds. In these remarks Whipple openly admitted that he was functioning not as a bishop but as a government agent, a mere pawn of the political structure. But he was clearly more than that in this case. The congressional act and the President's appointment were quite in line with the reformers' vision. Hence, Whipple pursued the task of the commission as his own.

Whipple's second task was to explain to the Sioux the superiority of white civilization and invite them to try to become like himself. Indeed, he gave them little choice, believing that his course was the only one that would ensure the survival of the tribes, that "instead of growing smaller and smaller until the last Indian looks upon his own grave, they might become, as the white man has become, a great and powerful people." In this cause he listed three things that accounted for white superiority:

> The first is that he [the white man] has a Government that protects him in his home, in his property, and in his life, and that Government is over him wherever he is, from one end of the land to the other. The second is that the white man lives by the use of the things which the Great Spirit has put in this world, and he always selects a home where he may find an abundance of everything that is necessary for himself and his children. The third thing is the education of his

children, training them up to be the true servants and friends of their own people, and the servants of the most high God.[54]

Unfortunately, Whipple's apologia for white culture did not extend to an explanation of the government's inability to control its own people's excesses against Indian peoples. At the same time, his own assumptions about white-Indian relationships prevented him from recognizing tribal governing structures as a valid form of true government. He might have argued that the Indian forms of government were inferior but chose instead to deny that they met any criteria for the category at all. His second point could be read as an outright reversal of reality, since tribal people in North America have always lived in intimate relationship to the land. Instead, Whipple presented a justification for consumption, a position that built on notions of "dominion" from Genesis 1. As to the third point, Whipple said "education," but what he meant was "white" education. He did not seem to recognize that Indian people surely did educate their children—within their own cultural context. Implicit, of course, was Whipple's and the reformers' hope for Indian assimilation, which was possible only through white education.

The Attack on Sovereignty

The whole of Whipple's reform notions was embodied in one of them, namely that Indian people should not be treated as if they were sovereign nations. Indeed, Whipple's bottom-line paternalism emerges most explicitly in his critique of Indian sovereignty. His arguments demonstrate explicit intentionality toward the destruction of the basic social structures of Indian community, from economies to kinship systems. Again and again, throughout his career he railed at the U.S. government's error in having conceded sovereignty in the first place. Indian sovereignty is a myth that never was a reality, according to Whipple, because Indian people have no government and no power to enforce a treaty. Thoroughly confusing the reality of nationhood with European notions of state, Whipple was incapable of seeing the enduring validity of traditional native social and political structures.

From the time of his arrival in Minnesota, Whipple saw Indian sovereignty as the critical issue that stood in the way of solving the "Indian problem." Ultimately, Whipple's early critique became the clarion call of the reform movement. A decade later it resulted in legislation to abolish treaty making with Indian tribes (1871) and eventually in legislation intentionally designed to destroy Indian community and tribal structures by eroding their land base and converting tribal lands held as joint tenure to individually owned private property.

As we have seen, the system of treaty making that defined Indian-white relationships in North America dates from early seventeenth-century New England. It persevered through the development of the U.S. Constitution and served as the primary vehicle for taking over Indian lands until 1871. Treaty making with tribes first came under attack only in the 1830s by Andrew Jackson's administration. Jackson, however, lost a crucial Supreme Court decision and succeeded in removing tribes from southeastern states only at the cost of disregarding both the Congress and the court.[55] But the real tide against sovereignty and treaty making developed only after Whipple began to publicize the issue.[56] Once again, we can see Whipple functioning as the catalyst for the later reform movement.

The "success" of the 1876 commission is readily apparent in the cover letter from John Q. Smith, commissioner of Indian affairs, to Zachariah Chandler, the secretary of the interior, forwarding the report of the commission upon the completion of its duty: "By reference to the instructions issued by this office, copy herewith, it will be seen that the commission has succeeded in the fullest and most satisfactory manner in performing the duties with which they were charged."[57]

Essentially, the commission accomplished three objectives: It reduced the Great Sioux Reservation de facto by more than half; in particular, it won the cession of the Black Hills, at least in the commissioners' understanding of the agreement. The U.S. government gained the right to build three roads through what was left of Sioux territory, from the Missouri to the newly ceded lands,[58] and the Sioux were forced to move to the Missouri River in order to receive all of their supplies and annuities.[59]

Although Whipple and other reformers had opposed the treaty-making process as a means of dealing with Indian people on principle, they were strong supporters of observing treaty proprieties for the sake of justice—until this particular opportunity, at least. Ironically, despite the injustice, winning new land cessions from the Sioux fit Whipple's and the other reformers' proposed solution to the "Indian problem." Whipple argued that the only hope for civilizing the Sioux, and hence ensuring their survival, lay in reducing their land base, which would limit their nomadic tendencies and force them to settle down in one place and take up the civilized occupation of tilling the earth (at least, it used to be a civilized occupation before the farm crisis of the 1980s).[60] Thus, the end justified the means, and the U.S. government's antitreaty theft of the Black Hills was legitimated with the help of the powerful presence of the church and one of its bishops. Of course, the reduction of the land base had an effect on tribal structures and the integrity of the tribes' cultures, which Whipple did not foresee in 1876 and which he ignored even up to his death in 1901.

Whipple held firmly to the goal of assimilation, the fundamental doctrine of the reform movement. His writings and the conduct of his missions clearly indicate that he had no overt sense of inherent white superiority other than cultural superiority. To those who harbored doubts, he continued to proclaim his resounding "Yes! Indians are capable of being civilized." All that was necessary was "fair treatment and acceptance by Indians of the values of Christianity and acquisitive capitalism."[61] Yet detribalization and the reduction of the land base hardly produced the anticipated assimilation. Rather, the Christianization of Indian peoples resulted in societal dissolution, alienation, and poverty.

If Whipple confused issues of gospel and culture in his reform commitments and in his role as pastor to the Indian mission congregations, his confusion was due in large measure to his overwhelming commitment to his own culture as an inherently superior form of human existence. In the final analysis, Whipple subscribed to an assimilationist position and helped to implement a cultural imperialism designed to destroy the cultural integrity of the very people he intended to protect. As such, he typifies the more subtle, systemic racism inherent in unbalanced cultural interrelationships. His was the sin of good intentions. Hoping to reform an oppressive system and curb some of its overt bigotry, he ended up serving that system and compounding its oppressiveness. A century later, Sioux people are still struggling to repair the damage done by Whipple's reforms and to regain the land to which they have every legitimate and moral claim.[62] They and all Native Americans continue to suffer from the cultural and spiritual dislocation furthered by Whipple and other well-meaning missionaries. With 60 percent unemployment, internalized self-despising, and a longevity of under fifty years, the genocide was still a reality as we celebrated the quincentenary of Christopher Columbus's misadventure.

The complicity is not just Whipple's, of course. The Reverend Samuel D. Hinman, for example, did the translating not only for this commission but for the 1882–83 Edmunds commission sent out to the Sioux to negotiate even further cessions of land and rights. When the Edmunds commission failed to garner enough signatures from Sioux leaders to convince Congress that at least a facade of justness had been maintained, Hinman was entrusted personally with a follow-up effort to continue the negotiation process until enough signatures had been collected. And as late as 1883, Bishop William H. Hare served as chair of a committee of missionaries who called out for further reductions in the Sioux reservation, in fact, for dividing and separating the Sioux into smaller bands. In a report to the Board of Indian Commissioners, they contended:

> The undersigned advocate the division in any just way, of the Great Sioux Res-
> ervation into a number of separate reserves for the several tribes, and the cession,
> on equitable terms, of a portion of the present reservation to the United States
> for settlement by the whites. The reservation in its present shape and size is, in
> their opinion, a serious hindrance to the prosperity and welfare of the whites, and
> a great impediment to the civilization of the Indians. But, while holding this
> opinion, they think that the method of a division provided for in the proposed
> agreement is not just, and that the consideration offered is not equitable.[63]

In an important way, Whipple—and the others involved in Indian missions— was as much a victim of Anglo arrogance as were Indian peoples. He really could not have done other than what he did, but this by no means excuses him. Indeed, it becomes all the more important for modern white America to learn from the traps and pitfalls of his valiant attempt to achieve the best for his people, including Indian people. It also becomes important for Indian people in Minnesota and the Dakotas to own this part of their past, even when it involves a certain amount of pain. Episcopal Indians, in particular, must come to acknowledge that their internalization of Whipple's heroism is to some real extent a participation in the general Indian dysfunctionality that we all experience as we live in the Indian community. Health and well-being come not from denying our past or even disassociating ourselves from it, but only from acknowledging and learning from it.

The Enduring Dilemma
Where Do We Go from Here?

All evangelism is in some sense subversion involving a change of loyalties from blood ancestors among whom historically and physically Jesus Christ is not.

—John Pobee, African theologian[1]

As Jack Forbes says of Western civilization, "Might makes right is the wétiko [Euroamerican conquest of the Americas] slogan, but it is often accompanied by self-serving doctrines of 'divine will,' 'manifest destiny,' 'the march of civilization,' or 'doing God's work.' "[2] Unfortunately, the missionary history of Christian churches among American Indians during the past five hundred years is filled with examples that attest to Forbes's point. Both implicitly and explicitly, wittingly and unwittingly, European and Euroamerican missionaries of all denominations have been a part of Europe's conquest of the Americas.

While these chapters have described four missionary stories that are quite different in their particularities, they are structurally similar. Each of these missionaries arrived with a genuine interest in the well-being of Indian people and an announced commitment to bring them the gospel message of salvation. At the same time, all came with implicit, largely unspoken commitments to their own cultural values and social structures. In the final analysis, these latter commitments proved to be the stronger and more pervasive. In every case, even for those like Bartolomé de Las Casas in Mexico and the Caribbean, Samuel Worcester who went to prison in the 1830s for his support of Cherokees in Georgia, or Samuel Kirkland among the Iroquois in eighteenth-century New York, the cultural commitments of the missionary leave even those with the best of intentions complicit in the European conquest of Indian people and complicit in the destruction of Indian societies, economies, and self-determining freedom.[3] Their own Euroamerican cultural blindness and self-righteous sense of cultural superiority meant that all missionaries inevitably assumed this posture. This inevitability, however, cannot excuse them from the devastation and death they caused. Perhaps the most fearful aspect of the missionary history of conquest and genocide is the extent to which it is a history of good intentions. None of the missionaries discussed here listed cultural genocide among his goals, yet the genocidal results are patently obvious in retrospect.

A recovering alcoholic, jokingly referring to the origins of his alcoholism, suggested that he had started with three strikes against him: he was, he announced, a priest, Irish, and the son of an alcoholic father. About the latter two he could have done nothing whatsoever, yet he readily acknowledged that he and only he was ultimately responsible for his actions. Every missionary who has served among native Americans, both past and, unfortunately, present, has been caught in a similar bind that has predicated his or her behavior in the mission context. Whether preaching to, disciplining, interpreting, or making judgments about Native Americans, the missionaries' concerns and actions have been shared by their European and Euroamerican cultural context and institutional commitments.

The missionary efforts of John Eliot, Junípero Serra, Pierre-Jean De Smet, and Henry Benjamin Whipple have demonstrated in some detail how the cultural values of the missionaries regularly became confused with the gospel they proposed to preach to Indian peoples. To the missionaries, conversion to Christianity meant conversion to Euroamerican economic and political structures, structures that entailed the long-term subjugation of tribal peoples to a conquering people. To Native Americans, it meant conversion to new and destructively alien social structures and patterns of behavior; conversion to alien concepts of morality that more often than not resulted in the erosion of native cultural values and community structures; and conversion to alien structures of intellectual thought and to religious understandings that left native people even weaker in their struggle for parity with the conqueror.

How did this happen? The question remains a complex puzzle, yet it is important for understanding ourselves and our contemporary context. As George Santayana is reputed to have said, "Those who cannot remember the past are condemned to repeat it." The question of how well-intentioned missionaries of the past could be so blind must eventually translate into an introspective questioning of our own modern blindness. It can be demonstrated that the cultural imposition of the missionaries continues today, even among the more sensitive and liberal-minded missionaries of our own time. Indeed, the problem is so systemic and so deeply ingrained that it has become part of the unarticulated foundation of all Western thought and behavior and goes unrecognized even by those whom one would expect to be most acutely sensitive.

Two important general observations emerge from the case studies of the missionaries presented here, raising issues for theological, moral, spiritual, and political reflection. The first involves the cultural reasons these missionaries were unable to see beyond their own culture and cultural commitments. The second concerns the effect of all-encompassing, systemic structures in determining peoples' (such as the missionaries' or our own) responses to the world.

Culture and the Missionary Impetus

To begin, we must come to an understanding of the pervasiveness of culture in determining structures of intellectual development as well as other, more physical patterns of behavior. This pervasiveness of culture comes to light if one assumes a definition of culture offered by Clifford Geertz: Namely, culture consists of habitual responses to the world.[4] That is, a culturally integral community of people will have a rather discrete, if enormously large, set of habitual responses to the world that function first of all to give social, spiritual, and intellectual cohesion to that community. Moreover, it is that set of habitual responses that makes the community identifiable as a discrete entity to those outside the community—e.g., to anthropologists and missionaries. The vast majority—perhaps nearly all—of the habitual behaviors that make up a community's culture remain unexamined and undifferentiated by the community as a whole. Rather, they are naively presumed to be "normal" behavior and "normal" perceptions of truth. As such, they form the foundation for what Wittgenstein identifies as "common sense knowledge." This is even true of the narrow subculture of the missionaries. Theirs was a culture of a people who for centuries had been given to careful theological and philosophical reflection on their perceptions of the world. That the missionaries, like the politicians and the soldiers, found their perceptions of the world to be definitive and universally true resulted from generations of ingrown isolation and should not be surprising. That Europeans became powerful enough to impose their notions of universality on the rest of the world was.[5]

At both lay and scholarly levels, cultural study too often is presumed appropriate only for people other than contemporary Euroamericans or for minority cultures (and subcultures) in the Euroamerican midst.[6] Thus, in academic fields such as anthropology, history of religions, or ethnohistory, scholars develop tools of critical analysis for intense reflection on culture at a theoretical level, while usually relying on some exemplary non-Euroamerican culture to demonstrate their case. Yet such studies rarely include any reflection on the cultural rootedness of the scholar's own methods, analyses, and conclusions.[7] At a more popular level in the United States, of course, culture is a category referencing the lifeways of nonwhites and is applied to white society only as a collective referent for museums, operas, and orchestras, excluding even rock concerts, let alone fork placement, dating rituals, and academic modes of discourse. Yet all of these, including "intellectual traditions," are discrete sets of habitual responses to the world.

The pervasiveness of a culturally ingrained sense of white superiority persists in the contemporary missionary context in spite of the best intentions of many modern, more sensitive missionaries. At the same time, the old, nineteenth-century style of colonial missionary endeavor also continues. Most so-called main-line denominations in the United States today still maintain one or more mission outposts that are committed to separating Indian people from their traditional cultures as quickly as possible. Much more common today, however, is the gentler liberalism that nevertheless takes paternalism as its most common form and functions to subvert and co-opt the culture of an Indian community. Perhaps the most blatant example of this mission posture is the proclivity for "liberal" and "open" white missionaries to usurp native cultural forms into their own repertoires. On many plains reservations, for instance, a sacred pipe can be found customarily placed on the altar next to holy communion on Sunday mornings. While this may seem sensitive to the needs of the community at a surface level, two deep structure messages are being spoken that are less than empowering, even disempowering, to Indian people.

First, placing a native religious symbol adjacent to the Christian focus of worship elevates the white religious expression of the gospel as superior to traditional native spiritual forms. The pipe is being used in this case to enhance the power of the missionary spiritual form, that is, holy communion. Most often, the pipe is used not as a sacrament in and of itself, but as a mere symbol of comfort to the people as they focus on the true sacramental presence in bread and wine. The behavior here is more subtle than that of missionaries a century ago, but white superiority is still implicitly emphasized even as the missionary attempts to affirm native culture.[8]

Second, since this misappropriation of native spirituality is usually performed in a context where the pastoral leadership is characteristically non-Indian, another very powerful message affirming white leadership is being demonstrated to the people. Namely, by placing the pipe, the native sacramental presence of spiritual power, on the altar, the priest is implicitly presenting himself as the new "traditional" spiritual leader of the people, the new "medicine man." Again, white priority is affirmed. It begins with a Euroamerican interpretation of the gospel, which is inherently culturally biased, and ends actualized in a white missionary presence, a person who is empowered as a white, who becomes the authority figure for an Indian congregation or even a whole tribe. For better or for worse, the role model taught to Indian peoples and internalized by them is that spiritual leadership, like economic leadership, has passed to white people.

Missionaries and Systemic Causation

A more powerful corollary to the cultural rootedness of the Euroamerican missionaries and the results of their preaching has to do with the role of all-encompassing, systemic structures in determining a people's existence. At stake here are those structures of Western, Euroamerican societies that generated the attitudes of the missionaries, as well as the attitudes of the political and military leaders who shared so many of the missionaries' beliefs and ultimate goals for dealing with the aboriginal inhabitants of North America. We can now begin to identify the structural web of a systemic *causal nexus*[9] in which these missionaries were firmly entrapped, even as we are more or less entrapped in it today.

Simply engaging in missionary bashing—the judgmental condemnation of missionaries, either individually or as a group—is to miss the point entirely. We dare not stop with an historical critique or moral judgment of the missionaries. Such a focus is simply too narrow. The trees, as it were, get in the way of seeing the forest. The missionaries were, after all, only a part of a much larger systemic whole that escaped their notice in large part even as they naively but clearly acted on behalf of significant objectives of that systemic whole.

By systemic I mean here the whole constellation of institutional and social structures that determine much of who we are individually and collectively. Of course, the systemic includes those gross institutional superstructures that are readily recognized by nearly all members of a society, but it must also encompass the more subtle and complex interconnections that might only be recognized at first by specialists. Perhaps we can begin to grasp the overwhelming nature of the systemic if we reduce it paradigmatically to economic and political terms.

From the renaissance world of ideas, Europeans were empowered to begin the ongoing process of imposing their political and economic structures on the rest of the world for their own political and economic gain. The beginning of this colonial process coincided with the voyage of Columbus and with the emergence of a new, and now pervasive, political idea, that of the modern nation-state. The old feudal kingdoms of medieval Europe gave way to a new world of centralized political order, which was capable of managing increasingly larger populations and territories. Over the past five hundred years, European colonialism and the emergence of the modern state as a political unit together have generated what Immanuel Wallerstein calls the "modern world-system."[10] The development of that world system, primarily an economic system with a strong political infrastructure, has continued to this day and is demonstrably experienced by most of the world as oppressive. The entire southern hemisphere today lives in immense poverty, even as North Americans enjoy unprecedented wealth. The fact that this wealth has been generated by the United States' exploitation of cheap labor and natural resources pillaged from the southern hemisphere is all too often ignored by U.S. citizens or excused with some rationalized line of argumentation.

Yet the wealth and comfort produced by this system, however oppressive to others, are a powerful sedative to the consciences of those who benefit directly from it. Indeed, if there are any doubts, the system itself becomes increasingly persuasive as it becomes more entrenched. The answers it offers finally become so much a part of a national community's larder of common sense knowledge that to question the system's propriety becomes unthinkable. At both conscious and subconscious levels, Euroamerican missionaries have, sometimes unthinkingly, found the political, social, and economic world system of European hegemony to be irresistible. Religious and theological reasoning became inevitably entwined with the political and economic. Even though most missionaries personally stood to gain little economically or politically, the political and economic well-being of the system continued to hold their allegiance.

Of course, one reason the systemic is so durable is that it cannot be limited so easily to the realm of the political and economic. To begin to grasp the full spectrum of the systemic, one must plot everything from cultural patterns of social behavior to institutional development and economic interaction, political structures and processes, and especially to intellectual patterns of thought. As such, the social structures of cognition that are the basis for all academic disciplines and theoretical reflection participate in the systemic whole. That is to say, the very theological discourse that propelled well-intentioned people into missionary outreach was already so systemically committed that it is unrealistic to expect any missionary to have acted apart from the common wisdom of the day. But two questions persist: How are our actions and thoughts today controlled by this same systemic whole? And how can we begin to stand apart from it with some intentionality?

Indian Dysfunctionality: The Continuing Legacy of the Missionary Effort

> Western Christian theology has been and is a most pernicious religious version of capitalist ruling-class ideology.
>
> —Itumeleng Mosala, South African theologian[11]

"The gospel," an acquaintance once suggested, "has not worked very well for native Americans." The continuing legacy of Indian evangelization can be traced today in the horrifying statistics of social well-being that chronically plague Indian peoples in North America. American Indians suffer a level of poverty marked by a per capita income that is the lowest of any ethnic group in the United States and an unemployment rate that hovers around 60 percent. In health statistics, longevity, rate of alcohol addiction, and educational achievement, American Indian peoples consistently rank far worse than any other ethnic community in the United States.[12] This *litany of woes* is part of the legacy of the missionary tradition and its participation in the conquest of Indian peoples. That traditional values and spiritual strengths continue at all is a testament to the endurance and will to survive of our tribal nations.

Yet native peoples have not survived intact. Each of our reservation or urban Indian communities is consistently plagued with individual and community dysfunctionalities that eat away at the well-being of the people. With far too much assistance and complicity from the missionaries, the U.S. government has carefully manipulated our nations into relationships of total dependence that are today best described as co-dependent. The economic viability of most reservations today depends not on natural resources, and certainly not on manufacturing, but rather on U.S. government-funded projects associated with tribal government, especially those that deliver social services, provide for health and education development, and pay the actual day-to-day expenses of running a tribal government. As a result, each reservation community is divided into the hopelessly unemployed have-nots and the few who live on more than ample government salaries.

Likewise, the various denominations that are present on reservations or in urban Indian communities are also hooked into co-dependent relationships with the Indian people they intend to serve. Very few of the hundreds of main-line denominational ministries in these contexts are self-supporting. Rather, they depend on outside charitable funding which continues to root Indian peoples in self-defeating co-dependency. While many denominations have successfully developed something of indigenous leadership, the actual power, which ultimately determines how Indian people will interpret Christianity and how they will function as churches, is almost always a white authority structure. Hence, the importance of native traditional faith ways, ceremonies, and teachings is always minimalized, even or perhaps especially by indigenous ministers.

This co-dependency takes its greatest toll on American Indian health and well-being, but its most pernicious elements are too often overlooked by both Indian and non-Indian observers. As a result, both all too often play the blame-the-victim game. One aspect of this dysfunctionality is apparent in the long excerpt from Leslie Silko's novel at the beginning of this book. In no small measure, Tayo's healing involves a self-confrontation with the *lie* of white superiority. At an intellectual level, of course, neither Indian people nor well-intentioned white friends would admit their belief in the superiority of white people. The problem is that both Indian and white act implicitly as if white culture, religion, economics, and political systems were superior, even as they both attempt to deny that they live out of this reality. Even those New Age adherents who tout the superiority of Indian spirituality finally reduce it to a commodity for individual consumption available in the white world's supermarket of spirituality.

In terms of Indian dysfunctionality, this reality can best be expressed as addictive behavior. Indian people, who suffer an interminable rate of alcohol addiction, suffer an even greater addiction. It is an addiction to the color white. More than Tayo's inability to recognize white thievery, this addiction to the color white involves a deeply ingrained need to be affirmed by perceived white authority figures and institutions. The erosion of Indian self-esteem, at a community-wide level, has meant that subconsciously and implicitly Indian people have acted as if Bureau of Indian Affairs policy, the word of a white bishop, or the affirmation of a New Age interloper into our traditional ceremonies were the critical ingredient for our well-being. So we all too readily submit to white hierarchies and cater to white friends and authority figures, hoping to win their support or approval, usually for the benefit of our own self-esteem.

A more critical form of missionary devastation exists in the modern context. Strangely enough, those denominations that have had the most success in recruiting and training Indian pastors for their congregations may also have been the most successful in blunting the cultural claims of traditional tribal existence. The conservative or even fundamentalist posture of many Indian-led congregations in nearly all Protestant denominations is a prime example of what Robert Thomas called "internal colonialism" and Annette Jaimes identifies as "auto-genocide."[13] Psychologically, both at the level of the individual and communally, American Indian people have so internalized the missionary critique of Indian culture and religious traditions and so internalized our own concession to the superiority of Euroamerican social structures that we have become complicit in our own oppression. Today, an Indian pastor is more likely than a white missionary to criticize the paganism of traditional spirituality. Just as the Euroamerican missionary cannot help but be bogged down in her or his own cultural reality, too many Indian leaders have likewise become stuck in the affirmation of white power and white structures, even to the point of strongly articulating self-criticism of traditional culture. Several generations of oppression and con-quest, along with persistently hearing the recitation of the superiority of all white forms of existence, have taken their toll on the cultural self-confidence of Indian peoples.

In spite of this recognition of Indian dysfunctionality, it should be apparent that the failure of the missionaries is not an Indian failure but the result of white, Euroamerican racism. This is not to presume that Europeans and North Americans of European descent have an inherent hatred of other people. More to the point, we are dealing with an inbred ideology that is systemically instilled from birth in both Indians and whites, although in different ways and with different results. As Robert Williams has so thoroughly demonstrated, the ide-ology has theological and juridical theoretical roots in the white European world that go back at least to the medieval European church and its enunciation of such foundational doctrines as that of "infidel dominium."[14] The resulting trium-phalism of Christianity is directly responsible for European and Euroamerican systemic notions of superiority and becomes a very useful cover, concealing and at the same time fueling the avaricious impetus for power and wealth. The notion of superiority, thoroughly infused in the Western psyche, becomes a rationale to justify colonial conquest at a political, economic, social, and religious level.

Missionaries and Colonialism

Colonization names a complex category. Historically, it identifies a political subunit of people who moved away from their home territory to a territory some distance away but nevertheless remain under the political jurisdiction of their home territory. This notion implicitly presumes that the colonizers moved to an unoccupied territory. Roman legends, for example, attributed the origins of Rome to a colony of Trojan peoples from a Greek-speaking cultural world. As such, the Romans often described themselves as having settled in an economically ideal but unoccupied site in Italy.[15] By the fifteenth century, colonization was explicitly associated with conquest, as the papal bulls so aptly attest.[16] The contemporary discussion focuses on the continuing legacy of fifteenth-century European colonization. With the benefit of hindsight, colonization is now iden-tified as a process involving an unhealthy relationship between two distinct peoples, the colonizer and the colonized.[17] More than just a convenient economic relationship, colonization has necessarily meant and continues to mean the domination of a people by another people. Furthermore, colonization has ne-cessitated and continues to necessitate the political, military, social, psycho-logical, and economic domination that virtually requires the elimination of the culture and value system of the colonized and the imposition of the values and culture of the colonizer. For the sake of economic control, the main impetus behind any colonization, the colonizer must devise ever new means of oppressing the colonized.

By and large, the Christian missionaries entered the fields of pagan harvest as an integral part of the colonizing effort of one European power or another.

Liberation theologian Justo Gonzales has argued that it has not always been the case that the missionaries functioned as agents of the colonial enterprise. Although he acknowledges that the expansion of Protestant missions in the west coincided with colonial expansion, he maintains that the complex relationship between the missionaries and colonialism has resulted in the two sometimes abetting and sometimes impeding each other. The relationship is complex, as he notes, and there are plentiful stories of missionaries of all denominations who sided with Indian peoples in disputes with governments and seemed to oppose the colonial impetus.[18] Against Gonzales, however, it must be recognized that the best of the missionaries, even when they may have avoided functioning explicitly as agents of colonialism, were always implicitly and de facto crucial to the success of colonial expansion. As Casely Hayford noted with respect to African missions nearly a century ago:

> It is the favorite practice with European nations to precede the Flag with the Gospel of Jesus Christ. . . . The missionary points to the cardinal lessons of truth, love and brotherhood as proclaimed by the Gospel, which are in accord with the higher impulses of the Native, and commands his ready respect and obedience. In the course of time, the Flag makes its appearance, and with it boldly emerges the merchant and tradesman, who before were merely sneaking round the corner.[19]

The argument of this book has been that Europe's colonial conquest of the Americas was largely fought on two separate but symbiotically related fronts. One front was relatively open and explicit; it involved the political and military strategy that drove Indian peoples from their land to make room for the more "civilized" conqueror and worked to deprive Indian peoples of any continuing self-governance or self-determination. The second front, which was just as decisive in the conquest if more subtle and less explicitly apparent, was the religious strategy pursued by missionaries of all denominations. In many instances, the missionaries arrived first, to be followed in due course by the flag, armies, farmers, and merchants. Yet it should be noted that the missionaries also stayed on and continue to this day to exert their more subtle social control over Indian communities. Williams argues that the colonial impetus means an impetus toward ensuring that the conquest is complete and decisive.[20] In the end, the conquest is not the conquest of a people by another people, but the systemic conquest of us all. In this conquest, as in the European conquest of Indian peoples, theology becomes a crucial ingredient, and the missionaries become an important strategic phalanx.

New Age and the Continuing Colonial Conquest

American Indian peoples need their white friends today more than ever. What we need, however, are genuine friends, not self-proclaimed friends who know what is best for us. We do not need so-called friends who would invite themselves in to pillage the remaining treasures of Indian spirituality, or well-meaning liberals who would try to show us how to make the system work for Indians. Rather, we need friends who will join us in the struggle against the continuing imperialism of Western, European-American culture. Genuine friends do not invade one another, physically or spiritually. Genuine friends do not prescribe for one another. But genuine friends do stand beside one another, supporting one another in times of need and crisis.

Yes, American Indians need friends today, but we need friends who will fight political battles within their own political system, not friends who have abandoned the political struggle in favor of a retreat to some reservation nirvana where all their problems dissipate into a cloud of spiritual smoke.

A curious reversal has seemingly occurred in the attitudes of many white Americans and Europeans toward Native American peoples. One of the more significant problems faced by Indian peoples today is not the intentional and overt imposition of European culture in the guise of Christianity. Nor is it the federal legislation or policy that made many tribal ceremonies illegal or the official church and state displeasure that made nearly all ceremonies difficult to sustain.[21] Rather, our modern problem is just the opposite of the problem the tribes confronted a century ago in the presence of the missionary. Nevertheless, in a subtle way, the systemic imposition of Euroamerican culture on Indian peoples persist. Paradoxically, the modern appeal of Indian spirituality to many white people has, I believe, become a major destructive force in our Indian communities. The withering of white Christian spirituality has so disillusioned people that many have engaged in a relatively intense search for something to fill the spiritual void, from Buddhism, Sufi mysticism, or Hindu meditation to Lynn Andrews hucksterism[22] or the so-called "men's council" movement, with channeling, astrology, and witchcraft falling somewhere in between. In this time of spiritual crisis, Indian spirituality, which just a short while ago was the anathema of heathenism, has now become an appealing alternative to many of the seekers.

The main difficulty is that Indian spiritual traditions are still rooted in cultural contexts that are quite foreign to white Euroamericans, yet Euroamerican cultural structures are the only devices Euroamericans have for any deep structure understanding of native spiritual traditions. Hence, those native traditions can only be understood by analogy with white experience. To use a paradigm devised by linguist Noam Chomsky over three decades ago, Indian and white people may see an identical surface structure, yet understand that surface structure in radically different ways because they are rooted in culturally disparate deep structures.[23] To make matters even more confusing, the two may go along for a long time without recognizing the deep structure differences in understanding. A simple example may suffice to demonstrate the potential for complex cultural differentiation. The sentence, "The girl hit the boy with the bat," is a single surface structure, yet it equally represents two quite different deep structure perceptions of reality. Without further investigation, one is left wondering whether the boy was struck with the bat or was holding the bat when he was struck. While this sort of confusion is a part of the intrinsic ambiguity of human language that becomes the basis for much humor and joke telling, it also has caused destruction and radical cross-cultural misunderstandings.

There is a New Age, liberal equivalent of this deep structure/surface structure dilemma. Both well-meaning New Age liberals and hopeful Indian spiritual traditionalists can easily be swept up into a modern process of imposed cultural change, without recognizing deep structure cultural imposition even when in its midst. The first Indian casualty today in any such New Age spiritual-cultural encounter is most often the strong deep structure cultural value of community and group cohesion that is important to virtually every indigenous people. As adherents of Western cultures, Europeans and Euroamericans live habitual responses to the world that are culturally rooted in an individualist deep structure rather than communitarian. In this "meeting" of cultures, the communal cultural value of Indian people is transformed by those who do not even begin to see the cultural imposition that has occurred, however unintended. Hence, dancing in a ceremony in order "that the people might live" gives way to the New Age, Euroamerican quest for individual spiritual power. What other reason would a New Yorker have for rushing out to South Dakota to spend eight days participating in a Sun Dance ceremony? Yet well-meaning New Agers drive in from New York and Chicago or fly in from Austria and Denmark to participate in annual ceremonies originally intended to secure the well-being of the local, spatially configured community. These visitors see little or nothing at all of the reservation community, pay little attention to the poverty and suffering of the people there, and finally leave having achieved only a personal, individual spiritual high. "That the people might live" survives as merely an abstract ideal at best.

The transformative, coyote twist here involves three things. The first is the impact of white participants on the thinking of younger Indians, many of whom are learning their own ceremonial traditions through increasingly individualist eyes. A second impact is the temptation of many Indians to convert their spiritual tradition into career and economic development opportunities. A certain wealth can be generated by catering to the individualist needs of white New Age aficionados, and the phenomenon has created a large number of what Churchill calls "plastic" medicine people.[24] The third effect is less immediately perceptible, but just as observable over time. It involves the shift in the thinking of the "traditional" people in an Indian community. Little by little, usually without them even perceiving it, their language about spiritual practices changes both to accommodate the participation of whites and to translate discrete cultural idiosyncracies for an alien culture in ways that can be more easily understood and appropriated (or rather, misappropriated).

Indian dysfunctionality—a result of the conquest, including the missionary endeavor—means in this case that Indian people are all too ready to participate in our own oppression and continuing conquest. Craving the approval of white acquaintances and hoping for a broader understanding of and appreciation for the validity of traditional ceremonial life, Indian people often rush to invite this new European invasion, the invasion of what remains of tribal ceremonies.

I am convinced that this meeting of cultures is in the final analysis harmful to Indian peoples and their tribal traditions. Yet, I would argue that it is equally harmful to those well-meaning white seekers who, having lost themselves back in some white community or white church, hope to find themselves on some Indian reservation. The conquest has always been spiritually harmful to Euroamericans, even when the damage has gone largely unrecognized due to the systemic camouflage of wealth and physical comfort. To their credit, many New Age adherents have seen through this part of the lie, yet they are so systemically ingrained that they fail to recognize their continued participation in acts of conquest.

NOTES

CHAPTER 1: Missionary Intentions, Missionary Violence

1. Leslie Silko, *Ceremony* (New York: Viking Press, 1977).
2. Ibid., 198ff.
3. Rollo May, *Power and Innocence* (New York: Dell, 1972), 50f.
4. See Ashis Nandy, *The Intimate Enemy: Loss and Recovery of Self under Colonialism* (Delhi: Oxford Univ. Press, 1983), v, xv, 2,7.
5. Sue and Kate McBeth, for example, Presbyterian lay missionaries in the late nine-teenth century, fully shared the commitment of their male counterparts to civilizing Indian people and bringing them "out of the blanket." See Allen Conrad Morrill and Eleanor Dunlop Morrill, *Out of the Blanket: The Story of Sue and Kate McBeth, Missionaries to the Nez Perces* (Moscow, Idaho: Univ. of Idaho Press, 1978); and Michael C. Coleman, *Presbyterian Missionary Attitudes toward American Indians, 1837–1893* (Jackson: Univ. of Mississippi Press, 1987).
6. See Clyde A. Milner, *With Good Intentions: Quaker Work among the Pawnees, Otos, and Omahas in the 1870s* (Lincoln: Univ. of Nebraska Press, 1972), for a treatment of Quaker missionary involvement during the period of Whipple's activity. There was substantial Episcopal-Quaker cooperation during these years as both pursued the same reform goals; see Rayner Wickersham Kelsey, *Friends and the Indians: 1655–1917* (Philadelphia: Associated Executive Committee of Friends on Indian Affairs, 1917), 164ff.
7. I have selected representative examples from different main-line denominations to avoid the appearance of any bias toward a particular denomination. The only church notably absent is my own denomination. The Lutherans seem to have somewhat avoided these pitfalls. Namely, in the United States, Lutherans avoided much of the missionary zeal of other churches, preferring instead simply to displace Indian people and occupy the best Indian lands in Minnesota, Iowa, Kansas, and the Dakotas. This gentle barb aside, there were indeed a few Lutheran efforts, which invariably fell into the same Euroamerican pattern of cultural arrogance. See, for example, Gerhard M. Schmutterer, *Tomahawk and Cross: Lutheran Missionaries among the Northern Plains Tribes, 1858–1866* (Sioux Falls: Augustana College, 1989), whose hagiographic content is heralded in the dedication at the beginning of the volume: "Dedicated to the memory of Moritz Braeuninger, Lutheran missionary martyr in

America. . . ." While many have assumed Braeuninger was murdered by Indians in 1860, he is just as likely to have been killed by a bear (p. 79) or drowned in the Powder River by accident. See also Erwin Fritschel, *A History of the Indian Mission of the Lutheran Iowa Synod, 1856 to 1866* (Fort Collins: Colorado State College of Education, 1939); Albert Keiser, *Lutheran Missions among the American Indians* (Minneapolis: Augsburg, 1922); Adam Schuster, *Von Indianern ermordert* (Neuendettelsau: Missionsverlag, 1929); Schmutterer and Charles Lutz, "Iowa 1854: Mission Martyr on the Western Frontier: Can Cross-cultural Mission Be Achieved?" in *Church Roots*, ed. Charles Lutz (Minneapolis: Augsburg, 1985), 117–42; and Oswald F. Wagner, "Lutheran Zealots among the Crows," *Montana: The Magazine of Western History* 22 (1972): 2–19.

8. See George Tinker and Paul Schultz, *Rivers of Life; Native Spirituality for Native Churches* (Minneapolis: Augsburg Fortress, 1988), chaps. 1 and 2, for a discussion of modern reservation realities with regard to Indian dysfunctionality and church participation.

9. Jack Norton, *When Our Worlds Cried: Genocide in Northwestern California* (San Francisco: Indian Historian Press, 1979), 137, offers a definition at its simplest: "Genocide is a modern word for an old crime. It means the deliberate destruction of national, racial, religious or ethnic groups."

10. Whipple argues that extermination was de facto policy throughout English occupation of what is now the United States: "For almost three centuries our nation has pursued the policy of extermination. . . ." Whipple, "On the Moral and Temporal Condition of the Indian Tribes on Our Western Border, 1868," Report to the Board of Mission, in *Lights and Shadows of a Long Episcopate: Being Reminiscences and Recollections of the Right Reverend Henry Benjamin Whipple, D.D., LL.D., Bishop of Minnesota* (New York: Macmillan, 1912), 521. Likewise De Smet argued in an 1859 letter: "Since the discovery of America a system of extermination, of moving the Indians, thrusting them farther back, has been pursued and practiced by the whites, little by little, at first—more and more as the European settlers multiplied and gained strength. At this day this same policy is marching with giant strides; the drama of spoliation has reached its last act, both east and west of the Rocky Mountains. The curtain will soon fall upon the poor and unhappy remnants of the Indian tribes, and they will henceforth exist only in history." The text of this letter is in Hiram Martin Chittenden and Alfred Talbot Richardson, *Life, Letters and Travels of Father Pierre-Jean De Smet, S.J., 1801–1873*, 4 vols. (New York: Francis P. Harper, 1905; reprint, New York: Arno Press and the New York Times, 1969), 4:1219.

The statistics for the Caribbean and Mexico during the first sixty years of European occupation underscore the history of genocide from the beginning of European-Indian relations. Entire native populations of most islands were indeed exterminated and not by disease alone. The native population of San Salvador, the island of Columbus's first beachhead, numbered some 100,000 when he arrived. Before his death in 1506, they had been completely exterminated. By 1522 some 300,000 had perished on the island of Española, and by the mid-sixteenth century the population of Mexico had been reduced by 80 percent. From an estimated 25 million at the time of the invasion, a mere five million had survived. See Bartolomé de Las Casas, *The Devastation of the Indies: A Brief Account*, trans. Herma Briffault (New York: Seabury, 1974), 37–41; Alfred W. Crosby, Jr., *The Columbian Exchange* (Westport, Conn.: Greenwood Press, 1972); and Sherburne F. Cook and Woodrow Borah,

Essays in Population Study, 2 vols. (Berkeley: Univ. of California Press, 1971, 1973).

Such systematic extermination was not spoken of officially in the United States or its predecessor colonies. Yet the cry was raised popularly, especially during the 1860s and 1870s in the West. For example, in July 1866, eighteen months after Sand Creek and still prior to the Red Cloud/Powder River War, a *Kansas Daily Tribune* editorial argued: "There can be no permanent, lasting peace on our frontier till these devils are exterminated. Our eastern friends may be slightly shocked at such a sentiment, but a few years' residence in the West, and acquaintance with the continued history of their outrages upon the settlers and travelers of the West, has dispersed the romance with which these people are regarded in the East." White bloodthirst was fueled again in the West after the defeat of Lt. Col. George Custer at the Greasy Grass in 1876. The *New York Times* (July 12, 1876) reported that civilians across the West were offering their own services "to avenge Custer and exterminate the Sioux." See also the *Boulder News* (July 7, 1876).

11. United Nations, "Official Records of the Third Session of the General Assembly, Part I," Sixth Committee: Annexes to the Summary Records of Meetings, 1948, Document A/C.6/288 (Geneva). My argument is largely in agreement with Ward Churchill, "Genocide: Toward a Functional Definition," *Alternatives* 11 (1986): 403–30. See also Egon Schwelb, "Human Rights," in *Encyclopaedia Britannica*, 15th ed.; and Norton, *When Our Worlds Cried*, 136–47, who also reprints the text of the convention. Helen Fein, *Accounting for Genocide* (New York: Free Press, 1979), argues that genocide is a premeditated act of "organized state murder" (p. 7). In a very helpful volume, she describes the genocide of Jews and Armenians in the twentieth century as a long history of being "decreed by the dominant group that was to perpetuate the crime to be outside the sanctified universe of obligation— that circle of people with reciprocal obligations to protect each other whose bonds arose from their relation to a deity or sacred source of authority" (p. 4).

12. Sherburne F. Cook, *The Conflict between the California Indian and White Civilization* (Berkeley: Univ. of California Press, 1976 [orig. 1943]); and Rupert and Jeanne Costo, eds., *The Missions of California: A Legacy of Genocide* (San Francisco: Indian Historian Press, 1987).

13. See Alfred W. Crosby, "Virgin Soil Epidemics as a Factor in the Aboriginal Depopulation in America," *William and Mary Quarterly*, 3d ser., 33 (1976): 289–99; Sherburne F. Cook, *The Indian Population of New England in the Seventeenth Century*, University of California Publications in Anthropology, no. 12 (Berkeley, 1976); and "The Significance of Disease in the Extinction of the New England Indians," *Human Biology* 45 (1973).

For American Indian scholarship on Indian demography, see Lenore A. Stiffarm and Phil Lane, Jr., "The Demography of Native North America: A Question of American Indian Survival," in *The State of Native America: Genocide, Colonization, and Resistance*, ed. M. Annette Jaimes (Boston: South End Press, 1992), 23–53.

14. The latter distinguishes cultural genocide, as I have defined it, from situations like that currently prevailing between Russia and Lithuania. For Lithuania, political viability much more than cultural viability is at stake. Perhaps some Wittgensteinian notion of family resemblance categorization needs to be worked out here to distinguish the sufficient cultural disparateness necessary to threaten the cultural viability of a weaker entity.

15. White reformers during the post–Civil War era, the so-called "friends of the Indian," commonly charged that the United States had failed to fulfill the obligations of a

single treaty signed with Indian people. Whipple, *Lights and Shadows of a Long Episcopate*, and Helen Hunt Jackson, *A Century of Dishonor: A Sketch of the United States Government's Dealing with Some of the Indian Tribes* (New York: 1881), are two prominent white spokespeople of that era who acknowledge this fact. Whipple repeats the allegation in his introduction to Jackson's volume.

16. On the Civilization Act (1819), see Francis Paul Prucha, *American Indian Policy in the Formative Years: The Indian Trade and Intercourse Acts, 1790–1834* (Cambridge: Harvard Univ. Press, 1962); and Bernard Sheehan, *Seeds of Extinction: Jeffersonian Philanthropy and the American Indian* (New York: W. W. Norton, 1974).

17. For a discussion of the Indian reform movement and the resulting "Peace Policy" of the Grant administration, see Robert Winston Mardock, *The Reformers and the American Indian* (Columbia: Univ. of Missouri Press, 1971); Francis Paul Prucha, *American Indian Policy in Crisis: Christian Reformers and the Indian, 1865–1900* (Norman: Univ. of Oklahoma Press, 1976); and Henry E. Fritz, *The Movement for Indian Assimilation, 1860* (Westport, Conn.: Greenwood Press, 1981).

18. For a detailed description of the uneasy but collusive relationship between the Mormon Church and the U.S. government in dealing with the native inhabitants of Utah, see Gustive O. Larson, "Brigham Young and the Indians," in *The American West: An Appraisal*, ed. Robert G. Ferris (Santa Fe: Museum of New Mexico, 1963), 176–87. See also Francis Paul Prucha, *The Great Father: The United States Government and the American Indians*, 2 vols. (Lincoln: Univ. of Nebraska Press, 1984), 1:374–80.

19. Antonio Fabié, *Vida y escritos de Don Fray Bartolomé de Las Casas* (Madrid, 1879), 2:83ff.; English translation in Benno M. Biermann, "Bartolomé de Las Casas and Verapaz," in *Bartolomé de Las Casas in History: Toward an Understanding of the Man and His Work*, ed. Juan Friede and Benjamin Keen (De Kalb: Univ. of Northern Illinois Press, 1971), 453.

20. For the establishment of the reservation policy, see Prucha, *The Great Father*, "Part Three: American Expansion and the Reservation System," 1:315–410; and Edmund Jefferson Danziger, Jr., *Indians and Bureaucrats: Administering the Reservation Policy during the Civil War* (Champaign: Univ. of Illinois Press, 1974).

21. Dee Brown, *Bury My Heart at Wounded Knee* (New York: Holt, Rinehart and Winston, 1970), 13–36.

22. See Richard Erdoes, *The Sun Dance People: The Plains Indians, Past and Present* (New York: Vintage, 1972), 175; and Vine Deloria, Jr., *Indians of the Pacific Northwest: From the Coming of the White Man to the Present Day* (Garden City, N.Y.: Doubleday, 1977), 9ff.

23. Brown, *Bury My Heart at Wounded Knee*, 414–45. For a contemporary account by an anthropologist, see James Mooney, *The Ghost-Dance Religion and the Sioux Outbreak of 1890* (Washington, D.C.: Bureau of American Ethnology, 1896). Nicholas Black Elk gives a Lakota eyewitness account, recorded in *Black Elk Speaks*, ed. John Neihardt (New York: Morrow, 1932); and a fine modern political analysis can be found in Ward Churchill, "The Earth Is Our Mother," in *The State of Native America*, 139–88.

24. Canadian history is likewise filled with examples of cultural genocide. The Canadian "Indian Act" of 1927 outlawed the potlatch ceremony, which has both social and religious aspects:

> Every Indian or other person who engages in, or assists in celebrating or encourages either directly or indirectly another to celebrate any Indian festival, dance or other ceremony of which the giving away or paying or giving

> back of money, goods or articles of any sort forms a part, or is a feature, whether such gift of money, goods or articles takes place before, at, or after the celebration of the same, or who engages or assists in any celebration or dance of which the wounding or mutilation of the dead or living body of any human being or animal forms a part or is a feature, is guilty of an offence and is liable on summary conviction to imprisonment for a term not exceeding six months and not less than two months.

Revised Statutes of Canada, 1927: vol. 2, chap. 98, no. 140, p. 2218.

25. See Robert F. Berkhofer, Jr., *The White Man's Indian* (New York: Knopf, 1978); Gary B. Nash, *Red, White, and Black: The Peoples of Early America* (Englewood Cliffs, N.J.: Prentice-Hall, 1974); James Axtell, *The European and the Indian: Essays in the Ethnohistory of Colonial North America* (Oxford: Oxford Univ. Press, 1981); and Francis Jennings, *The Invasion of America: Indians, Colonialism and the Cant of Conquest* (New York: W. W. Norton, 1975).

26. Robert H. Fuson, ed. and trans., *The Log of Christopher Columbus* (Camden, Maine: International Marine Publishing Company, 1987), 77, 80.

27. See Cornel West, *Prophesy Deliverance! An Afro-American Revolutionary Christianity* (Philadelphia: Westminster Press, 1982), especially chap. 2, "A Genealogy of Modern Racism." See also Lewis Hanke, *Aristotle and the American Indians: A Study in Race Prejudice in the Modern World* (Bloomington: Indiana Univ. Press, 1959). Hanke deals with the application of Aristotle's theory of "natural slaves" to native peoples of the Americas in the Sepúlveda/Las Casas debate in the Spanish court.

28. See, for example, the publication of the Women's National Indian Association, with Baptist affiliation and a nondenominational, evangelical stance: *Christian Civilization and Missionary Work of the Women's National Indian Association* (Philadelphia, 1887). Quite aside from the implications connoted by the phrases "Christian civilization" and "Christian culture," one might wonder how this might be compared with a Muslim or Buddhist civilization or culture.

29. Jennings, *The Invasion of America*, especially chap. 1, "Crusader Ideology," 3–14. See also Bernard W. Sheehan, *Savagism and Civility: Indians and Englishmen in Colonial Virginia* (New York: Cambridge Univ. Press, 1980), especially chap. 2, "Conversion."

30. For example, see Ward Churchill and Jim Vander Wall, *Agents of Repression: The FBI's Secret Wars against the Black Panther Party and the American Indian Movement* (Boston: South End Press, 1988); and Rex Weyler, *The Blood of the Land: The Government and Corporate War against the American Indian Movement* (New York: Vintage, 1984).

31. Henry Bowden, writing in 1981, explicitly recognizes the all-too-happy marriage between the gospel and culture in the work of the missionaries. But he continues to see this confusion as a virtue. Noting the rapid increase in mission outreach on the plains beginning with 1830, he says, "Protestants and Catholics contacted almost every aboriginal group to acquaint them with the teachings of the gospel and with white civilization. By 1835 most tribes knew that the missionaries wanted to alter their culture with schools, agriculture, and Christian morals." *American Indians and Christian Missions* (Chicago: Univ. of Chicago Press, 1981), 185. In discussing the development of schools under the guidance of ABCFM missionaries in the Dakotas, Bowden continues, "They struggled to change customary dress and general appearance, with Riggs [Rev. Return Riggs] assuring potential warriors that the 'gospel of soap was indeed a necessary adjunct and outgrowth of the Gospel of Salvation.'

Once reformed behavior had become ingrained in the students, together with a new work ethic, differentiated by sex roles, the missionaries hoped that aboriginal preferences for polygamy, subsistence hunting, communal property, and glorification of war would disappear" (pp. 188f.). Even Marla Powers, who attempts to write sympathetically about Oglala women, in a seemingly careless sentence calls the missionaries at Pine Ridge an "important civilizing agency." *Oglala Women: Myth, Ritual, and Reality* (Chicago: Univ. of Chicago Press, 1986), 108. While it is surely not the case that all cultural values are equal, it requires enormous cultural arrogance to assert so universally that one's own cultural values are invariably superior.

32. Prucha, *The Great Father*, 1:479–606, "Part Five: The Peace Policy," especially 512–27. The latter section discusses the policy of allotting Indian agencies to different churches.

33. Nevertheless, De Smet is finally accountable for having leaked that information to the American public. Despite his protestations of good intentions in keeping the information secret, in 1872 he did tell Charles Collins, editor of the *Sioux City Times*, a frontier South Dakota newspaper, that there was gold in the Black Hills. It seems more than a simple mistake to share such a *secret* with someone who buys ink by the barrel. See Churchill and Vander Wall, *Agents of Repression*, 106, 413; and Donald Jackson, *Custer's Gold: The United States Cavalry Expedition of 1874* (Lincoln: Univ. of Nebraska Press, 1966), 8.

34. From a letter written about a month later to the father general of the Jesuit order, July 20, 1838. Published in Chittenden and Richardson, 1:162f.

35. A Blackfeet Sioux band. Chittenden and Richardson, 1:251ff. De Smet quite wrongly identifies these people as related to the Blackfeet of northern Montana. So does Howard L. Harrod, *Mission among the Blackfeet* (Norman: Univ. of Oklahoma Press, 1971), 28. This incident occurred somewhere in the middle of the Dakotas as the party was headed toward Fort Pierre. The band was clearly Sioux.

36. One of De Smet's traveling companions was a Canadian, "who could speak the Sioux language a little better." Chittenden and Richardson, 1:252. De Smet, curiously enough, tries to leave the impression here that he could speak some Sioux, even though he had had only one very short encounter with Sioux peoples some years before. His confusing the two tribes is all the more curious since he had had slightly more contact with Blackfeet, a distinctly different language family. De Smet was not especially proficient linguistically.

37. Chittenden and Richardson, 1:253. Another version of the event appears in Pierre-Jean De Smet's *Letters and Sketches*, Letter IX, reprinted in Reuben Gold Thwaites, *Early Western Travels: 1748–1846*, vol. 27 (Cleveland: Arthur H. Clark, 1906), 285; and Chittenden and Richardson, 1:319.

38. The alienation of human beings from the natural world in European culture is well known: Kirkpatrick Sale, *The Conquest of Paradise: Christopher Columbus and the Columbian Legacy* (New York: Knopf, 1990), 75ff., describes the European sense of fear and enmity toward nature. "This separation from the natural world, this estrangement from the realm of the wild, I think, exists in no other complex culture on earth" (p. 78).

39. Chittenden and Richardson, 1:253f. It is equally possible, of course, that De Smet's interpreter supplied the "worms" language and did so because he already knew quite a bit of De Smet's own context and what would make sense to him.

40. By the end of his career, De Smet seems to have had a somewhat better, if still unsophisticated, understanding of such a ceremonial act. He still misses the point

of the reciprocal dualism of the sacred (e.g., male/female, above/below, sky/earth) respected by most North American Indian tribes. Reporting a Pipe ceremony in which he participated in 1868, De Smet said: "Then he raised the calumet solemnly to heaven and lowered it to earth; thus invoking, by the Indian interpretation, heaven and earth as his witnesses." Rather, Black Moon was invoking the spiritual powers of the Creator as Sky and Earth. Chittenden and Richardson, 3:915.

41. Reuben Gold Thwaites, ed., *The Jesuit Relations and Allied Documents* (Cleveland: Clark and Company, 1897), 2:89; 1:163; see also Marcel Trudel, *Beginnings of New France*, trans. Patricia Claxton (Toronto: McClelland and Stewart, 1978); and Neal Salisbury, *Manitou and Providence: Indians, Europeans, and the Making of New England, 1500–1643* (New York: Oxford Univ. Press, 1982).

42. For a discussion of this first Pilgrim-Indian treaty, see Salisbury, *Manitou and Providence*, 110–25.

43. From the opening verse of Woody Guthrie's famous song, "This Land Is Your Land."

44. There are examples of the contrary. For instance, Jason Lee, the Methodist missionary who today is called the Father of Oregon, benefited from the acquisition of extensive landholdings.

45. See Magnus Morner, *The Political and Economic Activities of the Jesuits in the La Plata Region: The Hapsburg Era*, trans. by Albert Read (Stockholm: Patterson, 1953); and Morner, ed., *The Expulsion of the Jesuits from Latin America* (New York: Knopf, 1965).

46. Bartolomé de Las Casas, *Historia de las indias*, ed. Augustín Millares Carlo, 3 vols. (Mexico City: Fondo de Cultura Económica, 1951); George Sanderlin, ed., *Witness: Writings of Bartolomé de Las Casas* (Maryknoll: Orbis Press, 1992 [1971]).

47. See Lesley Byrd Simpson, *The Encomienda in New Spain: The Beginning of Spanish Mexico*, 2d ed. (Berkeley: Univ. of California Press, 1950). John H. Elliott, *Imperial Spain: 1469–1716* (New York: St. Martin's, 1963), 59ff.; Sale, *The Conquest of Paradise*, 156f.; and Lewis Hanke, *The Spanish Struggle for Justice in the Conquest in America* (Philadelphia: Univ. of Pennsylvania Press, 1949), especially the bibliography, 182–89. Las Casas came to Española in 1502, where he was himself an *encomendero* for some eight years before taking his religious vows.

48. Leonardo Boff clearly and briefly details the cultural complicity of the early missionaries in the European conquest of the Americas:

> All missionaries, even the most prophetic, like Pedro de Córdoba (author of *Christian Doctrine for the Instruction and Formation of the Indians, after the Manner of a History*, 1510) and Bartolomé de Las Casas (*The Sole Manner of Drawing All Peoples to the True Religion*, 1537) begin with the presupposition that Christianity is the only true religion: the Indians' religions are not only false, they are the work of Satan. Method alone is open to discussion: whether to use violence and force (the common method, which went hand in hand with colonialism), or a "delicate, soft, and sweet" method (in the words of Las Casas). Either method was calculated to achieve the same effect: conversion. . . . All persons must be compelled to assimilate this religious order, which is also a cultural one."

From *New Evangelization: Good News to the Poor* (Maryknoll: Orbis Press, 1991), 15.

49. Toribio de Motolinía, *Historia de los indios de la Nueva España* (Mexico: Editorial Salvador Chávez Hayhoe, 1941) (*History of the Indians of New Spain*, trans. and

ed. by Elizabeth Andros Foster [Berkeley: Cortés Society, 1950]); Gerónimo de Mendieta, *Historia eclesiástica indiana*, 4 vols. (Mexico: Chávez Hayhoe, 1945). See also John Leddy Phelan, *The Millennial Kingdom of the Franciscans in the New World* (Berkeley: Univ. of California Press, 1970).

50. So Mendieta, *Historia*, 3:156–63, 167–72.
51. See ibid., 2:64, 96–99, 124–26, *et inter alia*; and Motolinía, *History*, 194.

CHAPTER 2: John Eliot

1. Cotton Mather, *Triumphs of the reformed religion in America: The Life and Death of the Renown'd Mr. John Eliot, Who Was the First Preacher of the Gospel to the Indians in America*, 2d ed. (London, 1691), 28.

2. John Eliot, in Henry Whitfield, ed., *The Light Appearing More and More Towards the Perfect Day. Or, a Farther Discovery of the Present State of the Indians in New-England* (1651), Massachusetts Historical Society (MHS) *Collections*, 3d ser., vol. 4 (Cambridge, Mass., 1834), 131.

3. Samuel E. Morrison, *The Intellectual Life of Colonial New England* (New York: New York Univ. Press, 1956), 306.

4. For example, Francis Jennings, "Goals and Functions of Puritan Missions to the Indians," *Ethnohistory* 18 (1971): 197–212, rewritten as "Apostle to the Indians," for his quite remarkable volume, *The Invasion of America: Indians, Colonialism, and the Cant of Conquest* (New York: W. W. Norton, 1975), 228–53; Neal Emerson Salisbury, "Conquest of the 'Savage': Puritans, Puritan Missionaries, and Indians, 1620–1680 (Ph.D. diss., University of California, Los Angeles); and "Red Puritans: The 'Praying Indians' of Massachusetts Bay and John Eliot," *William and Mary Quarterly*, 3d ser., 31 (1974): 27–54; Alden T. Vaughn, *New England Frontier: Puritans and Indians, 1620–1675*, rev. ed. (New York: W. W. Norton, 1979); and James Axtell, *The Invasion Within: The Conquest of Cultures in Colonial North America* (Oxford: Oxford Univ. Press, 1985), especially 218–41.

5. Jennings, *Invasion of America*, 232ff.

6. Ibid., 286–87. Jennings describes how Eliot was entrusted with arms and ammunition bought with mission money and how in 1669 these arms and ammunition were used by a large force of Indians to attack the Mohawks. Jennings writes: "John Eliot and Daniel Gookin disclaimed responsibility for the march, but the evidence is strong that they must have shared some sort of complicity, possibly under protest."

7. See Richard W. Cogley, "The Millenarianism of John Eliot, Apostle to the Indians," Ph.D. diss. (Ann Arbor: University Microfilms International, 1983); "John Eliot and the Origins of the American Indians," *Early American Literature* 21 (1986–87): 210–25; and J. F. Maclear, "New England and the Fifth Monarchy: The Quest for the Millennium in Early American Puritanism," *William and Mary Quarterly*, 3d ser., 32 (1975), 223–60. Cogley and Maclear attempt to explain the process of mission in New England in terms of a millenarianism overlooked by both Vaughn (a pro-Eliot historian) and Jennings (a critic of Eliot and the history written about him). Timothy J. Sehr, "John Eliot, Millennialist and Missionary," *The Historian* 46 (1984): 187–203; James A. deJong, *As the Waters Cover the Seas: Millennial Expectations in the Rise of Anglo-American Missions, 1640–1810* (Kampen: J. G. Kok, 1970); and James Holstun, "John Eliot's Empirical Millenarianism," *Representations* 4 (1983): 128–53.

8. So Jennings, *Invasion of America*, and Salisbury, "Conquest of the 'Savage.'"

9. See Carl Ortwin Sauer, *Sixteenth Century North America: The Land and the People as Seen by the Europeans* (Berkeley: Univ. of California Press, 1971), especially 231–69.

10. See again Sauer, *Sixteenth Century North America*, 231–68; Neal Salisbury, *Manitou and Providence: Indians, Europeans, and the Making of New England, 1500–1643* (Oxford: Oxford Univ. Press, 1982), 50–109; James Axtell, "Europeans, Indians and the Age of Discovery in American History Textbooks," *American Historical Review* 92 (1987): 621–32; and *After Columbus: Essays in the Ethnohistory of Colonial North America* (Oxford: Oxford Univ. Press, 1988), 144–81.

11. There is growing scholarly consensus regarding an epidemic depopulation figure of 90 percent. See Alfred W. Crosby, "God . . . Would Destroy Them, and Give Their Country to Another People," *American Heritage* 29 (1978): 38–43; "Virgin Soil Epidemics as a Factor in the Aboriginal Depopulation in America," *William and Mary Quarterly*, 3d ser., 33 (1976): 289–99; Sherburne F. Cook, *The Indian Population of New England in the Seventeenth Century*, University of California Publications in Anthropology no. 12 (Berkeley, 1976); "The Significance of Disease in the Extinction of the New England Indians," *Human Biology* 45 (1973); and Herbert U. Williams, "The Epidemic of the Indians of New England, 1616–1620, with remarks on Native American Infections," *Bulletin of the Johns Hopkins Hospital* 20 (1909): 340–49.

   On the other hand, the figure of 90 percent depopulation accords so closely with Daniel Gookin's own early estimates for New England that the figure may have been considerably higher. See Gookin, *Historical Collections* (London, 1674; new ed. by Jeffrey H. Fisk [Towtowa, N.J.: 1970]), 8–12, *inter alia*.

12. Salisbury, *Manitou and Providence*, 109. For the European (and especially English) penchant for kidnapping native peoples, see David Beers Quinn, ed., *New American World: A Documentary History of North America to 1612*, 5 vols. (New York: Arno Press, 1979), 1:110, 157, and 293.

13. William Bradford, *Of Plymouth Plantation*, ed. Samuel Eliot Morrison (New York: Knopf, 1952).

14. Edward Winslow, "Good Newes from New England" (1624), in *Chronicles of the Pilgrim Fathers of the Colony of Plymouth, from 1602 to 1625*, ed. Alexander Young (Boston, 1841), 304f., 308f.

15. Winslow, "Good Newes," 330–343; Thomas Morton, *New England Canaan*, (1632), in Peter Force, comp., *Tracts and Other Papers, Relating Principally to the Origin, Settlement, and Progress of the Colonies in North America, from the Discovery of the Country to the Year 1776* (Washington, D.C., 1836), 253f.; Phineas Pratt, "A Declaration of the Affairs of the English People that First Inhabited New England" (1662), in MHS, *Collections*, 4th ser. (1858) 4:485f.; and Bradford, *Plymouth*, 118. It should be noted in passing that the good residents of Wessagusset, unrestrained by their countrymen at Plymouth, had been stealing corn from the Indians. While there was no overt movement toward reprisal by the Indians, the English no doubt felt they had something to fear. See Winslow, "Good Newes," 302; and Salisbury, *Manitou and Providence*, 110–40.

16. Winslow, "Good Newes," 336–43.

17. Bradford, *Plymouth*, 77–79.

18. Ibid., 80f.; Dwight B. Heath, ed., *A Journal of the Pilgrims at Plymouth: Mourt's Relation* (New York: Citadel Press, 1963), 56f.; Nathaniel Morton, *New Englands*

Memorial (1669), ed. Howard J. Hall (New York, 1937), 24; and William S. Simmons, "Cultural Bias in the New England Puritans' Perception of Indians," *William and Mary Quarterly*, 3d ser., 38 (1981): 56–72.

19. Heath, *A Journal of the Pilgrims*, 60f. See the discussion by Salisbury, *Manitou and Providence*, 110–40.

20. See Heath, *A Journal of the Pilgrims*, 60f.

21. Jennings, *Invasion of America*, 226.

22. Ibid., 222. See the firsthand reports, from the English point of view, of Mason, the commander of the English troops at Mystic, and Underhill: John Mason, *A Brief History of the Pequot War: Especially of the Memorable Taking of the Fort at Mistick in Connecticut in 1637* (Boston: Kneeland and Green, 1736); and John Underhill, *Newes from America; or A New and Experimental Discoverie of New England* (London, 1638). Underhill reports three to five hundred dead (p. 39). Mason, using Pequot survivor testimony, puts the number at seven hundred. Alden T. Vaughn's attempt to rescue the reputation of New England in this encounter reads consistently as modern Puritan defensiveness: *New England Frontier*; and "Pequots and Puritans: The Causes of the War of 1637," in *Puritan New England: Essays on Religion, Society and Culture*, ed. Alden T. Vaughn and Francis J. Bremer (St. Martin's Press, 1977), 201–12.

23. Roger Williams, "Christenings Make Not Christians," in Perry Miller, ed., *The Complete Writings of Roger Williams* (New York: Russell and Russell, 1963), 7:36; *A Key Unto the Language of America* (London: G. Dexter, 1643), ed. with a critical introduction, notes, and commentary by John J. Tenuissen and Evelyn H. Hinz (Detroit: Wayne State Univ. Press, 1973), 163. See also the critique of Williams by John Cotton in the extensive Williams/Cotton debate materials, e.g., John Cotton, *A Reply to Mr. Williams His Examination*, in *Complete Writings of Roger Williams*, 2:45–47.

24. Williams to Massachusetts General Court, October 1651, in John Russell Bartlett, ed., *Letters of Williams: 1632–1682*, Narragansett Club, *Publications* (Providence: Narragansett Club, 1874), 6:231f. See also *Winthrop Papers* (Boston: Massachusetts Historical Society, 1929), 3:502f., 508, 511.

25. Bartlett, *Letters of Williams*, 6:231f., 338f., letters to the Massachusetts General Court (October 1651) and to Major Mason (June 22, 1670).

26. Jennings, *Invasion of America*, 213.

27. Rich Mather's "Preface" to John Eliot, "A Brief Relation of the Proceedings of the Lord's Work among the Indians, in Reference unto their church-Estate; the Reasons of the not Accomplishing thereof at Present: With Some of Their confessions; Whereby It May Be Discerned in Some Measure, How Far the Lord Hath Prepared among Them Fit Matter for a Church," in Eliot and Thomas Mayhew, *Tears of Repentance; or, A Further Narrative of the Progress of the Gospel amongst the Indians in New-England: setting forth, not only their present state and condition, but sundry confessions of sin by diverse of the said Indians, wrought upon by the saving power of the gospel; together with the manifestation of their faith and hope in Jesus Christ, and the work of grace upon their hearts* (London: 1653), in MHS, *Collections*, 3rd ser., 4 (1834): 205f.

28. Ibid., 215f.

29. Mather affirms Eliot's instinct that civilizing had to precede conversion and that coming to church estate required evidence of Europeanization: "But if there be any work of Grace amongst them, it would surely bring forth, and be accompanied with

the Reformation of their disordered lives, as in other things, so in their neglect of Labor, and their living in idleness and pleasure." His response, based on what he witnessed at Natick, is to cite the accomplishments of the Indian town, pointing to the "Grounds that they have fenced in, and clawed and broken up, and especially their capacious Meeting-house, the Dimensions whereof are expressed in the Relation" (from Mather's preface to Eliot, "A Brief Relation"). His praise extends to the judgment that the workmanship of the church building was so fine that it could have been built by English labor alone. Eliot reaffirmed his instinct in a 1655 tract: "But I declared unto them; how necessary it was, that they should first be Civilized, by being brought from their scattered and wild course of life, unto civill Co-habitation and Government, before they could, according to the will of God revealed in the Scriptures, be fit to be betrusted with the sacred Ordinances of Jesus Christ, in Church-Communion." Eliot, *A Late and Further Manifestation of the Progress of the Gospel amongst the Indians in New-England* . . . (Cambridge, 1671), 1f. The title of chapter 5 in Daniel Gookin, *Historical Collections of the Indians in New England* (1674), ed. Jeffrey H. Fiske (Towtowa, N.J.: 1970), 45, is also instructive: "Of the Instruments and Means that God hath used, for the Civilizing and Conversion of some of the New England Indians."

30. [Thomas Shepard], *The Day-Breaking, If Not The Sun-Rising of the Gospel with the Indians in New England* (London, 1647), in MHS, *Collections*, 3d. ser., vol. 4 (Cambridge, Mass.: 1834), 20, nos. 5 and 7; Shepard, *The Clear Sun-Shine of the Gospel Breaking Forth upon the Indians in New-England; Or, An historicall narration of Gods wonderful workings upon sundry of the Indians, both chief governors and common-people* (London: R. Cotes, 1648), in MHS, *Collections*, 3d ser., vol. 4, no. 15, p. 40; Eliot and Mayhew, *Tears of Repentance*, 234, 239; William Wood, *New Englands Prospect* (1634), in Prince Society Publications, vol. 1 (Boston: Prince Society, 1865), 85; and J. Franklin Jameson, ed., *Narratives of New Netherland, 1609–1664: Original Narratives of Early American History* (New York, 1909; reprint, New York, 1974), 173.

31. Shepard, *Clear Sun-Shine*, 45; Henry Whitfield, ed., *Strength Out of Weaknesse: or A glorious manifestation of the further progresse of the gospel amongst the Indians in New-England. Held forth in sundry letters from divers ministers and others to the corporation established by Parliament for promoting the gospel among the heathen* (London: Corporation for the Promoting and Propagating of the Gospel of Jesus Christ in New England, 1652; reprint, New York: J. Sabin, 1830–39), 178; and Gookin, *Historical Collections*, 40.

32. Shepard, *Clear Sun-Shine*, 40.

33. John Winthrop reports Eliot's modus operandi in this regard: "A third question was, if a man had two wives, (which was ordinary with them,) seeing he must put away one, which he should put away. To this it was answered, that by the law of God the first is the true wife, and the other is no wife; but if such a case fell out, they should then repair to the magistrates, and they would direct them what to do, for it might be, that the first wife might be an adulteress, etc., and then she was to be put away." James K. Hosmer, ed., *Winthrop's Journal* (New York: Scribner's, 1908), 320.

34. Reuben Gold Thwaites, ed., *The Jesuit Relations and Allied Documents* (Cleveland: Clark and Company, 1897), 25:247: "Of all the laws we propound to them, there is not one that seems so hard to them as that which forbids polygamy, and does

not allow them to break the bonds of lawful marriage" (1644). See Axtell, *Invasion Within*, 123f.

35. Given his anti-Catholic bias, Eliot would not acknowledge openly that he had borrowed his principal mission strategy from the Spanish experience in the southern hemisphere and the French in Canada. For the French effort to "reduce the Indians to civility," see Axtell, *Invasion Within*, 43–70.

36. Shepard, *Clear Sun-Shine*, 40, 50; Eliot, *A Brief Narrative of the Progress of the Gospel amongst the Indians in New-England in the Year 1670. Given in by the Reverend Mr. John Eliot, minister of the gospel there, in a letter by him directed to the right worshipful the commissioners under His Majesties Great-Seal for propagation of the gospel amongst the poor blind natives in those United Colonies* (London: Company for the propagation of the gospel in New England and the parts adjacent in America, 1671), 8.

37. Gookin describes the "Praying Indians" as living in a forty-mile radius "from us on every side," *Historical Collections*, 4:9 (p. 40). See the map included in Fiske's edition, 67.

38. Whitfield, *Strength Out of Weaknesse*, 182; Eliot, *A Further Account of the Progress of the Gospel amongst the Indians in New England: Being a Relation of the Confessions Made by Several Indians* (London, 1660), 9.

39. "Goals and Functions of Puritan Missions to the Indians" and "Apostles to the Indians," in *Invasion of America*, 228–53.

40. George Edward Ellis, "The Indians of Eastern Massachusetts," in *The Memorial History of Boston, Including Suffolk County, Massachusetts, 1630–1880*, ed. Justin Winsor, 4 vols. (Boston, 1880–81), 1:241–74.

41. *Records of the Court of Assistants of the Colony of the Massachusetts Bay, 1630–1692* (Boston, 1901), 1:17, quoted in Jennings, *Invasion of America*, 230. Eliot goes so far as to assert that the English immigration to New England was part of God's intended strategy for converting Indian peoples: "It is plainly to be observed, That one end of Gods sending so many Saints to New-England, was the Conversion of these Indians." This resonated with Richard Hakluyt's charge to Queen Elizabeth more than a century earlier: "The people of America crye oute unto us . . . to come and helpe them and bringe unto them the gladd tidings of the gospell." In E. G. R. Taylor, *The Original Writings and Correspondence of the Two Richard Hakluyts* (London: Hakluyt Society, 1935), 2:216. At least the sentiment received graphic illustration in the Massachusetts Bay Colony seal, created in 1629, the year before the departure to America. It depicts a native person crying out, "Come over and help us."

42. Thomas Lechford, *Plain Dealings; or, News from New England* (1642), ed. J. Hammond Trumbull (1867), with a new introduction by Darrett B. Rutman (New York, 1969), 56. Writing nearly three decades after the fact, Gookin, *Historical Collections*, 5:4 (p. 48), illustrates the sensitive nature of this issue. One of Eliot's three key motives was "the accomplishment and fulfilling the covenant and promise, that New England people had made unto their king, when he granted them their patent or charter, viz. that one principal end of their going to plant these countries, was, to communicate the gospel unto the native Indians; which in truth is a clause in the charter. . . ."

43. Jennings, *Invasion of America*, 207f.

44. The discrepancy in dating the event is between July 5 and September 15, 1646. See Jennings, *Invasion of America*, 238f.

There is also a discrepancy whether Eliot preached first to Cutshumoquin or

Waban. Just as Jennings points out, Winthrop's July 5 entry is left incomplete: "Three of our elders, viz., Mr. Mather, Mr. Allen and Mr. Eliot, took with them an interpreter, and went to the place where Cutshamekin, the Indian sachem [lived]." See Hosmer, *Winthrop's Journal*, 2:276. In chapter 4 of *Historical Collections*, Gookin says "Kuchamakin . . . was the first sachem and his people to whom Mr. Eliot preached . . ." (p. 40). In chapter 5, however, Gookin says: "The first place he [Eliot] began to preach at, was Nonantum, near Watertown mill, upon the south side of Charles river, about four or five miles from his own house; where lived at that time Waban, one of their principal men, and some Indians with him" (p. 46). It was "Within a short time after this first attempt," that Eliot "set up another lecture at a place, called Neponsitt, within the bounds of Dorchester, about four miles from his house southward; where another company of Indians lived, belonging unto the sachem Kuchamakin" (p. 46).

The author of "Day-Breaking" clearly dates the first mission attempt, involving Cutshumoquin, at six weeks prior to the Nonantum event of October 28.

45. Jennings, *Invasion of America*, 235ff.
46. Ibid., 233. Gookin tries to argue the contrary, that Eliot functioned as a missionary without the encouragement of any external reward. *Historical Collections*, 47. That the claim is hagiographic hyperbole can be illustrated from Gookin's own text where he reports a more than inconsiderable reward, 5:4 (pp. 48f.): "For after some years' travail in this work, the Lord was pleased to stir up divers worthy and pious persons in Old England . . . to be benefactors unto this good work; and from that beneficence this blessed instrument had some annual encouragement. . . . Hereby he was enabled to educate his five sons . . . both at the schools, and after in the college at Cambridge . . . to take their degrees of bachelors and masters of art."
47. Nathaniel B. Shurtleff, ed., *Records of the Governor and Company of the Massachusetts Bay in New England* (Boston: 1853–54), 2:55f.; Hosmer, *Winthrop's Journal*, 2:156–157.
48. [Shepard], *Day-Breaking*, 4, 11. Gookin excludes any mention of the Dorchester Mill event.
49. *Massachusetts Colonial Records*, 2:176–79: ". . . for the honor of the eternal God, whom only we worship & serve, that no person within the jurisdiction, whether Christian or pagan, either by wilfull or obstinate denying the true God, or His creation or government of the world, or shall curse God, or reproach the holy religion of God, as if it were but a politic device to keep ignorant men in awe, nor shall utter any other eminent kind of blasphemy, of the like nature & degree. . . ."
50. Ibid. "It is ordered & decreed by this Court, that no Indian shall at any time powwow, or perform outward worship to their false gods, or to the Devil, in any of our jurisdiction, whether they be such as dwell here, or shall come hither."
51. See Hosmer, *Winthrop's Journal*, 2:319, for Winthrop's 1647 entry; for Eliot's characterization, see [Wilson], *Day-Breaking*, 3:3–4.
52. Jennings, *Invasion of America*, 239ff.
53. Shurtleff, *Records of the Governor and Company*, 2:84, 134, 166, 176–79; 3:6f., 56f.; William H. Whitmore, ed., *The Colonial Laws of Massachusetts, Reprinted from the Edition of 1660, with the Supplements to 1672* (Boston, 1889), 55.
54. Fiske, in his Introduction to Gookin, *Historical Collections*, p. xi. Gookin did relinquish his position for a few years during this time due to a lengthy return to England.
55. Gookin, *Historical Collections*, 79.

56. Ibid., 80.
57. Ibid., 83f.
58. Mather, *Life and Death of John Eliot*, 40.
59. Axtell, *Invasion Within*, 159. One wonders, of course, what it is about the color "tawny" that Axtell finds "undignified," unless of course he finds the entire farming profession to be so.
60. There were other motives for pressing toward a relationship of economic dependency. More than a century and a half later, Jefferson noticed a growing reluctance on the part of Indians to concede further landholdings to the white immigrants and thereupon began to advocate "the establishment of trading houses that would get the Indians used to the white man's goods and lead them away from their primitive life." Cited from Francis Paul Prucha, *American Indian Policy in the Formative Years, 1790–1834* (Lincoln: Univ. of Nebraska Press, 1962), 215.
61. Gary C. Anders, "Theories of Underdevelopment and the American Indian," *Journal of Economic Issues* 14 (1980): 681–701, describes the modern context of Indian dependent economics.
62. Gookin, *Historical Collections*, 73f.
63. For surface structure/deep structure transformational analysis, see the transformational-generative linguistic theory of Noam Chomsky: *Aspects of the Theory of Syntax* (Cambridge, Mass.: MIT Press, 1965).
64. Axtell, *After Columbus*, 100. Cf. 100–21 (chap. 7: "Were Indian Conversions Bona Fide?").
65. See Salisbury, *Manitou and Providence*; Kenneth M. Morrison, " 'That Art of Coyning Christians': John Eliot and the Praying Indians of Massachusetts," *Ethnohistory* 21 (1974): 89, argues that contact with Europeans slowly eroded the confidence of the Indian people in their culture and in themselves.
66. Eliot, *A Late and Further Manifestation of the Progress of the Gospel amongst the Indians in New-England: Declaring that constant Love and Zeal to the Truth: With a redinesse to give Accompt of the Faith and Hope; as of their desires in church Communion to be Partakers of the Ordinances of Christ; Being a Narrative of the Examinations of the Indians, about their Knowledge in Religion, by the Elders of the Churches* (London, 1655; reprint, MHS, *Collections*, 3d ser., vol. 4 (1834). The quotation comes from the beginning of Eliot's treatise titled "A Brief Narration of the Indians Proceedings in Respect of Church-Estate, and How the Case standeth at the present," 269.
67. Eliot, "A Brief Relation," 1.
68. The presumed berbata of the 1652 confessions made by several Natick converts, in Eliot, "A Brief Relation." The catechetical exam questions asked of the Natick converts at the Roxbury examination in 1654 is published in Eliot, *A Late and Further Manifestation*, 261–87.
69. Mayhew was to have assisted in the translation duties but did not arrive. He was, however, present for the second, catechetical examination of the Natick converts two years later in 1654. This second examination was qualitatively different from the examination of the confessions made by the converts in 1652. In the earlier confessions, the converts were evidently quite free to say whatever was on their minds, although I have argued that Eliot's translation must have shaped the responses considerably in terms of Puritan idioms, metaphors, and so on. In the more catechetical exercise of 1654, the converts' responses took the form of short, memorized answers recited verbata. In any case, my analysis would not differ remarkably had

Mayhew been present for the 1652 examination. For the 1654 occasion, see Eliot, *A Late and Further Manifestation*.

Eliot does bemoan his singular service as translator for the occasion:

> . . . though I had fully used all fit means, to have all the interpreters present that I could, that so the interpretation might not depend upon my single testemony, yet so it was that they all failed, and I was alone as I have been wont to be in this work which providence of God was not to be neglected in so solemn a business (p. 25).

70. See Rich Mather's "To the Christian Reader," in the introductory materials to Eliot's "A Brief Relation."
71. Eliot, *A Further Accompt of the Progresse of the Gospel amongst the Indians in New-England* (London, 1659), 8f. Jennings compares the rather sophisticated theological language that Eliot attributed to Waban with a far less complimentary tradition relating a different level of articulation on the part of the comprador Waban. See Samuel G. Drake, *Biography and History of the Indians of North America from its First Discovery*, 11th ed. (Boston, 1856), 179f.
72. In "A Brief Relation," commenting on his translation of Ponampam's confession, Eliot says that he was "oft . . . forced to inquire of my interpreter (who sat by me) because I did not perfectly understand some sentences, especially of some of them . . ." (p. 24). After Ponampam's confession, Eliot says:

> I have been true & faithful unto their souls, and in writing and reading their Confessions, I have not knowingly, or willingly made them better, than the Lord helped themselves to make them, but am verily purswaded on good grounds, that I have rather rendered them weaker (for the most part) than they delivered them; partly by missing some words of weight in some Sentences, partly by my short and curt touches of what they more fully spake, and partly by reason of the different Idioms of their Language and ours. (pp. 26–27)

After Nishohkou's confession, Eliot says: ". . . many things he spoke that I missed, for want of through (sic) understanding some words and sentences . . ." (p. 33). By "through" Eliot must mean "thorough."

73. All quotations are from Eliot, "A Brief Relation," 5, 30, 28, 33, 38.
74. Axtell, *After Columbus*, 100–124.
75. Eliot, *A Late and Further Manifestation*, 277–84; and Axtel, *Invasion Within*, 224.
76. Eliot, "A Brief Relation," 37, 38.
77. Nataous (Wiliam of Sudbury), "The Confession Which He Made on the Fast Day before the Great Assembly," in Eliot, "A Brief Relation," 10.
78. A number of years ago, I helped prepare adult curriculum material for Indian Lutheran congregations. The intent was to present Indian Christianity using the conceptual world and modes of discourse that would be as compatible as possible with Native American cultures. Far from being merely a culturally compatible restatement of classical Lutheran theology, it was an initial attempt to recast the gospel wholly within the parameters of an Indian world, shifting fundamental metaphors, for instance, from temporal to spatial categories. Before publication, the material was tested in manuscript in a variety of Native American contexts, including among Stockbridge/Munsee peoples who once lived in southern New England and New York. Although they were not among Eliot's converts, they were

a part of the general mix of that era and were missionized early. One member of the tribe, upon reading the manuscript, allowed as how the manuscript really reflected what she had always believed. She went as far as to say that she had always believed there was something wrong with her for thinking the way she had thought. See G. Tinker and Paul Schultz, *Rivers of Life: Native Spirituality for Native Churches* (Chicago: Evangelical Lutheran Church in America, 1988).

79. Cf. John Josselyn, *An Account of Two Voyages to New-England Made during the years 1638, 1663* (London, 1674; reprint, Boston, 1865), (1896: 103): "They dye patiently both men and women, not knowing of a Hell to scare them, nor a Conscience to terrifie them."

80. *Invasion Within*, 231.

81. Whitfield, *Light Appearing*, 110f., 115f.

82. Eliot, *Brief Narrative*, 5; Whitfield, *Strength Out of Weaknesse*, 170f.

CHAPTER 3: Junípero Serra

1. *Diary of Fra Junípero Serra, O.F.M.: Being an Account of His Journey From Loreto to San Diego, March 28 to June 30, 1769* (North Providence, R.I.: Franciscan Missionaries of Mary, 1936), 32.

2. See Jack Norton (Hupa-Cherokee), "The Path of Genocide: From El Camino Real to the Gold Mines of the North," in *The Missions of California: A Legacy of Genocide*, ed. Rupert and Jeannette Costo (San Francisco: Indian Historian Press, 1987), 111–25. According to Norton, "The Franciscan period of mission rule, from 1769–1834, baptized 53,600 adult Indians and buried 37,000, a mortality rate of nearly 70 percent" (p. 113). Cf. Robert F. Heizer and Alan J. Almquist, *The Other Californians: Prejudice and Discrimination under Spain, Mexico, and the United States to 1920* (Berkeley: Univ. of California Press, 1971), 121. Evidently, when nonadult Indian baptisms are included, the statistics are even more devastating: "In the brief span of 65 years of mission operation, extending from the first founding in 1769 to the secularization of the missions in 1834, 81,000 Indians were baptized in the missions and 60,000 deaths were recorded to 1834. In 1834 there remained about 15,000 resident neophytes in the 21 missions, who were then released from the care of the mission fathers." Robert F. Heizer and Albert Elsasser, *The Natural World of the California Indian* (Berkeley: Univ. of California, 1980), 226.

Sherburne F. Cook, *The Population of the California Indians, 1769–1970* (Berkeley: Univ. of California, 1976), argues that the birth and death rates for California Indians were in an equilibrium in the mid-eighteenth century that was "profoundly disturbed" by the arrival of the Europeans and the introduction of Serra's missions. ". . . after missionization had begun, . . . conversion operated upon not a residual equilibrium population, but upon one which was itself diminishing" (p. 24). He offers an estimate for the relationship between the birth and death rates for the missions themselves during the 1769–1834 period (p. 107):

> The birth rate was high by modern standards, for it appears to have ranged between 30 to 50 births per thousand per year. Meanwhile the crude death rate was extremely high, from 70 to 90 deaths per thousand per year. The birth-death ratio was of course less than unity [ranging from .399 to .654].

In his article, "Historical Demography," in *California*, vol. 8 of *Handbook of North American Indians*, ed. Robert F. Heizer (Washington, D.C.: Smithsonian Institution, 1978), 91–98, Cook estimates an even higher peak death rate of "nearly 100 per 1,000 adults and 150 per 1,000 children" (p. 92).

3. In an ironic Franciscan reversal, Francisco Palóu appears to have played Brother Junípero to Junípero Serra's Brother Francis.

4. Francisco Palóu, *Palóu's Life of Fray Junípero Serra*, translated and annotated by Maynard J. Geiger (Washington, D.C.: Academy of American Franciscan History, 1955). Englebert says: "Except for Sulpitius Severus, who got matters under way while St. Martin was still alive, no disciple was ever in greater haste than was Francisco Palóu to see his master canonized." Omer Englebert, *The Last of the Conquistadors: Junípero Serra* (New York: Harcourt, Brace and Co., 1956), 341.

5. Palóu, *Life of Serra*, 28f., 37.

6. See Costo and Costo, *Missions of California*, especially "Part Five: The Indian Testimony," 131–70; including the essay by Father (Dr.) Michael Galvan (Ohlone), a member of the Indian tribal group that flourished around the *reduccion* at Mission San Jose, "No Veneration for Serra," 168–70.

7. Herbert E. Bolton, *The Mission as a Frontier Institution in the Spanish-American Colonies* (El Paso: Academic Reprints, 1960), 4, 13.

8. Fr. Diego Miguel Bringas, O.F.M., writing in 1796–97 in a report to the Spanish monarch on the Franciscan missions of northern Sonora, announced with a clear conscience that the primary goal of their work was "the extension of our Holy Faith and the dominion of Your Majesty over the frontier nations" [i.e., Indian communities of what was then the northern frontier of Spanish occupation in Sonora and modern Arizona]. *Friar Bringas Reports to the King: Methods of Indoctrination on the Frontier of New Spain in 1796–97*, trans. and ed. Daniel S. Matson and Bernard L. Fontana (Tucson: Univ. of Arizona Press, 1977), 39.

9. See Nancy M. Farriss, *Crown and Clergy in Colonial Mexico, 1759–1821*, University of London Historical Studies, vol. 21 (London: Athlone Press, 1968), 7, 115.

10. Matson and Fontana, in *Friar Bringas Reports to the King*, 6. See also Farriss, *Crown and Clergy in Colonial Mexico*, 7–15; and Lillian E. Fisher, *Viceregal Administration in the Spanish-American Colonies*, University of California Publications in History, vol. 15 (Berkeley, 1926), 197.

11. Junípero Serra, *Writings of Junípero Serra*, ed. Antonine Tibesar, O.F.M., vol. 3 (Washington, D.C.: Academy of American Franciscan History, 1956), 49.

12. Francisco Palóu, *Historical Memoirs of New California*, ed. Eugene Bolton (Berkeley: Univ. of California Press, 1926), 3:59–66.

13. Teodoro de Croix, upon assuming his office as commandant general, charged the Franciscans with founding two missions on the lower Colorado River, "not only for the conversion of those pagans but also to make secure the passage that had been discovered [by the Anza expeditions], in order that contact between those provinces and this one be made." Palóu, *Life of Serra*, 216.

14. Serra, *Diary*, 3.

15. Despite his severe critique of the missions, Sherburne F. Cook readily acknowledges the good intentions of Serra and his missionaries: "The mission environment was in large measure conditioned by the desire of the invading race to convert the other to a new way of thinking, a new religion. Economic and political factors were undoubtedly involved, but the driving force was provided by a group of men inspired primarily by religious, not material zeal." *The Conflict between the California Indian*

and White Civilization (Berkeley: Univ. of California Press, 1976 [1943]), 2. While the religious zeal of the missionaries must be noted, I would argue that economic and political factors were systemically involved.

16. Herbert E. Bolton, *Fray Juan Crespi: Missionary Explorer on the Pacific Coast, 1769–1774* (Berkeley: Univ. of California Press, 1927), xviiif., xxxif. Viceroy Croix received a royal order to resist the Russian incursion on January 23, 1768.

17. Francis Guest, "Mission Colonization and Political Control in Spanish California," *Journal of San Diego History* 24 (1978): 100ff., discusses the conquest of the Sierra Gorda under the leadership of José de Escandón.

18. Palóu, *Life of Serra*, 35. See also Maynard J. Geiger's naive description of the Pame mission in *The Life and Times of Fray Junípero Serra, O.F.M.: Or the Man Who Never Turned Back* (Washington, D.C.: Academy of American Franciscan History, 1959), 1:106ff.

19. See Geiger, *Life and Times of Serra*, 116.

20. Palóu, *Life of Serra*, 26.

21. Ibid., 16, and fn. 26.

22. Serra left San Diego in October 1772; stayed in Mexico City from early February until September 1773, and arrived back in California in March 1774. See Palóu, *Life of Serra*, 134–45; and Geiger, *Life and Times of Serra*, 412–19.

23. Juan de Solórzano Pereira, *Política Indiana* (Amberes, 1703), 115. Solórzano was a Spanish jurist who developed a theory of social change that provided much of the foundation upon which the missionaries built. The argument for "hispanicization" had already been articulated by Juan Gines de Sepúlveda in his well-known court debate with Bartolomé de Las Casas in 1550–51, *Democrates segundo: o, De las justas causes de la guerra contra los indios*, ed. Angel Losada (Madrid: Consejo Superior de Investigaciones Cientificas, Instituto Francisco de Vitoria, 1951), 82–112.

24. Galvan (Ohlone), "No Veneration for Serra," in Costo and Costo, *Missions of California*, 168.

25. Serra, *Diary*, 27.

26. Herbert Eugene Bolton, ed., *Font's Complete Diary of the Second Anza Expedition*, vol. 4 of *Anza's California Expeditions* (New York: Russell and Russell, 1966 [1930]), 73f.

27. Solórzano Pereira, *Política Indiana*, 115 and fn. 25.

28. Palóu, *Life of Serra*, 54.

29. Ibid., 54 and 55.

30. Ibid., 29.

31. Geiger, *Life and Times of Serra*, 127ff. describes the relationship between the missionaries and the military government in the Sierra Gorda during Serra's tenure there.

32. Adalbert von Chamisso, a visitor to the San Francisco area in 1816, observed that the native peoples of the region lived free lives until they received baptism. From that moment on, he allows, they belonged to the church. See August C. Mahr, *The Visit of the Rurik to San Francisco in 1816* (Palo Alto: Stanford Univ. Press, 1932), 174. Even Francis Guest, mission apologist, admits that "in accordance with Spanish law, baptized Indians could not live outside the reductions to which they belonged." "An Examination of the Thesis of S. F. Cook on the Forced Conversion of Indians in the California Missions," *Southern California Quarterly* 61 (1979): 5. See also his biography of Lasuén: *Fermín Francisco de Lasuén, 1736–1803: A Biography* (Washington, D.C.: Academy of American Franciscan History, 1973), 204f.; and

"Cultural Perspectives on California Mission Life," *Historical Society of Southern California Quarterly* 65 (1983): 34. For the Spanish law at stake, see *Recopilación, ley* xix, *título* iii, *libro* vi.

33. Palóu, *Life of Serra*, 32, describes the strategy for the Sierra Gorda in some detail:

> In order to obtain this spiritual fruit [the principal purpose of the conquest], the servant of God put into execution the instructions laid down for temporal government as soon as he came to the Mission Santiago de Xalpan. He used all available means to provide food and clothing for the Indians and to have them come to the mission rather than be absent in their search for necessary sustenance. To bring this about, he obtained through the syndic an increase of bulls, cows and other animals such as pigs and sheep; and maize and beans in order to plant a crop immediately. In this transaction were spent not only the balance of the three hundred pesos of the stipend supplied by His Majesty to each of the missionaries for his maintenance, but also the alms for saying Masses and those alms which he obtained from certain benefactors. By this means in a short time he obtained some kind of harvest, which increased year by year. This was distributed daily after the recitation of Christian doctrine. When, at the price of meticulous industry and with the blessings of heaven, these harvests increased and became so abundant that there was some left over and above the needs of sustenance, he instructed the Indians to sell the remainder of the seeds under the direction of the fathers. With this money more yoke of oxen were bought, while the tools and other necessary articles for work were increased. From Mexico City blankets, cloth and apparel with which to clothe the Indians were brought. He always presented the tillers with a special gift to reward them for special work and to attract the rest to this form of labor, which is the most difficult and also the most necessary.

See also Serra, et al., "Report on the Sierra Gorda Mission," Mexico, January 11, 1762, cited by Geiger in Palóu, *Life of Serra*, 349, n. 33.

34. Palóu, *Life of Serra*, 66.
35. Enrique Dussel, *History and the Theology of Liberation: A Latin American Perspective,* trans. John Drury (Maryknoll: Orbis, 1976), 93.
36. Heizer and Elsasser, *Natural World of the California Indians*, pp 1–27.
37. Palóu, *Life of Serra*, 128f.; cf. 195, 226.
38. Cook, *Conflict*, 82–83.
39. Robert Ricard, *The Spiritual Conquest of Mexico* (Berkeley: Univ. of California Press, 1966, French ed., 1933), 288ff.
40. See M. Annette Jaimes, "La Raza and Indigenism: Alternatives to Autogenocide in Native North America," *Global Justice* 3 (1992): 4–19; Francis Paul Prucha, *The Great Father: The United States Government and the American Indian* (Lincoln: Univ. of Nebraska Press, 1984), 687–715; and *Americanizing the American Indian: Writings by "Friends of the Indian," 1880–1900* (Cambridge, Mass.: Harvard Univ. Press, 1973), 197–206. Jerry Krammer, *The Second Long Walk: The Navajo-Hopi Land Dispute* (Albuquerque: Univ. of New Mexico Press, 1980), describes the damaging effects of government- and church-imposed education on the integrity of Hopi culture.
41. Jack Forbes, *A World Ruled by Cannibals: The Wetiko Disease of Aggression, Violence, and Imperialism* (Davis, Calif.: D-Q Univ. Press, 1979), 23.

42. Cook, *Conflict*, 95.
43. Edwin A. Beilhartz, *Felipe de Neve, First Governor of California*, California Historical Society, Special Publication no. 49 (San Francisco: California Historical Society, 1971), 52.
44. Quoted from H. H. Bancroft, *History of California*, 7 vols. (San Francisco: The History Company, 1886–1890), 1:593.
45. Although Cook, *Conflict*, is very critical of "the mental and moral aspects of labor" (p. 95) Serra and the others imposed on Indian converts, he would reject the use of the word "slavery" because there was "no implication of personal ownership whatever" (p. 96). Though "mental or bodily exertion of the type demanded by white civilization was completely new to . . . [Indian converts]" (p. 95), they were used to a labor system in their own native economy that was based on extensive, if intermittent, physical exertion (pp. 98f.).

   Cook is most incisive in describing the results of imposing a new culture of work in California. Indian converts found themselves "in a so-called civilized environment, surrounded by a race with an utterly different tradition . . ." (p. 99), one with a value of labor that made them appear to be incompetent—"stupid and ignorant"—and characterized them as "lazy and indolent" (p. 98).
46. Edward D. Castillo, "The Impact of Euro-American Exploration and Settlement," in *California*, vol. 8 of *Handbook of North American Indians*, ed. Robert F. Heizer (Washington, D.C.: Smithsonian Institution, 1978), 99–127; Cook, *Conflict*; and James J. Rawls, *The Indians of California: The Changing Image* (Norman: Univ. of Oklahoma Press, 1984).
47. See *Supra*, n. 32.
48. So acknowledges Fr. Zephyrin Engelhardt, a modern Franciscan apologist. *San Gabriel Mission and the Beginnings of Los Angeles* (San Gabriel: San Gabriel Herald Press, 1927), 34. See also Cook, *Conflict*, 56–91.
49. See Serra, *Writings*, 3:255.
50. Palóu, *Life of Serra*, 17. This recalls the idealism of Gerónimo de Mendieta in the late sixteenth century. Mendieta hoped the new order of the kingdom of God could be established in Mexico, built on the pristine innocence of his Indian converts. Arguing in terms of pre- and post-Constantinian eras of the church, he saw Europe as the post-Constantinian, degenerate church, while his Indian converts represented the purity of the pre-Constantinian age. Mendieta, *Historia eclesiástica indiana*, 4 vols. (Mexico: Chávez Hayhoe, 1945); see also Phelan, *The Millennial Kingdom of the Franciscans in the New World* (Berkeley: Univ. of California Press, 1970), 41–57.
51. Palóu, *Life of Serra*, 32.
52. Kirkpatrick Sale, *The Conquest of Paradise: Christopher Columbus and the Columbian Legacy* (New York: Knopf, 1990), 145f., 155, describes this reality for the early invasion. Those who came were searching for easy wealth and had no aversion to the use of force to accumulate it.
53. Palóu, *Life of Serra*, 33.
54. That the *reduccion* with its imposed European agricultural technologies experienced periodic famines is apparent from the beginning. Mendieta already acknowledges this in the sixteenth century. *Historia*, 3:184–85.
55. So argue Iris Engstrand, John Johnson, Harry Kelsey, and Doyce B. Nunis in interviews with scholars who have been supportive of the canonization of Serra. The interviews are printed verbatim in Costo and Costo, *Missions of California*,

191–222. Francis Guest, "Cultural Perspectives," 35, also explicitly makes this claim: "Some [converts] had come to the mission for the wrong reasons . . . to secure more abundant food in periods of scant rainfall when the seeds of the forest were less abundant. . . ."

56. Lester R. Rowntree, "Drought during California's Mission Period, 1769–1834," *Journal of California and Great Basin Anthropology* 7 (1985): 17.

57. See Rowntree's tables, "Drought during California's Mission Period, 1769–1834" 16ff. Cook, *Population of the California Indians*, argues that hunger only became a major concern for California Indians after the establishment of the missions.

58. Cook, *Conflict*, 55.

59. Heizer and Elsasser, *Natural World of the California Indians*, 73. "Testimony from the [California] Indians is clear on the point that they were well aware of the beneficial effects of burning off chaparral areas at intervals to increase the deer supply . . . as land managers, the Indians were in some ways far ahead of us today."

60. A. H. Gayton, "Yokuts and Western Mono Ethnography," *Anthropological Records* vol. 10, no. 2 (Berkeley: Univ. of California Press, 1948); Chester D. King, "Chumash Inter-Village Economic Exchange," *The Indian Historian* 4 (1971): 30–43; and Elizabeth Colson, "In Good Years and Bad: Food Strategies of Self-Reliant Societies," *Journal of Anthropological Research* 35 (1979): 18–29.

61. Edwin M. Loeb, *Pomo Folkways*, University of California Publications in Archaeology and Ethnology, vol. 19, no. 2 (Berkeley, 1926); and Andrew Vayda, "Pomo Trade Feasts," in *Tribal and Peasant Economies*, ed. G. Dalton (Garden City, N.Y.: Natural History Press, 1967), 494–500.

62. Serra, *Diary*, 61. That this was a general condition of native peoples along the California coast is supported by a diary entry of Fray Juan Crespi, a Serra disciple, during the Pérez expedition further up the coast in 1774. He likewise found the natives to be "fat" and of a "good appearance." See Bolton, *Fray Juan Crespi*, lif. See also the complimentary descriptions of native peoples given by Fray Pedro Font in his diary of the second (1775–76) Anza expedition. Bolton, *Font's Complete Diary*, e.g., 4:254. Even in the desert regions of the Gila River and the lower Colorado River, Indians were evidently well fed. Font describes the Gilas as "corpulent" (4:45) and as "quite fat and robust" (4:49), while the Yumas were "well-formed, tall, robust, not very ugly, and have good bodies," the women being "corpulent and of very good stature" (4:101).

63. Palóu, *Life of Serra*, 193f. Crespi, in his diary of the Fages expedition to San Francisco Bay in 1772, also describes the considerable abundance of the region and the extensive population it supported. For instance, he records that wintering geese in the San Francisco Bay area were "uncountable." Bolton, *Fray Juan Crespi*, 277–304. Otto von Kotzebue, *Voyage of Discovery into the South Sea and Bering's Straits, 1815–1818*, vol. 3 (London: Longman, 1921), speaks of the "superfluity of game" around San Francisco Bay. See also Malcolm Margolin, *The Ohlone Way: Indian Life in the San Francisco–Monterey Bay Area* (Berkeley: Heyday, 1978), 7–12.

There is also evidence of abundance in the less hospitable environments of the California interior, including the San Joaquin Valley. In the context of the same expedition, Palóu describes the flat barrenness of the "vast plain" the Spanish encountered as they moved inland from the coastal mountains and notes that there were no "pagan settlements," presumably because water and wood were in such short supply. Eventually, however, they found extensive settlements even in the hot and arid plain. Native settlements were nestled along the large rivers where wood and food were as plentiful as they seemed absent in the valley only a short ways from the river bank. Here, protecting themselves

> . . . in the shade of the abundant trees against the excessive heat of those immense plains, as well as to fish in the river, where fish were numerous, and to kill deer. There is such an abundance of deer that they seem like great herds of cattle. They feed close to the river, both because there the pasture is greener and the water is at hand, and because they have means of escape, when pursued, by jumping into the river and swimming across. However, the pagans are clever in catching them, and they maintain themselves through a great part of the year on that meat. (Palóu, *Life of Serra*, 190)

64. Palóu, *Life of Serra*, 201f., see 202. Font, in Bolton, *Font's Complete Diary*, likewise acknowledges the more than adequate agricultural production of the Yumas in the hot desert of the lower Colorado River (p. 99), and yet he would teach them to "till the soil" (p. 73).
65. Margolin, *Ohlone Way*, 40, makes this precontact claim: "There is no record of starvation anywhere in central California." Cook, *Conflict*, chap. 3, esp. 45–53; Heizer and Elsasser, *Natural World of the California Indians*, 82–113; and Colson, "In Good Years and Bad: Food Strategies of Self-Reliant Societies."
66. Serra, *Diary*, 10.
67. Margolin, *Ohlone Way*, 58–63, describes the peaceful isolation that characterized central California coastal villages because plentiful resources were immediately available for sustenance.
68. Ibid., 40, *et inter alia*; see also Heizer and Elsasser, *Natural World of the California Indians*.
69. Palóu, *Life of Serra*, 139, 144f. Geiger, Palóu's editor, writes that California (meaning the Spanish missions and presidios) suffered "semi-starvation" through these eight months (p. 416); Palóu called it the "greatest want yet experienced" (p. 139).
70. Rowntree, "Drought during California's Mission Period," 7–20.
70. Serra, *Writings*, 3:51.
72. Francis F. Guest, "The Indian Policy under Fermín Francisco de Lasuén, California's Second Father President," *California Historical Society Quarterly* 45 (1966): 207; and *Fermín Francisco de Lasuén*, 203, 236–41. See also Causa criminal de Nazario, San Diego, December 18, 1811, Archive of California, vol. 17:191–96, Bancroft Library.
73. E.g., Serra, *Diary*, 32.
74. For a somewhat later native explanation for desertion in relation to the severity of punishment, see Julio Cesar, "Cosas de Indios de California, reletados a Thomas Savage en Tres Pinos (San Benito Co.) por Julio Cesar, natural de San Luis Rey, para la Bancroft Library, 1878" (manuscript in Bancroft Library); Provincial State Papers, Benicia Military, 72:11 (manuscript in Bancroft Library). Cook, *Conflict*, 70f.
75. Serra's letter to Pangua (October 1776). Serra, *Writings*, 3:55.
76. Serra, *Writings*, 3:35 and 209.
77. Quoted from Guest, "Indian Policy under Lasuén," 195–224.
78. Again, there is a long history of military support for mendicant friars imposing discipline on Indian converts. In the sixteenth century, Franciscan Pedro de Azuaga saw native peoples as "timid, opportunistic and hypocritical." Without a coercive military presence, Azuaga argued that Indian converts might rebel against the tutelage of the friars and reject Christianity. Phelan, *Millennial Kingdom*, pp. 46f.

79. Serra, *Writings*, 3:205, 349, and 365.
80. Guest, "Cultural Perspectives," 14.
81. Ibid., 22.
82. Milton Meltzer, *Columbus and the World around Him* (New York: Franklin Watts, 1990), 31f. Cf. J. R. Hale, *Renaissance Europe* (Berkeley: Univ. of California Press, 1977).
83. Robert A. Williams, Jr., *The American Indian in Western Legal Thought: The Discourses of Conquest* (New York: Oxford Univ. Press, 1990), describes the European strategy of creating legal fictions to facilitate the conquest and legitimate the use of violence against Indian peoples. This process began with early Roman Catholic canon law, but it was continued just as readily by Protestant colonizers from the late sixteenth century on.
84. See, for instance, the native testimonies in the final section of Costo and Costo, *Missions of California*, 131–70.
85. Palóu, *Life of Serra*, 74ff.; and *Historical Memoirs*, 2:261f.
86. Palóu, *Life of Serra*, 160–66, with a fuller account in his *New California*. Pedro Font, in Bolton, *Font's Complete Diary*, 186–234, recounts a version he heard from Fr. Fray Vicente Fuster upon arriving at San Diego only two months after the uprising. Font acknowledges that "many of the rebellious Indians . . . were reduced Christians" (p. 204).
87. Bolton, *Font's Complete Diary*, 4:197 and 205.
88. Palóu, *Life of Serra*, 216ff., 223ff. For the Quechan uprising, see Bancroft, *History of California*, 1:684; and Jack Forbes, *The Warriors of the Colorado: The Yumas of the Quechan Nation and Their Neighbors* (Norman: Univ. of Oklahoma Press, 1965), 175–205.
89. Palóu, *Life of Serra*, 223f.
90. Ibid., 224.
91. Ibid., 228.
92. Ibid., 129.
93. Jack Forbes, *Native Americans of California and Nevada* (Healdsburg, Calif.: Naturegraph, 1969), 215.
94. Serra, *Diary*, 55.
95. Bolton, *Fray Juan Crespi*, e.g., 244, 245.
96. See Bolton, *Font's Complete Diary*, e.g., 4:31, where a runaway muleteer (native) was publicly whipped; and 4:235–43:

> . . . we heard the news that last night a soldier of Monterey who was in the mission guard, and four others, two servants and two muleteers of the expedition, deserted with thirty saddle animals belonging to the mission and to some private individuals, taking other things which they stole at the camp; and that the lieutenant of the expedition had set forth with nine soldiers in pursuit of them. (p. 238)

97. Serra, *Diary*, 51; cf. 43.
98. For a description of the ongoing problem of desertion through the mission period, see Heizer and Almquist, *The Other Californians*, 6ff. For contemporary sources, see Lasuén, "Representacion: San Carlos Mission, Nov. 12, 1800," Santa Barbara Mission Archives (SBMA); G. H. von Langsdorff, *Langsdorff's Narrative of the Rezanov Voyage to Nueva California in 1806*, trans. Thomas C. Russell (San Francisco: T. C. Russell, 1927); F. W. Beechey, *Narrative of a Voyage to the Pacific, 1825–28*, 2 vols.

(London, 1832), 170f.; Estevan Tapis to José Joaquinde Arrillaga, Santa Barbara, March 1, 1805 (SBMA); Narcisco Durán to the President of Mexico, San Jose Mission in Alta California, Sept. 23–26, 1830 (SBMA). Also, Theodore Henry Hittell, *History of California* (San Francisco: Occidental, 1885), 1:563–65; and Cook, *Conflict*, 57–64, 69, 70f.

99. "This [a delay in the arrival of supplies from Mexico] had caused many of the soldiers to desert, and they took refuge among the pagans, whose depraved habits they adopted." Palóu, *Life of Serra*, 131; cf. Serra, *Diary*.

100. Palóu, *Life of Serra*, 132.

101. Cortés favored the use of the religious orders because of their vow of poverty and economic disinterest and involved them in the earliest evangelizing of Mexico. Francis A. MacNutt, *Letters of Cortés*, 2 vols. (New York: Putnam, 1908), 2:214–16; Phelan, *Millennial Kingdom*, 36ff. Succeeding administrations of Mexico, however, increasingly began to see the *reducciones* as a threat to the state's political control. Mendieta likewise participated in this ongoing debate during the latter half of the sixteenth century. Phelan, 54f., 86–91; Matson and Fontana, in *Friar Bringas Reports to the King*, 3–23. In the mid-eighteenth century in Nuevo Santandar, José de Escandón initiated the first real break from the Spanish mission policy of segregating native peoples into mission compounds. Instead of a chain of missions, Escandón preferred to construct Spanish towns, pueblos, whose inhabitants would include Indians and settlers from other frontier towns. As governor of the Sierra Gorda, Escandón was necessarily in dialogue with Serra about these strategies. Guest, "Mission Colonization and Political Control."

102. Guest, "Mission Colonization and Political Control," 103, reports an old Spanish missionary adage in this regard: ". . . the shadow of the Spaniard meant the death of the Indian."

103. As viceroy, Bucareli had become a firm supporter of mission segregation in California. Bucareli and the Royal Council of War and Exchequer, in an order issued in Mexico on May 6, 1773, had decreed "that the management, control, and education of the baptized Indians pertains exclusively to the missionary fathers, it was declared that it ought to be thus in all economic matters, just as a father of a family has charge of his house, and of the education and correction of his children, and that the governor of California should be advised to preserve harmonious relations and communication with those missionary fathers." Palóu, *Historical Memoirs*, 3:50; cf., Serra, *Writings*, n. 220, 3:460.

104. Serra, *Writings*, 3:255.

105. Serra to Father Lasuén (March 1779), *Writings*, 3:293ff. and 295.

106. This lack of respect accords with the earliest Franciscan tradition of European contact with American natives. Gerónimo de Mendieta, despite or perhaps because of his tendency to romanticize the pristine nature of native peoples, did not think them capable of ruling themselves or serving as priests. See, for example, Mendieta, *Historia*, 3:103, 105. Ricard, *Spiritual Conquest of Mexico*, 217–35, includes a lengthy discussion of the sixteenth-century missionary debate over whether the Indians' intelligence or nature would enable them to be candidates for ordination to the priesthood. See also Phelan, *Millennial Kingdom*, 53, 140.

107. Serra to Felipe de Neve (January 1780), *Writings*, 3:407 and 409.

108. Serra, *Writings*, 3:205.

109. Serra, *Diary*, 61. Cf. *Diary*, 34f., 45, 60, and *inter alia*, and *Writings*, 137, 221.

110. See, e.g., Mariano Payeras to Estevan Tapis, La Purisima, January 13, 1810, Santa Barbara Mission Archives (SBMA): "As God provides everything for us, we receive annually from Mexico, in addition to the usual assistance in clothing for all and skirts for the women, cloth, silk handkerchiefs, blue cloth for jackets and trousers, shirts and cotton underwear, etc., so that every year we are able to dress thirty or forty from head to foot and to mend others." Also Narcisco Durán to the President of Mexico, San Jose Mission in Alta California, September 23–26, 1830, SBMA, in accounting for desertions and describing the "repugnance [Indians] have for becoming civilized," reported the following: ". . . comparing the new state of artificial needs in food and clothing, of civilization, and of work with the ancient natural state in which they did not have these things and in which nature spontaneously assisted them, without work, in the few needs they had, and comparing further the immense difference, for them, between a rational political liberty and that of their wandering or savage life, they would try very quickly to dispossess themselves of everything artificial and let it go to rack and ruin and would exchange with great pleasure a repugnant state of life for one that they desire." Translations from Guest, "Cultural Perspectives," n. 130.

111. Williams, *American Indian in Western Legal Thought*, describes the development of European legal notions, beginning with canon law, to rationalize the conquest of culturally divergent peoples.

112. Serra was explicitly involved in destroying Indian religious ceremonials in the Sierra Gorda, however. He went so far as to steal a native deity figure for display at the Franciscan college in Mexico City.

113. Serra, *Diary*, 34, 38. On one occasion after the expedition had encountered natives and subjected them (through coercion) to mass, the Indians responded with a spiritual act of their own that went unrecognized as such by Serra. At the conclusion of mass, as Serra records the incident, the Indians immediately loaded and smoked a pipe (p. 34).

114. Williams, *American Indian in Western Legal Thought*, 13–58, argues that Europeans had preconceived notions about the Other (i.e., infidels) and the superiority of their own cultural and religious world that became evident in medieval discussions of crusades and the canon law doctrine of "infidel dominium."

115. I am not proposing a Marxist critique but rather an indigenous peoples' resistance to both socialist and capitalist alternatives. See Ward Churchill, ed., *Marxism and Native Americans* (Boston: South End Press, 1983).

116. See Palóu's "Final Chapter: Wherein Are Gathered Together the Virtues which Shone Forth in a Singular Manner in the Servant of God Fray Junípero," *Life of Serra*, 259–95.

117. Geiger, in Palóu, *Life of Serra*, 483, n. 1.

118. Norton, "Path of Genocide," 112.

CHAPTER 4: Pierre-Jean De Smet

1. Pierre-Jean De Smet, *Letters and Sketches*, quoted from Reuben Gold Thwaites edition, *The Jesuit Relations and Allied Documents: Early Western Travels, 1748–1846*, vol. 27 (Cleveland: Arthur H. Clark, 1906), 394f. Also included in Hiram Martin Chittenden and Alfred Talbot Richardson, *Life, Letters and Travels of Father Pierre-Jean De Smet, S.J., 1801–1873*, 4 vols., in *Religion in America*, ed. Edwin S. Gaustad

(New York: Francis P. Harper, 1905; reprint, Arno Press and the New York Times, 1969), 1:395f. (hereafter cited as C&R). The context is De Smet's encounter with a camp of Crow Indian peoples.

2. Pierre-Jean De Smet, *Origin, Progress, and Prospects of the Catholic Mission to the Rocky Mountains* (Philadelphia: Fithian, 1843).

3. Edward J. Kowrach, "Foreword," in Pierre-Jean De Smet, *Oregon Missions and Travels over the Rocky Mountains in 1845–46* (Fairfield, Wash.: Ye Galleon Press, 1978; reprint from New York: Dunigan, 1847), ix.

4. Helene Magaret, *Father De Smet: Pioneer Priest of the Rockies* (New York: Farrar and Rinehart, 1940).

5. E. Laveille, S.J., *The Life of Father De Smet, S.J. (1801–1873)*, trans. Marian Lindsay, S.J. (New York: P. J. Kenedy and Sons, 1915; reprint, Chicago: Loyola Univ. Press, 1981).

6. C&R. Laveille mentions Chittenden and Richardson's commentary with great appreciation, noting that even non-Catholics have recognized De Smet's greatness.

7. Gilbert J. Garraghan, S.J., *The Jesuits of the Middle United States* (New York: America Press, 1938), 3:66–107.

8. Laveille, *Life of De Smet*, 59f.

9. John Upton Terrell, *Black Robe: The Life of Pierre-Jean De Smet: Missionary, Explorer, and Pioneer* (New York: Doubleday, 1964), 34, says that this was De Smet's assignment on the university faculty, but cites no evidence. Garraghan, *Jesuits*, 1:299, reports that De Smet was appointed "procurator or treasurer" of the college in 1830. Laveille, *Life of De Smet*, 59, reports that De Smet was only sent to the college in 1830 from Florissant to fill "the offices of Procurator, Prefect of Studies, and Professor of English." The latter accords with the listing of St. Louis faculty in *Woodstock Letters* 14 (1885): 309–13.

10. Garraghan, *Jesuits*, 3:93.

11. The First Amendment to the U.S. Constitution prohibits the establishment of a religion. Yet the Trade and Intercourse Acts of the early nineteenth century consistently did so for Indian peoples, as did the so-called Grant Peace Policy (1869–1876). See Francis Paul Prucha, *The Great Father: The United States Government and the American Indians*, 2 vols. (Lincoln: Univ. of Nebraska Press, 1984), 1:89–114, 479–533.

12. See C&R, 1:4–7; Terrell, *Black Robe*, 26; and Garraghan, *Jesuits*, 1:45–55. The funding tapped by Calhoun in this instance was the "civilization fund" created by the so-called Civilization Act (March 3, 1819), which set aside funds to support activity aimed toward civilizing Indian peoples, even and especially if it meant imposing established religion on them. In actuality, the fund was used extensively to support the missionary activity (under the guise of education) of various denominations. See 3 *United States Statutes*, 516–17; cf. the report of Calhoun, January 15, 1820, *American State Papers: Indian Affairs*, 2 vols. (Washington, D.C.: Gales and Seaton, 1832–34), 2:200–01; also, the circular of September 3, 1819, ibid., 201. For a discussion of the act, see Prucha, *The Great Father*, 1:151–54.

13. Garraghan, *Jesuits*, 1:444; and C&R, 1:31.

14. C&R, 4:1463: "Here, in this veritable corner of the world, remote from our brothers and friends, surrounded with all sorts of miseries, poor as hairless rats, constantly witnessing the most revolting scenes, which are at the same time irremediable, in the midst of strangers and infidels, I will tell you plainly, every letter that we receive

makes a great feast-day for us. . . ." From an unaddressed letter written by De Smet in French on December 18, 1839.

15. Ibid., 1:157: "Of the 2,000 Potawatomies who were at the landing, not a single one seemed to have the slightest knowledge of our arrival among them, and they all showed themselves cold or at least indifferent toward us."

16. Ibid., 1:158.

17. Garraghan, *Jesuits*, 1:422–25.

18. C&R, 1:158. "This nation is divided into different bands, living five to twenty-five miles apart. We try to visit them once a week. . . ."

19. Garraghan, *Jesuits*, 1:444, suggests this rather explicitly.

20. See the brief discussion in C&R, 1:14. De Smet's report from the fall of 1840 is in C&R, 1:258. For the opening of the mission, see C&R, 1:157. Garraghan, *Jesuits*, 1:445f., notes the date of closing.

21. Garraghan, *Jesuits*, 1:422–25.

22. James A. Clifton, *The Prairie People: Continuity and Change in Potawatomi Indian Culture, 1665–1965* (Lawrence: Regents Press of Kansas, 1977), 389ff.

23. See the discussion by Garraghan, *Jesuits*, 2:183ff., 203ff.; 3:57–61; and *inter alia*.

24. Garraghan, *Jesuits*, 3:65.

25. Garraghan, *Jesuits*, 3:93, 95, 96, notes that De Smet's superiors criticized him for engaging in too much exploratory travel such as his excursion into Canada.

26. The number comes from reading De Smet's narrative of the journey. He is careful to record every meeting with Indian people, acknowledging their tribal affiliation. Chittenden and Richardson include De Smet's description of the journey from August 9, 1845, to the end of May, 1846. C&R, 2:484–552. His encounter with Blackfeet is reported in 2:523, 526, and his failure to locate them thereafter is clear in 2:526–28, 530.

27. C&R, 1:58f.

28. It should be noted that later, in 1868, the Jesuits did reinstitute a mission among the Flatheads, which built upon the work of the earlier missionaries. At least some of the early converts remained faithful to the new way of praying, and eventually Christianity did "take" among those peoples. Nevertheless, any suggestion of a positive effect of Christianity must be questioned in terms of the long-term destabilizing effects that evangelization had on the people. See Garraghan, *Jesuits*, 2:386–91.

29. December 10, 1858, cited from Garraghan, *Jesuits*, 2:386.

30. See Garraghan, *Jesuits*, 2:375–92, for a useful discussion, as far as it goes, of the failure of the Flathead mission. Particularly good at citing excuses is L. B. Palladino, *Indian and White in the Northwest; or, A History of Catholicity in Montana* (Baltimore: John Murphy, 1894), 50.

31. See C&R, 1:228, 487; 4:1457.

32. E.g., see C&R, 3:1198: "Far be it from us, however, to accuse the noble Republic of injustice and inhumanity in her late treaties. . . . If any one must be blamed on this point, it is rather private persons, new colonists, who act and place themselves in direct opposition with the good intentions of the Government in behalf of the savages." Letter to Mrs. S. Parmentier (Brooklyn, New York), February 24, 1858. The sentiment De Smet expresses in this letter is strangely contradictory to one written three years earlier, but to a European audience, for publication in *Précis Historiques* (December 30, 1854). In that piece, De Smet argued that bringing Indians under the jurisdiction of the United States meant that "their ruin appears

certain." C&R, 3:1205. Similar in sentiment is a letter addressed to "Gustave and Marie" in April 1855: "Since the discovery of America a system of extermination, of moving the Indians, thrusting them farther back, has been pursued and practiced by the whites. . . . The curtain will soon fall upon the poor and unhappy remnants of the Indian tribes. . . ." C&R, 4:1219. The apparent discrepancy in his thinking leads one to wonder if De Smet articulated different responses for European and American audiences, a question worthy of further research.

33. De Smet wrongly exonerates the Hudson Bay Company (HBC) from any trade in alcohol, "The Hudson Bay Company does not belong to this class of traders. By them the sale of all sorts of liquors is strictly forbidden." C&R, 4:1394. See Peter C. Newman, *Caesars of the Wilderness: Company of Adventurers*, vol. 2 (Ontario: Viking Press, 1987), 109–19. Newman reports that the HBC imported "as much as fifty thousand gallons of liquor" into fur trading country each season (p. 110). As late as 1857, hearings before the British House of Commons confirmed that the HBC was still using large quantities of rum in its fur trade with Indians. One witness blamed "its necessity on American competition" (p. 348).

34. Laveille, *Life of De Smet*, 245.

35. Ibid., 247; cf. *Woodstock Letters* 16 (1887): 96.

36. Cf. C&R, 4:1479.

37. See chap. 1, 11–14.

38. C&R, 1:163.

39. De Smet, *Origin, Progress, and Prospects*, 11. Cf. C&R, 1:366: ". . . we will strive to inspire all with the love of peace, which may be accomplished if each party remains at home. For this purpose we must create among them a greater taste for agriculture than for hunting."

40. I should acknowledge that "culture" was not a particularly important category of cognition for De Smet, nor does it appear to have been generally in vogue in contemporary discourse. I have used it here and throughout the book as an artificial organizing device to clarify how the missionaries functioned. A generation later Whipple clearly and openly articulated the need to teach Indians a "Christian culture."

41. Schaeffer, commenting on the imposition of monogamy on the Flatheads, said that "it is very probable that with a less well disposed people, they would not have succeeded." Claude Schaeffer, "The First Jesuit Mission to the Flatheads, 1840–1850, A Study in Culture Conflicts," *Pacific Northwest Quarterly* 28 (1937): 236.

42. On a second visit to the Kalispels, De Smet found them in a state of continued religious fervor, faithful to the disciplines of prayer that they had learned from the missionaries. Nevertheless, he did not consider them ready for baptism and said that the two principal obstacles to their conversion were "the plurality of wives" and their affection for native gambling games. Of the first, he said, ". . . many have not the courage to separate themselves from those by whom they have children." C&R, 1:370.

43. Ibid., 1:332: "We are then agreed on this principle, that among them, even to the present time, there has been no marriage, because they have never known well in what its essence and obligation consisted." See also 1:333, 335, 341.

44. Janie L. Gustafson, *Never to Turn Back: The Controversy between Junípero Serra, OFM, Fermin Francisco de Lasuén, OFM, and Commander Fernando De Rivera y Moncada and Its Effects on the Evangelization/Acculturation of the California Indians at Missions San Diego de Alcala and San Carlos Borromeo de Carmelo in the Years 1774–*

1777 (Ph.D. diss., Univ. of Michigan, 1986), in a dissertation written in the form of a historical novel, gives a narrative description of how native California families were disrupted by missionary insistence on monogamy.

45. John D. Hunter, *Manners and Customs of Several Indian Tribes* (1832; reprint, Minneapolis: Ross and Haines, 1957), 206f. See also Richard Drinnon, *White Savage: The Case of John Dunn Hunter* (New York: Schocken, 1972).

46. Louis F. Burns, *Osage Indian Customs and Myths* (Fallbrook, Calif.: Ciga Press, 1984), 73. Burns also notes that the survival rate of older women was between three and four times that for males. See also Burns, *The Osage Annuity Rolls of 1878, First Roll, Second Roll, and Third Roll* (Fallbrook, Calif.: Ciga Press, 1980). For Burns's comment on Osage polygamy, see his *History of the Osage People* (Fallbrook, Calif.: Ciga Press, 1989), 466ff.

47. This does not mean that the tribes treated children as illegitimate, but rather that the technical category of illegitimacy came into existence at this time.

48. Again this modern critique of De Smet benefits from analytical descriptions unavailable to him in the mid-nineteenth century. Neither De Smet nor any of his contemporaries would have understood what was meant by the "infrastructure" of a society.

49. See Richard Forbis, "The Flathead Apostasy, an Interpretation," *Montana: The Magazine of Western History* 1 (1951): 35–40. See also Robert Ignatius Burns, *The Jesuits and the Indian Wars of the Northwest* (New Haven: Yale Univ. Press, 1966), 66ff.

50. See Ravelli's letter to the father general, quoted in Garraghan, *Jesuits*, 2:376ff.

51. Ibid., 3:379f.; Palladino, *Indian and White in the Northwest*, 50; and Laveille, *Life of De Smet*, 245.

52. Gregory Mengarini, S.J., "The Rocky Mountains, the Memoirs of Fr. Gregory Mengarini," *Woodstock Letters* 17 (1888): 298–309; 18 (1889): 25–43, 142–52? See also, J. C. Ewers, *The Blackfeet, Raiders on the Northern Plains* (Norman: Univ. of Oklahoma Press, 1958), 186.

53. See C&R, 2:773; cf. 2:634, where De Smet describes a Sioux chief as regarding a gift of a medal of Pope Pius IX as "War-Manitou." A very improbable conversation, of course, since "manitou" is an Algonquian word and has no place on the lips of a Sioux-speaking person.

54. See C&R, 1:220f., 365f., 319f.

55. Schaeffer, "First Jesuit Mission to the Flatheads," 227–50.

56. Ibid., 250.

57. See Leslie Spier, *The Prophet Dance of the Northwest and Its Derivatives; the Source of the Ghost Dance*, American Anthropological Association, General Series in Anthropology, no. 1 (Menasha, Wis.: 1935).

58. C&R, 3:886.

59. Letter of Father Roothaan to De Smet, April 15, 1852, in Garraghan, *Jesuits*, 2:438.

60. C&R, 1:306: "I engaged Father Point, who is skilled in drawing and architecture, to trace the plan of the missionary stations. In my mind, and still more in my heart, the material was essentially connected with the moral and religious plan. Nothing appeared to us more beautiful than the Narrative of Muratori. We had made it our Vade Mecum." Cf. Garraghan, *Jesuits*, 2:438 n. 196. Muratori, the historian of pre-1757 Jesuit missions in Paraguay, described the development of the Jesuit "reduction" system there beginning in 1610. Cf. C&R, 1:317, 327–30, 366; 2:469; 4:1240f., *inter alia*.

61. This was less than forty years after the first incursion of Europeans into the Northwest under the leadership of Lewis and Clark.

63. C&R, 1:327, 360ff. The missionaries tried at first to accompany the hunting parties on their forays onto the plains. They began to pull back fairly soon, however, after Fr. Point almost died during a winter hunt. See Palladino, *Indian and White in the Northwest*, 40f.

64. C&R, 1:177.

65. So said Mahlon Wilkinson, an Indian agent on the upper Missouri River, in the fall of 1864. See Mahlon Wilkinson to James Harlow, July 14, 1864, Letters Received, OIA, RG 75, NA; or M. Wilkinson to N. Edmunds, August 31, 1864, or Depositions Taken by M. Wilkinson, July 5, 1864, Dakota Superintendency Field Papers, Office of Indian Affairs, Record Group 76, National Archives, Washington, D.C. See also John E. Sunder, *The Fur Trade on the Upper Missouri, 1840–1865* (Norman: Univ. of Oklahoma Press, 1965), 258f.

66. By 1844 Astor reportedly had acquired a fortune of $20 million. The total private-sector economy in the United States in this period amounted to only $200 million. See Newman, *Caesars of the Wilderness*, 2:104. See also Lucy Kavaler, *The Astors: A Family Chronicle of Pomp and Power* (New York: Dodd and Mead, 1966). In 1834 Astor sold the company to Pierre Chouteau, Jr., and a powerful group of investors in St. Louis. See William E. Foley and C. David Rice, *The First Chouteaus: River Barons of Early St. Louis* (Champaign: Univ. of Illinois Press, 1983).

67. Newman, *Caesars of the Wilderness*, 2:104. David J. Wishart, *The Fur Trade of the American West, 1807–1840: A Geographical Synthesis* (Lincoln: Univ. of Nebraska Press, 1979), 207, reports that $200,000 to $300,000 in furs passed annually through St. Louis alone during the period he discusses. Sunder, *Fur Trade on the Upper Missouri*, 18, reports an annual value of $500,000 to $600,000 for the fur trade during the following two decades.

68. Newman, *Caesars of the Wilderness*, 2:25–49; Shepard Krech III, ed., *The Subarctic Fur Trade: Native Social and Economic Adaptations* (Vancouver: Univ. of Brit. Columbia Press, 1984).

69. For example, Thomas F. Schliz, "The Gros Ventres and the Canadian Fur Trade, 1754–1831," *American Indian Quarterly* 12 (1988): 41–56; Rennie Warburton and Stephen Scott, "The Fur Trade and Early Capitalist Development in British Columbia," *The Canadian Journal of Native Studies* 5 (1985): 27–46; Ron G. Bourgeault, "The Indians, the Metis and the Fur Trade: Class, Sexism and Racism in the Transition from 'Communism' to Capitalism," *Studies in Political Economy* 12 (1983): 45–80; J. Brown, "Changing Views of Fur-Trade Marriage and Domesticity: James Hargrave, His Colleagues and 'the Sex,' " *Western Canadian Journal of Anthropology* 6 (1976): 92–105; and David Wishart, "Cultures in Cooperation and Conflict: Indians in the Fur Trade on the Northern Great Plains, 1807–1840," *Journal of Historical Geography* (1976): ca. 311.

70. Both Simpson and McLoughlin seem genuinely to have wanted to end liquor trading in Indian country, but found that HBC's continued participation was necessary to compete with other fur traders. All good intentions aside, the HBC invested heavily in liquor trade with Indians well into the 1860s. George Simpson, *Fur Trade and Empire: George Simpson's Journal, Entitled "Remarks Connected with the Fur Trade in the Course of a Voyage from York Factory to Fort George and Back to York Factory, 1824–25, rev. ed., ed. Frederick Merk (Cambridge, Mass.: Harvard Univ. Press,

1968), 109f., 182ff., 320f., 334f.; John McLoughlin, *Letters of Dr. John McLoughlin: Written at Fort Vancouver, 1829–1832*, ed. Burt Brown Barker (Portland, Ore.: Binfords and Mort, for the Oregon Historical Society, 1948), 16f., 215f., 237; Newman, *Caesars of the Wilderness*, 2:221f., 348; and E. E. Rich, *The Fur Trade and the Northwest to 1857*, Canadian Centenary Series (Toronto: McClelland and Stewart, 1967), 276.

71. Sunder, *Fur Trade on the Upper Missouri*, 9, 47–51, 70f., 89–92, 112–16, 224, 226–28, 258; cf. Wishart, *Fur Trade of the American West*, 69–74. Like his HBC competitors, Chouteau claimed competitive necessity as the reason for using liquor as a trade item for Indian furs. For Chouteau and the American Fur Company, this meant consistently circumventing U.S. laws prohibiting liquor trade with Indians and using a variety of subterfuges to avoid detection by government agents. More than once Chouteau and his company found themselves in court defending themselves against liquor-trading allegations.

72. Simpson, *Fur Trade and Empire*, 108. It should be noted here that Simpson's exploitation imposed significant changes on the earlier hunting economy of tribal peoples (see 14f., above). The dramatic shift was from a balanced male/female subsistence economy toward a predominantly male-oriented economy dedicated to generating an economic surplus. Moreover, it was a shift that necessarily created a dependent relationship. The independent subsistence economy had been self-sufficient. The new relationship created a dependence on European trade goods that could be satisfied only by depleting natural resources. Dependent on new signifiers of wealth such as metal knives, pots, trade cloth, and the like, Indian people were forced to harvest animals for fur pelts in unprecedented numbers, which soon resulted in the near eradication of those animals in many regions. The more the tribes adopted this new economy and its addictions, the more they became locked into a dependent relationship.

73. Simpson, *Fur Trade and Empire*, 108.

74. Note the letters of John McLoughlin to De Smet included in C&R, 4:1554ff. McLoughlin, born a Protestant, had become a Catholic and found the combination of personal piety and business quite convenient. His relationship with the missionaries clearly involved more than casual acceptance or even support but extended to technical assistance, advice, and material support. Eventually, the Catholic presence in the Northwest followed this advice from McLoughlin, expressed in a September 27, 1841, letter to De Smet:

> . . . I am fully convinced that the most effectual mode to diffuse the doctrines of the Roman Catholic Church in this part of the world is by establishing it on a good foundation in the Willamette and Cowlitz among the settlers— as the Indians will form themselves on what they see done by the whites. . . . (C&R, 4:1555)

75. Ibid., 4:1554.

76. Ibid., 3:803.

77. Ibid., 1:294f., a letter to the father provincial; written on August 16, 1841, from Fort Hall. For acute examples of De Smet's symbiotic relationship with these fur companies, see ibid., 1:201, 244, 294f., 356f., 388; 2:478, 518f., 607f., 609f., 628, 653, 772, 783; 3:819, 836f.; 4:1234, 1311, 1551–57.

78. Immanuel Wallerstein, *The Modern World-System: Capitalist Agriculture and the Origins of the European World-Economy in the Sixteenth Century* (New York: Academic Press, 1974).

79. Wishart, *Fur Trade of the American West*, 69, in an understatement says, ". . . the indiscriminate use of alcohol in the fur trade may have damaged the Indian societies as seriously as the smallpox epidemics." Newman, *Caesars of the Wilderness*, 109, more realistically acknowledges, ". . . the unrestrained use of liquor in the Canadian fur trade ranks as one of history's more malevolent crimes against humanity."

80. C&R, 1:172–76.

81. Ibid., 4:1214f., a letter to the father general, undated but supposed by the editors to have been written in 1839. De Smet also reports having written a letter to the "Government" in 1839 complaining about the alcohol trade; ibid., 1:184f.

82. See ibid., 2:595; 4:1343, 1537f.

83. See C&R's note, 1:171. They argue that his letters were "carefully pruned by his superiors of whatever savored too much of hostile criticism of the Government": 1:17.

84. The dubious honor for this ingenuity goes to Kenneth McKenzie, chief factor for the Upper Missouri Outfit of the American Fur Company at Fort Union, near the Canadian line. Importing a still to manufacture whiskey on site was an attempt to circumvent U.S. law, which made it illegal to ship liquor into Indian territory. Of course, in this endeavor McKenzie had the full support of Pierre Chouteau, the director of the Western Division of the American Fur Company in 1833 and head of the company after 1834. See Paul Chrisler Phillips, *The Fur Trade*, vol. 2 (Norman: Univ. of Oklahoma Press, 1961), 426ff. See also Hiram Martin Chittenden, *The American Fur Trade of the Far West*, 2 vols. (New York: Press of the Pioneers, 1935; reprint, Lincoln: Univ. of Nebraska Press, 1986), 1:358f. For a brief survey of U.S. laws regulating the liquor trade with Indian peoples, see Phillips, 2:377–88.

85. C&R, 1:172–76. Fifty barrels of whiskey were unloaded for Indian trade at Council Bluffs on May 30, 1839. At 30 gallons per barrel (C&R, 1:172), that amounts to 1,500 gallons! De Smet reports that other shipments arrived throughout the summer. In 1844 the American Fur Company claimed that 400–500 gallons of liquor were needed in the spring to maintain business with the Blackfeet and Assiniboins tribes, since other companies were using alcohol as a trade good. See Sunder, *Fur Trade on the Upper Missouri*, 71f. In 1822 the American Fur Company steamer *Chippewa* blew up on its way to Fort Benton with 22 barrels (660 gallons) of illicit liquor on board (Sunder, 224–28).

86. Hiram Martin Chittenden tells with considerable delight of the great lengths to which American Fur Company boats (captain and crew) went to conceal their liquor cargoes to avoid detection by government agents at the two checkpoints along the Missouri River. One incident involved John James Audubon, the famed naturalist and ornithologist. As a passenger, he helped delay an army inspection of the steamboat *Omega* and then further assisted in distracting the army captain just prior to his inspection by wining and dining him on board. *History of Early Steamboat Navigation on the Missouri River: Life and Adventures of Joseph La Barge, Pioneer Navigator and Indian Trader for Fifty Years with the Commerce of the Missouri Valley*, 2 vols. (New York: Francis P. Harper, 1903), 1:141–48. Chittenden has another account in *American Fur Trade of the Far West*, 2:669ff.

87. Sunder, *Fur Trade on the Upper Missouri*, 23–25, 98–100.

88. De Smet made this comment on hearing that a German prince intended to establish a German settlement in the territory of modern Wyoming, in the midst of Crow, Blackfeet, Sioux, Cheyenne, Arapaho, and Snake peoples, "the most feared and warlike of the desert." Cited from C&R, 2:686.

89. Cited from Chittenden and Richardson's introduction, C&R, 1:127. Cf. 2:645f.: "Will not the President of the Republic, like some of his predecessors, pluck some plumes from the Indian eagle, once the emblem of their greatness and power, to place them in the crown composed of the trophies of his administration? In the limits which I trace he will bind an extent of country vast enough to be represented by three or four stars more of the first magnitude, which will enhance the lustre of the galaxy of the flag of the Union. This great territory will hold an immense population, destined to form several great and flourishing states. But then, what will become of the Indians?"

90. Garraghan, *Jesuits*, 3:94, offers another explanation for De Smet's fame, although he recognizes that De Smet's time in direct mission service was short. He goes a step further in arguing that De Smet was temperamentally unsuited to missionary service.

91. In the midst of his 1864 peace mission on behalf of the U.S. government, De Smet suddenly abandoned his efforts when he encountered Alfred Sully's army ready to attack the same Sioux bands as punishment for their involvement in the Little Crow uprising of 1862: "In consequence of the general's declaration . . . , my errand of peace, though sanctioned by the Government, became bootless and could only serve to place me in a false position: namely, that of being face to face with the Indians without being able to do them the least service." C&R, 3:834.

92. Melodie Beattie, *Co-Dependent No More: How to Stop Controlling Others and Start Caring for Yourself* (San Francisco: Harper and Row, 1987); Ann Wilson Schaef, *When Society Becomes an Addict* (San Francisco: Harper and Row, 1987).

93. C&R, 3:1195ff., 1202; 4:1219.

94. Ibid., 1:119; cf. 3:1198, where De Smet says, "Far be it from us, however, to accuse the noble Republic of injustice and inhumanity in her late treaties. It seems to us, on the contrary, that no nation has ever furnished them more means of civilization. If any one must be blamed on this point, it is rather private persons, new colonists, who act and place themselves in direct opposition with the good intentions of the Government in behalf of the savages."

95. Compare the second quotation at the beginning of this section with similar language extolling the virtues of the United States: C&R, 3:1198; 4:1422f., 1427f., 1447f., 1455f., *inter alia*.

96. Ibid., 2:485–87 and 645. "Every time that I have traveled over these plains, I have found myself amid a painful void; Europe's thousands of poor, who cry for bread and wander without shelter or hope, often occur to my thoughts. 'Unhappy poor,' I often cry, 'why are ye not here: Your industry and toil would end your sorrows. Here you might rear a smiling home, and reap in plenty the fruit of your toil.' Yes, this void exists; and when I say it must be filled by an industrious and persevering population, I concur with the experience of all travelers." C&R, 2:647.

97. Ibid., 2:719f.

98. "Were I authorized to suggest a plan, I would propose to have all the upper lands evacuated by the whites, and form of it a territory exclusively of Indians. . . ." Ibid., 4:1240f.

99. Letter of September 27, 1841, from McLoughlin to De Smet, C&R, 4:1555.

100. Ibid., 2:676.

101. See ibid., 2:740ff.; 4:1570ff.

102. Ibid., 2:732 and 763.

103. Ibid., 1:72.

104. For Pleasonton's letters, see ibid., 4:1572 and 1577f.; for Harney's letter, see 4:1579.

105. Ibid., 3:816.

106. Ibid., 3:812 and 1514.

107. Ibid., 3:879ff.

108. Ibid., 3:860, 861, 878. In an 1866 letter, De Smet offers a long catalog of the injustices suffered by Indian peoples. See ibid., 3:1200f. Cf. 3:1201–11. "It is rarely . . . that he [the Indian] is the aggressor; surely, not once out of ten provoking cases." Ibid., 2:727.

109. Ibid., 3:859.

110. Ibid., 4:1585.

111. Neal Salisbury, *Manitou and Providence: Indians, Europeans, and the Making of New England, 1500–1643* (Oxford: Oxford Univ. Press, 1982), 261, n. 59.

112. See De Smet's letter to the mother superior of the Termond Orphanage, July 1839, written from the Potawatomi mission at St. Joseph, C&R, 1:185: "I visit the Indians in their wigwams, either as a missionary, if they are disposed to listen to me, or as a physician to see their sick. When I find a little child in great danger, and I perceive the parents have no desire to hear the word of God, I spread out my vials: I recommend my medicines strongly. I first bathe the child with a little camphor; then taking some baptismal water, I baptize it without their suspecting it. . . ."

113. C&R, 2:630ff.

114. De Smet himself told the story. References in later writings attest to the ongoing friendship of Red Fish and De Smet. Ibid., 2:791f.; 3:809f., 835.

115. The story is reported in several versions. Sunder has a short account in *Fur Trade on the Upper Missouri*, 139. A fuller, more revealing version is reported by Chittenden, based on a conversation with La Barge, in *History of Early Steamboat Navigation on the Missouri River*, 1:196ff.

116. See Chittenden, *History of Early Steamboat Navigation*, 1:197 and 198, for the two quotations.

117. De Smet's own account of the incident, written to the editor of *Précis Historiques*, perhaps for publication, is somewhat more modest. Of the rain that came he says, "This fortunate circumstance filled all hearts with respect for the word of God" and "made a deep impression on these simple-minded Indians." C&R, 3:831.

118. Columbus's initial impression of the first natives he encountered was voiced repeatedly by Europeans during the first two centuries of contact. In his log entry for October 12, 1492, Columbus asserted, "[T]hey seem to have no religion." Robert H. Fuson, ed. and trans., *The Log of Christopher Columbus* (Camden, Maine: International Marine Publishing Company, 1987), 77.

119. C&R, 4:1216.

120. Ibid., 1:227: "Is it these people whom the civilized nations dare to call by the name of savages?"

CHAPTER 5: Henry Benjamin Whipple

1. From the closing lines of Whipple's book, *Lights and Shadows of a Long Episcopate: Being Reminiscences and Recollections of the Right Reverend Henry Benjamin Whipple, D.D., LL.D., Bishop of Minnesota* (New York: Macmillan, 1912), 494.

2. The population of the state at the time of Whipple's arrival in 1859 was around 170,000. At his death (1901) the state's population neared two million. See Phillips

Endecott Osgood, *Straight Tongue: A Story of Henry Benjamin Whipple, First Episcopal Bishop of Minnesota* (Minneapolis: T. S. Denison, 1958), 283.

3. Whipple, *Lights and Shadows*, 29.

4. Every writer on Whipple cites what seems to be the obligatory quotation from President Lincoln after the two had discussed the Little Crow War and Indian reform: "He [Whipple] came here the other day and talked with me about the rascality of this Indian business until I felt it down to my boots. If we get through this war, and I live, this Indian system shall be reformed!" The comment is preserved only by Whipple himself, in ibid., 137.

5. See ibid., 50ff. and 136f. For a discussion of the Indian reform movement see Robert Winston Mardock, *The Reformers and the American Indian* (Columbia: Univ. of Missouri Press, 1971); Francis Paul Prucha, *American Indian Policy in Crisis: Christian Reformers and the Indian, 1865–1900* (Norman: Univ. of Oklahoma Press, 1976); Henry E. Fritz, *The Movement for Indian Assimilation, 1860–1890* (Westport, Conn.: Greenwood Press, 1981); Frederick E. Hoxie, *A Final Promise: The Campaign to Assimilate the Indians, 1880–1920* (Lincoln: Univ. of Nebraska Press, 1985); and Valerie Sherer Mathes, "Nineteenth Century Women and Reform: The Women's National Indian Association," *American Indian Quarterly* 14 (1990): 1–18.

6. Robert H. Keller, Jr., *American Protestantism and United States Indian Policy, 1869–82* (Lincoln: Univ. of Nebraska Press, 1983) calls Whipple "the church's most effective advocate of Indian reform during the 1860s and '70s." Photo caption between 166 and 167.

7. William Watts Folwell comments that Whipple was "the one man in Minnesota who was not swept off his feet by the tide of passion" after the Little Crow War when angry anti-Indian sentiment was the rule among Minnesota whites. *A History of Minnesota*, 4 vols. (Minneapolis: Minnesota Historical Society, 1924), 2:206; cf. 4:472–77.

8. See, for example, the St. Paul *Pioneer*, December 6, 1862; and the Faribault *Central Republican*, June 10, 1863.

9. Whipple, *Lights and Shadows*, 554 and 318. Custer's death at the Greasy Grass was not a "massacre," but the result of a fair fight, in which Custer actually made a surprise attack on the allied camp of Sioux, Arapaho, and Cheyenne. They just turned out to be the superior force. Likewise, Sand Creek was no "battle." The rhetoric of "massacre" language was already clear to the abolitionist and Indian reform advocate Wendell Phillips. See his letter to the editor of the *Boston Evening Transcript*. Also, Richard R. McMahon, *The Anglo-Saxon and the North American Indian* (Kelly, Pict & Company, 1876), 41ff.

10. Henry Benjamin Whipple, "The Indian System," *North American Review* 99 (October 1864): 449.

11. Whipple knew the trials were unjust and that at least some of those hanged were clearly innocent. "Three hundred were condemned to death by Military Court. The President commuted the sentences of all but thirty-nine, who were hanged at Mankato. The Rev. Dr. Riggs, who was present at the trial, said that it was conducted with haste and that forty men were tried in one day. An officer told me that one man was hanged for lying, the circumstance having been that the man, who was not at Yellow Medicine during the outbreak boasted upon his return that he had killed Garvey, an Indian trader, with an arrow. 'As we knew,' said the officer, 'that Garvey had been killed by a bullet, we hung the rascal.' " *Lights and Shadows*, 131.

For a full analysis of the Little Crow War, see the account in Dee Brown, *Bury My Heart at Wounded Knee* (New York: Holt, Rinehart and Winston, 1970), 37–66.

12. Reprinted in Whipple, *Lights and Shadows*, 127f.: "There is no man who does not feel that the savages who have committed these deeds of violence must meet their doom. The law of God and man alike require it. . . . As citizens, we have the clear right to ask our rulers to punish the guilty." A similar opinion was held by other "friends" of Indian people. To wit, De Smet wrote in December 1862, "that thirty-nine of the Indian prisoners in Minnesota would be executed on the 20th instant, on account of the numerous murders and cruelties they have committed against the white settlers along the frontiers. Surely they deserve no better lot." Hiram Martin Chittenden and Alfred Talbot Richardson, *Life, Letters and Travels of Father Pierre-Jean De Smet, S.J., 1801–1873*, 4 vols., in *Religion in America*, ed. Edwin S. Gaustad (New York: Francis P. Harper, 1905; reprint, Arno Press and New York Times, 1969), 4:1510.

13. James B. Finley, *My Life among the Indians* (Cincinnati: Cranston and Curtis; New York: Hunt and Eaton, n.d. [c. 1850]), 450–53. Finley, a Methodist missionary in the Ohio region during the late eighteenth and early nineteenth centuries, voiced similar concerns. To his credit, he seems to have been one of the few who saw white encroachment as a negative force to be resisted by people of conscience.

14. Cited from Francis Paul Prucha, *The Great Father: The United States Government and the American Indian*, abridged edition (Lincoln: Univ. of Nebraska Press, 1984, 1986), 109f. Robert M. Kvasnicka, "George W. Manypenny, 1853–1857," in *The Commissioner of Indian Affairs, 1824–1977*, ed. Kvasnicka and Herman J. Viola (Univ. of Nebraska Press, 1979), 57–67.

15. Whipple, *Lights and Shadows*, 510.

16. The annual proceedings are published; note, for example, "Address of Bishop Whipple," *Proceedings of the Eleventh Annual Meeting of the Lake Mohonk Conferences of Friends of the Indian* (1893), ca. p. 34. For general information about the Lake Mohonk Conferences, see Clyde A. Milner II, "Albert K. Smiley: Friend to Friends of the Indians," in *Churchmen and the Western Indians: 1820–1920*, ed. Milner and Floyd A. O'Neil (Norman: Univ. of Oklahoma Press, 1985), 143–76. The conferences were annual meetings where the community of reformers assembled to read papers and engage in the informal discussions that kept the movement alive. The meetings began in 1883 and continued to 1912. The most exhaustive studies are by Larry E. Burgess, "The Lake Mohonk Conferences on the Indian, 1883–1916" (Ph.D. diss., Claremont Graduate School, 1972); "We'll Discuss It at Mohonk," *Quaker History* 40 (1971): 14–28; *The Lake Mohonk Conference of Friends of the Indian: Guide to the Annual Reports* (New York: Clearwater Publishing, 1975); and *Mohonk, Its People and Spirit: A History of One Hundred Years of Growth and Service* (New Paltz, N.Y.: Mohonk Mountain House, 1980).

17. Stephen Jay Gould, *The Mismeasure of Man* (New York: W. W. Norton, 1981), 30–72; Reginald Horsman, "Scientific Racism and the American Indian in the Mid-Nineteenth Century," *American Quarterly* 37 (May 1975): 152–68; John S. Haller, Jr., *Outcasts from Evolution: Scientific Attitudes of Racial Inferiority, 1859–1900* (Champaign: Univ. of Illinois Press, 1971); and William R. Stanton, *The Leopard's Spots: Scientific Attitudes toward Race in America, 1815–1859* (Chicago: Univ. of Chicago Press, 1960).

18. Finley, *My Life among the Indians*, argued strongly for the unity of humankind, explicitly mentioning white, Indian, and Black in this context. His missionary work

among Wyandot people was conducted with a Black missionary partner, John Stewart. It should be noted, however, that their missionary outreach did not prevent the removal and eventual destruction of the Wyandots as a nation.

19. See Horsman, "Scientific Racism and the American Indian"; also, Reginald Horsman, *Race and Manifest Destiny: The Origins of American Racial Anglo-Saxonism* (Cambridge, Mass.: Harvard Univ. Press, 1981), 189–207; Russel B. Nye, *Society and Culture in America, 1930–1960* (New York: Harper and Row, 1974); and Thomas F. Gossett, *Race: The History of an Idea in America* (Dallas: Southern Methodist Univ. Press, 1963).

20. Francis Paul Prucha, "Scientific Racism and Indian Policy," in *Indian Policy in the United States: Historical Essays* (Lincoln: Univ. of Nebraska Press, 1981). For examples of the American School of Ethnology, see Samuel George Morton, *Crania Americana: or, a Comparative View of the Skulls of the Various Aboriginal Nations of North and South America, to Which Is Prefixed an Essay of the Varieties of the Human Species* (Philadelphia: J. Dobson, 1839); and J. C. Nott and George R. Gliddon, *Types of Mankind: or, Ethnological Researches, Based upon the Ancient Monuments, Paintings, Sculptures, and Crania of Races, and upon Their Natural, Geographical Philological, and Biblical History* (Philadelphia: Lippincott, Grambo and Company, 1854). Gould, *Mismeasure of Man*, offers a modern critique of this nineteenth-century racist science.

21. Commission of Indian Affairs Report, 1851, Serial 613, 274.

22. Commission of Indian Affairs Report, 1855, Serial 610, 338.

23. Whipple, *Lights and Shadows*, 512. Of course, the enduring judgment of Canada's relationship with American Indian peoples within the borders it claims is not nearly as sanguine as Whipple suggests. See Robert Davis and Mark Zannis, *The Genocide Machine in Canada: The Pacification of the North* (Toronto: Black Rose Books, 1973).

24. See Whipple, "The Indian System," 454: "The first step in the change from barbarism to civilization must be so distinct and marked that it will admit of no return. The civilized Indian consents to have his hair cut after the fashion of the white man."

25. Letter to Miss Edwards, December 9, 1851, in Charles Breck, comp., *The Life of the Reverend James Lloyd Breck, D.D., Chiefly from Letters Written by Himself* (New York: E. and J. B. Young & Co., 1883), 182.

26. Letter to Miss Edwards, July 12, 1852, in Breck, *Life*, 215.

27. "Letter from Rev. J. J. Enmegahbowh," *Spirit of Missions* 39 (1874): 226, cited from Martin N. Zanger, " 'Straight Tongue's Heathen Wards': Bishop Whipple and the Episcopal Mission to the Chippewas," in *Churchmen and the Western Indians: 1820–1920*, ed. Clyde A. Milner II and Floyd A. O'Neil (Norman: Univ. of Oklahoma Press, 1985), 197. The article has a full description of the momentous event, including a generous dose of Indian humor.

28. Enmegahbowh to Rev. Breck, September 6, 1862, HBW Papers, cited from Zanger, "Straight Tongue's Heathen Wards," 203.

29. Letter to Miss Edwards, April 20, 1852, in Breck, *Life*, 206, 208.

30. E.g., his letter to Miss Edwards, July 12, 1852, in Breck, *Life*, 215.

31. Whipple, "The Indian System," 459: "The next question that we shall ask is, 'Are the Indian races of North America capable of receiving a Christian civilization?' We answer, unhesitatingly, Yes."

32. Ibid., 454.

33. Ibid., 456.

34. Whipple, "What Shall We Do with the Indian?" Written for the public press, in *Lights and Shadows*, 514.
35. Letter to President Grant, in ibid., 558–61.
36. Francis Paul Prucha, ed., *Americanizing the American Indian: Writings by the "Friends of the Indian," 1880–1900* (Cambridge, Mass.: Harvard Univ. Press, 1973), 3. By the 1880s the reform theme could be summarized in this outline of doctrine as Prucha recites it: ". . . first, to break up the tribal relations and their reservation base and to individualize the Indian of a 160 acre homestead by the allotment of land in severalty; second, to make the Indian citizens and equal with the whites in regard to both the protection and the restraints of law; and third, to provide a universal government school system that would make good Americans out of the rising generation of Indians." Prucha omits Christianization here, but it is implicit in the whole of the reform discussion and explicit in the Grant Peace Policy.
37. U.S. Senate, *Executive Documents: Second Session of the Forty-Fourth Congress, 1876–1877*, vol. 1, document 9.
38. Ward Churchill, "The Earth Is Our Mother," in *The State of Native America*, ed. Annette Jaimes (Boston: South End Press, 1992), 139–88, provides a compelling political analysis of the Sioux peace commission of 1876 and its explicit task of dispossessing Sioux peoples from their landholdings.
39. Ibid., 8.
40. It should not go unnoticed that "friends of the Indian" was a self-proclaimed title assumed by the reformers of the era. See Prucha, *Americanizing the American Indian*, 1 and *inter alia*.
41. Whipple, *Lights and Shadows*, 166ff., 307ff., 519f., 530–46.
42. U.S. Congress, Joint Special Committee, "Condition of the Indian Tribes," 39th Cong., 2d sess., 1866–1867, Senate Rep. 156, 3–10.
43. "Indian Peace Commission, Report to the President, January 7, 1868, *Annual Report of the Commissioner of Indian Affairs, 1868, Annual Report of the Secretary of the Interior*, 40th Cong., 3d sess., 1868–69, House Executive Document 1 (Serial 1366), 502 (full report, 486–510). Also quoted in the Sioux commission report in 1876.
44. "Indian Peace Commission," 503f.
45. Lydia Maria Child, *An Appeal for the Indians* (New York: William P. Tomlinson, 1868).
46. Prucha, *The Great Father*, 1:490.
47. Ibid., 1:492.
48. Quoted from Whipple, *Lights and Shadows*, 167.
49. U.S. Indian Commission, "Memorial, July 14, 1868," *Annual Report of the Commissioner of Indian Affairs, 1868, Annual Report of the Secretary of the Interior*, 41st Cong., 2d sess., 1869–70, House Executive Document 1 (Serial 1414), 538.
50. U.S. Indian Commission, "Memorial," 10f.
51. H. B. Whipple, Preface to Helen Hunt Jackson, *A Century of Dishonor: A Sketch of the United States Government's Dealing with Some of the Indian Tribes* (New York: Harper, 1881), viii–ix.
52. General Sibley, an old friend and ally of Whipple's, had to decline service due to his health. See his letter attached to the commission's report, Senate, *Executive Documents, 1876–77*, 86–90.
53. Ibid., 31.
54. Ibid.

55. Prucha, *The Great Father*, 1:191–213, and William McLoughlin, *Cherokees and Missionaries: 1789–1839* (New Haven: Yale Univ. Press, 1984), 239–99.
56. Implicit in the discussion here is the fact that if Indian tribal sovereignty was admitted up to this point in U.S. and North American history, then Americans must face the realization that an important part of their history is false. Namely, they must confront their denial that, "We never conquered other peoples whose land and fate we now control."
57. Executive Document 9, 2.
58. Remember that the Red Cloud/Powder River War of 1866–68 had been fought over the building of a single road, the Bozeman Trail. While this road does not seem to have been in violation of the 1851 Fort Laramie Treaty, the government's cessation of annuities in 1866 was.
59. The terms of the agreement are spelled out in brief in Smith's letter to Chandler (Executive Document 9, 2) and in more detail in the "Articles of Agreement" signed by the commissioners and the Sioux leaders who participated (pp. 21ff.).
60. Again, Whipple repeats a theme sounded already by Eliot in seventeenth-century New England and by Finley in the early nineteenth century in Ohio as he encouraged Indians to "abandon the hunt."
61. Zanger, "Straight Tongue's Heathen Wards," 182; and Whipple to H. H. Montgomery, July 1, 1901, H. B. Whipple papers, Minnesota Historical Society.
62. The struggle of the Sioux peoples to regain aboriginal landholdings, the Black Hills in particular, is analyzed in numerous books and articles. See Churchill, "The Earth Is Our Mother"; Russell Means, "The Black Hills: They're Still Not For Sale!" *Oyate Wicaho* (May 1980); and Steven C. Hanson, "United States vs. Sioux Nation: Political Questions, Moral Imperative and National Honor," *American Indian Law Review* 8 (1980): 459–84. See also the materials prepared for the 1986 Senate hearings on the proposed Black Hills Bill.
63. Report of the Board of Indian Commissioners, 1883, 34f.

CHAPTER 6: The Enduring Dilemma

1. African theologian John Pobee, quoted from Ogbu U. Kalu, "Church Presence in Africa: A Historical Analysis of the Evangelization Process," in *African Theology Enroute: Papers from the Pan African Conference of Third World Theologians*, ed. Kofi Appiah-Kubi and Sergio Torres (Maryknoll: Orbis Press, 1979), 20.
2. Jack Forbes, *A World Ruled by Cannibals: The Wétiko Disease of Aggression, Violence, and Imperialism* (Davis, Calif.: D-Q Univ. Press, 1979), 24. Forbes actually applies *wétiko* to every historical urge to empire and conquest, from the ancient Assyrians to the Aztecs and Incas in the Americas.
3. Leonardo Boff, *New Evangelization: Good News to the Poor* (Maryknoll: Orbis Press, 1991), 15, offers a firm corrective against heroizing Las Casas (see chap. 1, n. 49. For Worcester, see William McLoughlin, *Cherokees and Missionaries: 1789–1839* (New Haven: Yale Univ. Press, 1984), 239–99. A man of considerable courage who defended the Cherokees in the face of removal and willingly served time in the Georgia state penitentiary for the Cherokee cause, Worcester nevertheless was firmly committed to the missionary goal of "civilizing" the Cherokees. For Kirkland, see Donald A. Grinde, Jr., *The Iroquois and the Founding of the American Nation* (San Francisco: Indian Historian Press, 1977), 43–94. Kirkland was loved by many

and respected by most of the Iroquois, yet Grinde reports, "This New England Puritan, with 'New Light' principles, was a patriot to the core" (43). Grinde describes the extent to which Kirkland functioned as an American agent in his capacity as missionary among the Iroquois to facilitate Iroquois cooperation in the American revolution. See also Samuel Kirkland Lothrop, *Life of Samuel Kirkland* (Boston, 1847).

4. Clifford Geertz, *The Interpretation of Cultures* (New York: Basic, 1973); and *Local Knowledge: Further Essays in Interpretive Anthropology* (New York: Basic, 1983). Geertz's definition builds by extension on the classic definition offered by E. B. Tylor in 1871: ". . . that complex whole which includes knowledge, belief, art, morals, law, custom, and any other capabilities and habits acquired by man as a member of society." *Primitive Culture* (New York: Holt, 1889), 1.

5. For an accessible and useful description of European desperateness on the eve of the conquest in the fifteenth century, see Kirkpatrick Sale, *The Conquest of Paradise: Christopher Columbus and the Columbian Legacy* (New York: Penguin, 1990), 28–46 (also 74–91). Pre-Columbian Europe was fractured into a multitude of small, relatively insignificant feudal fiefdoms that were only beginning to coalesce into larger, more centralized nation-states.

6. E.g., the work of Mary Douglas on the substrata of British and London society.

7. For a brilliant exception, see Lawrence E. Sullivan, *Icanchu's Drum: Orientation to Meaning in South American Religions* (New York: Macmillan, 1988).

8. William Stolzman, *The Pipe and Christ* (Pineridge, S. Dak.: Red Cloud Indian School, 1986), makes this relationship perfectly clear. Stolzman, the paradigm of the modern, sensitive, liberal missionary, argues for the validity of the native Lakota religious forms and attempts to show that they are not necessarily at odds with Christianity, especially Catholicism. At the same time, he is clear that Catholic doctrine, Christ, and the Catholic sacraments are implicitly superior to native expressions of spirituality. The latter are to be accepted where they do not contradict or come into opposition with the former. And by the former, we should note, he implicitly means not just Christianity, but a Euroamerican interpretation of Christianity.

9. The term here refers to that interconnected systemic whole that in itself has become causative or determinative of subsequent actions, where all actions are to a significant extent determined by all previous actions. Who each one of us is as a human being is not a matter of complete freedom; rather, the parameters of our behavior are determined by our culture, the structures of society around us, when we live, who our parents are, and so forth. I am not arguing here for complete determinism, either. The limitations to human freedom, however, must be recognized in order to press those limits to allow for greater freedom.

10. Immanuel Wallerstein, *The Modern World-System* (New York: Academic Press, 1974). Wallerstein, however, believes the world economic system is now threatening the sovereignty of the nation-state. See also his essay, "The Rise and Future Demise of the World Capitalist System," *Comparative Studies in Society and History* 16 (1974): 387–415.

11. Itumeleng Mosala, "African Independent Churches: A Study in Sociotheological Protest," in *Resistance and Hope: South African Essays in Honour of Beyers Naude*, ed. Charles Villa-Vincencio and John W. De Gruchy (Grand Rapids: Eerdmans, 1985), 101.

12. See G. Tinker and Loring Bush, "Native American Unemployment: Statistical Games and Cover-ups," in *Racism and the Underclass in America*, ed. George W. Shepherd, Jr., and David Penna (New York: Greenwood Press, 1991); Tinker, "Does 'All People' Include Native Peoples?" in *God, Goods and the Common Good*, ed. Charles Lutz (Minneapolis: Augsburg, 1986), 125–36; and "American Indian Unemployment: Confronting a Distressing Reality," A First Friday Report, issued by the Full Employment Action Council and the Lutheran Council U.S.A. Office for Governmental Affairs and the Rural Coalition, et al., ed. John Lillie, Taly Rutenberg, Sarah Shella, and Janice View, Washington, D.C., October 4, 1985.

13. See Ward Churchill, "Indigenous Peoples of the United States: A Struggle Against Internal Colonialism," *Black Scholar* (1985): 29–35; and M. Annette Jaimes, "La Raza and Indigenism: Alternatives to Autogenocide in Native North America," *Global Justice* (October, 1992).

14. Robert Williams, *The American Indian in Western Legal Thought: Discourses of Conquest* (New York: Oxford Univ. Press, 1990), especially 29–47.

15. See J. Whatmough, *The Foundations of Roman Italy* (London: Methuen, 1937); and H. H. Howard Hayes Scullard, *The Etruscan Cities and Rome* (Ithaca, N.Y.: Cornell Univ. Press, 1967).

16. See Williams's chapter, "The Perfect Instrument of Empire: The Colonizing Discourse of Renaissance Spain," *The American Indian in Western Legal Thought*, 58–118.

17. Ashis Nandy, *The Intimate Enemy: Loss and Recovery of Self under Colonialism* (Delhi: Oxford Univ. Press, 1983).

18. Jeremiah Evarts, *Cherokee Removal: The William Penn Essays and Other Writings*, ed. Francis P. Prucha (Knoxville: Univ. of Tennessee Press, 1981), and McLoughlin, *Cherokees and the Missionaries*, give examples of missionary courage in supporting an Indian cause at the time of the Cherokee removal in the 1830s.

19. J. E. Casely Hayford, *Gold Coast Native Institutions, with Thought upon a Healthy Imperial Policy for the Gold Coast and Ashanti* (London: Cass, 1970), 232. Cf. Glyndwr Williams, *The Expansion of Europe in the Eighteenth Century: Overseas Rivalry, Discovery and Exploitation* (New York: Walker, 1967), 34–38; and now the very fine analysis of Luis N. Rivera, *A Violent Evangelism: The Political and Religious Conquest of the Americas* (Louisville: Westminster/John Knox, 1992).

20. Williams, *The American Indian in Western Legal Thought*, 193–205. Williams implicitly demonstrates the deep, symbiotic relationship between theology and both European and English civil law and the beginnings of international legal theory in the sixteenth century. Both the Catholic Franciscus de Victoria in Spain and the Protestant Alberico Gentili in England accepted the fundamental principle that "Europeans could lawfully wage war against *normatively divergent peoples* who violated Eurocentrically conceived natural law" (195f.). It was only a small step from such a European discourse of conquest to a liberal, well-intentioned missionary discourse of conversion that identified Native American societies as culturally divergent and in need of conversion to the gospel of their own superior European culture and social structures.

21. Francis Paul Prucha, *The Great Father: The United States Government and the American Indian* (Lincoln: Univ. of Nebraska Press, 1984), 2:646f., 800–05; Vine Deloria, Jr. and Clifford M. Lytle, *American Indians, American Justice* (Austin: Univ. of Texas Press, 1983), 230ff. For an example of explicitly articulated federal policy, see

Prucha, ed., *Documents of United States Indian Policy* (Lincoln: Univ. of Nebraska Press, 1975), 186ff.

22. Ward Churchill, *Fantasies of the Master Race: Literature, Cinema and the Colonization of American Indians*, ed. M. Annette Jaimes (Boston: South End Press, 1992), 187ff. and 215ff., describes the charlatanism of the likes of Lynn Andrews and Carlos Casteneda with their made-up, pseudo-Indian affectations, as well as the charlatanism of Native American would-be spiritual leaders like Sun Bear and Wallace Black Elk who purport to sell access to Indian ceremonies to non-Indian people. See also Alice B. Kehoe, "Primal Gaia: Primitivists and Plastic Medicine Men," in *The Invented Indian: Cultural Fictions and Government Policies*, ed. James A. Clifton (New Brunswick, N.J.: Transaction Books, 1990), 193–209.

23. Noam Chomsky, *Syntactic Structures*, Janua Linguarum, Series Minor, no. 4 (The Hague: Mouton, 1957); and *Aspects of the Theory of Syntax* (Cambridge, Mass.: MIT Press, 1965).

24. See his essay, "Spiritual Hucksterism: The Rise of the Plastic Medicine Men," in Churchill, *Fantasies of the Master Race*, 215–30.

SELECTED BIBLIOGRAPHY

CHAPTER 2: John Eliot

Primary Sources (Seventeenth Century)

BOWDEN, Henry W., and James P. Rhonda, eds. *John Eliot's Indian Dialogues: A Study in Cultural Interaction.* Westport, Conn.: Greenwood Press, 1980 [originally printed in Cambridge, 1671].

ELIOT, John. *A Late and Further Manifestation of the Progress of the Gospel amongst the Indians in New-England: Declaring their constant Love and Zeal to the Truth: With a redinesse to give Accompt of the Faith and Hope; as of their desires in church Communion to be Partakers of the Ordinances of Christ; Being a Narrative of the Examinations of the Indians, about their Knowledge in Religion, by the Elders of the Churches.* London, 1655. Pp. 261–87. This pamphlet includes the catechetical exam questions asked of the Natick converts at the Roxbury examination of April 13, 1654.

———. *A further Accompt of the Progresse of the Gospel amongst the Indians in New-England, and of the means used effectually to advance the same.* London: Corporation of New England, 1659.

———. *A further Account of the Progress of the Gospel amongst the Indians in New England: Being a Relation of the Confessions Made by Several Indians.* London, 1660.

———. *The Christian Commonwealth: or, The Civil Policy of the Rising Kingdom of Jesus Christ.* London: 1660. In Massachusetts Historical Society, *Collections,* Third Series, 9:127–64. Boston, 1846.

———. *A Brief Narrative of the Progress of the Gospel amongst the Indians in New-England in the Year 1670. Given in by the Reverend Mr. John Eliot, minister of the gospel there, in a letter by him directed to the right worshipful the commissioners under His Majesties Great-Seal for propagation of the gospel amongst the poor blind natives in those United Colonies.* London: Company for propagation of the gospel in New England and the parts adjacent in America, 1671.

———. "An Account of Indian Churches in New England" (1673). In Massachusetts Historical Society, *Collections,* First Series, 10:124–29. Boston, 1809.

ELIOT, John, and Thomas Mayhew. *Tears of Repentance; or, A Further Narrative of the Progress of the Gospel amongst the Indians in New-England: setting forth, not only their present state and condition, but sundry confessions of sin by diverse of the said Indians, wrought upon by the saving power of the gospel; together with the manifestation of their faith and hope in Jesus Christ, and the work of grace upon their hearts.* London: 1653. In Massachusetts Historical Society, *Collections*, Third Series, 4:197–260. Boston, 1834. This includes a 47-page transcription by Eliot of the presumed verbata of the 1652 confessions made by several Natick converts: "A Brief Relation of the Proceedings of the Lord's Work among the Indians, in Reference unto their church-Estate; the Reasons of the not Accomplishing thereof at Present: With Some of Their confessions; Whereby It May Be Discerned in Some Measure, How Far the Lord Hath Prepared among Them Fit Matter for a Church."

GOOKIN, Daniel. *Historical Collections of the Indians in New England* (1674). In Massachusetts Historical Society, *Collections*, First Series, 1:141–226. Boston, 1792. New edition, ed. Jeffrey H. Fiske. Towtowa, N.J.: 1970.

———. "History of the Christian Indians." In *Transactions and Collections of the American Antiquarian Society*. Vol. 2. Cambridge: Cambridge Univ. Press, 1836. Pp. 424–525.

MATHER, Cotton. *Triumphs of the reformed religion in America: The Life and Death of the Renown'd Mr. John Eliot, Who Was the First Preacher of the Gospel to the Indians in America.* Second ed. London, 1691.

SHEPARD, Thomas. *The Clear Sun-shine of the Gospel Breaking Forth upon the Indians in New-England: Or, An historicall narration of Gods wonderful workings upon sundry of the Indians, both chief governors and common-people.* London: R. Cotes, 1648. In Massachusetts Historical Society, *Collections*, Third Series, 4:25–67. Cambridge, Mass., 1834.

WHITFIELD, Henry, ed. *The Light Appearing More and More Towards the Perfect Day. Or, a farther Discovery of the present state of the Indians in New-England.* London: Corporation for the Promoting and Propagating of the Gospel of Jesus Christ, 1651. In Massachusetts Historical Society, *Collections*, Third Series, 4:100–47. Cambridge, Mass., 1834.

———, ed. *Strength Out of Weaknesse: or A glorious manifestation of the further progresse of the gospel amongst the Indians in New-England. Held forth in sundry letters from divers ministers and others to the corporation established by Parliament for promoting the gospel among the heathen.* London: Corporation for the Promoting and Propagating the Gospel of Jesus Christ in New England, 1652. Reprint, New York: J. Sabin, 1830–39.

WILLIAMS, Roger. *Christenings Make Not Christians, or A Briefe Discourse Concerning That Name Heathen, Commonly Given to the Indians.* (1645). In *Rhode Island Historical Tracts* 14:1–21. Providence, 1881.

[WILSON, John ?] *The Day-Breaking, If Not The Sun-Rising of the Gospel with the Indians in New England.* London, 1647. In Massachusetts Historical Society, *Collections*, Third Series, 4:1–23. Cambridge, Mass., 1834.

WINSLOW, Edward. *The Glorious Progress of the Gospel, amongst the Indians of New England: Manifested by three letters under the hand of that famous instrument of the Lord, Mr. John Eliot, and another from Mr. Thomas Mayhew, Jun., both preachers of the word, as well to the English as Indians in New England.* London: 1649. In Massachusetts Historical Society, *Collections*, Third Series, 4:69–98. Cambridge, Mass., 1834.

Secondary Sources

COGLEY, Richard W. "John Eliot and the Origins of the American Indians." *Early American Literature* 21 (1986–87): 210–25.

————. "The Millenarianism of John Eliot, Apostle to the Indians." Ph.D. Dissertation. Ann Arbor: University Microfilms International, 1983.

JENNINGS, Francis. "Goals and Functions of Puritan Missions to the Indians." *Ethnohistory* 18 (1971):197–212.

————. *The Invasion of America: Indians, Colonialism and the Cant of Conquest.* New York: W. W. Norton, 1975.

KELLAWAY, William. *The New England Company, 1649–1776, Missionary Society to the American Indians.* London: Longmans, Green, 1961. See esp. ca. pp. 103–5.

MACLEAR, J. F. "New England and the Fifth Monarchy: The Quest for the Millennium in Early American Puritanism." *William and Mary Quarterly,* Third Series, 32 (1975): 223–60.

MORRISON, Kenneth M. " 'That Art of Coyning Christians': John Eliot and the Praying Indians of Massachusetts." *Ethnohistory* 21 (1974): 77–92.

SALISBURY, Neal Emerson. "Conquest of the 'Savage': Puritans, Puritan Missionaries, and Indians, 1620–1680." Ph.D. Dissertation, Univ. of California, Los Angeles.

————. *Manitou and Providence: Indians, Europeans, and the Making of New England, 1500–1643.* Oxford: Oxford Univ. Press, 1982.

————. "Prospero in New England: The Puritan Missionary as Colonist," *Papers of the Sixth Algonquian Conference, 1974.* Ed. William Cowan. National Museum of Man, Mercury Series, Canadian Ethnology Service. Vol. 23. Ottawa, 1975.

————. "Red Puritans: The 'Praying Indians' of Massachusetts Bay and John Eliot." *William and Mary Quarterly,* Third Series, 31(1974): 27–54.

SHUFFELTON, Frank. "Indian Devils and Pilgrim Fathers: Squanto, Hobomok, and the English Conception of Indian Religion." *New England Quarterly* 49(1976): 108–16.

THOMAS, G. E. "Puritanism, Indians and the Concept of Race." *New England Quarterly* 48(1975).

WEIS, Frederick. "The New England Company of 1649 and Its Missionary Enterprises." *Publications of the Colonial Society of Massachusetts* 38(1947–51).

CHAPTER 3: Junípero Serra

Primary Sources

BOLTON, Herbert Eugene, ed. *Anza's California Expeditions.* 5 vols. Berkeley: Univ. of California Press, 1930.

————, ed. and trans. *Fray Juan Crespi: Missionary Explorer on the Pacific Coast, 1769–1774.* Berkeley: Univ. of California Press (reprint of AMS, 1929).

FONT, Pedro. *Font's Complete Diary: A Chronicle of the Founding of San Francisco, 1775–1776.* Herbert Eugene Bolton, ed. Berkeley: Univ. of California Press, 1933.

VON KOTZEBUE, Otto. *A New Voyage Round the World: 1823–26.* London, 1830.

PALÓU, Francisco. *Palóu's Life of Fray Junípero Serra.* Translated and annotated by Maynard J. Geiger, O.F.M. Washington, D.C.: Academy of American Franciscan History, 1955.

DE PORTOLA, Gaspar. *Diary of Gaspar de Portola during the California Expedition of 1769–70.* Donald E. Smith and Frederick J. Teggart, eds. Berkeley: Publications of the Academy of Pacific Coast History, 1909. Pp. 31–89.

SERRA, Junípero. *Diary of Fra Junípero Serra, O.F.M.: Being an Account of His Journey From Loreto to San Diego, March 28 to June 30, 1769.* The Documentary Preface to the History of the Missions of California. North Providence, R.I.: The Franciscan Missionaries of Mary, 1936.
———. *The Writings of Junípero Serra.* Antonine Tibesar, O.F.M., ed. 4 vols. Washington, D.C.: Academy of American Franciscan History, 1950–66.

Secondary Sources

BORAH, Woodrow W. "The California Mission." In *Ethnic Conflict in California History.* Charles Wollenburg, ed. Los Angeles: Tinnon Brown, 1970.
CASTILLO, Edward D. "The Impact of Euro-American Exploration and Settlement." In *Handbook of North American Indians.* Vol. 8 (California). R. F. Heizer, ed. Washington, D.C.: Smithsonian, 1978. Pp. 99–127.
COOK, Sherburne F. *The Conflict Between the California Indian and White Civilization: The Indian Versus the Spanish Mission.* Ibero-American, no. 21. Berkeley: Univ. of California Press, 1943. Reprint, Berkeley: Univ. of California Press, 1976.
———. *The Population of the California Indians, 1769–1970.* Berkeley: Univ. of California Press, 1976.
COSTO, Rupert, and Jeanette Henry Costo, eds. *The Missions of California: A Legacy of Genocide.* San Francisco: Indian Historian Press, 1987.
GUEST, Florian F. "The Indian Policy under Fermín Francisco de Lausén, California's Second Father President." *California Historical Society Quarterly* 45 (1966): 195–224.
———. "Mission Colonization and Political Control in Spanish California." *Journal of San Diego History* 24 (1978): 97–120.
———. "An Examination of the Thesis of S. F. Cook on the Forced Conversion of Indians in the California Missions." *Southern California Quarterly* 61 (1979): 1–77.
———. "Cultural Perspectives on California Mission Life." *Historical Society of Southern California* 65 (1983): 1–65.
HEIZER, Robert F., and Alan F. Almquist. *The Other Californians: Prejudice and Discrimination Under Spain, Mexico, and the United States to 1920.* Berkeley: Univ. of California Press, 1971.
PHELEN, John Leddy. *The Millennial Kingdom of the Franciscans in the New World.* Berkeley: Univ. of California Press, 1970.
PHILLIPS, George H. "Indians and the Breakdown of the Mission System." *Ethnohistory* 21 (1976): 201–301.
ROWNTREE, Lester. "Drought During California's Mission Period, 1769–1834." *Journal of California and Great Basin Anthropology* 7 (1985): 7–20.

Ethnographic Material

BANCROFT, Hubert Howe. *The Native Races of the Pacific States of North America.* 5 vols. San Rafael, Calif.: Bancroft Press, 1967.
BAUMHOFF, Martin A. *Ecological Determinants of Aboriginal California Populations.* University of California Publications in American Archaeology and Ethnology. Vol. 49, no. 2 (1963).
HEIZER, Robert F., and Albert B. Elsasser. *The Natural World of the California Indians.* California Natural History Guide No. 46. Berkeley: Univ. of California Press, 1980.

HEIZER, Robert F. and Albert B. Elsasser, eds. *Aboriginal California: Three Studies in Culture History.* Published for the University of California Archaeological Research Facility. Berkeley: Univ. of California Press. Second printing, 1966.

KROEBER, A. L. *Handbook of the Indians of California.* New York: Dover, 1976. Reprint of Bulletin 78, American Bureau of Ethnography. Smithsonian, 1925.

STRONG, William D. "Aboriginal Society in Southern California." *University of California Publications in American Archaeology and Ethnology* 29 (1926): 1–358.

CHAPTER 4: Pierre-Jean de Smet

Primary Sources

BLANCHET, F. N. "Oregon Grapeshot." Elizabeth Vaughan, trans. In *Oregon Historical Quarterly* 69, no. 3 (1968): 269–71. Letter by vicar general of missions in Oregon Territory to bishop at Quebec 1844 describing arrival of De Smet and nuns in settlement of St. Paul on Willowotter Ridge(?), mission and school.

CHITTENDEN, Hiram M., and A. T. Richardson. *Life, Letters and Travels of Father Pierre-Jean De Smet, S.J., 1801–1873.* 4 vols. In *Religion in America,* ed. Edwin S. Gaustad. New York: Francis P. Harper, 1905. Reprint, New York: Arno Press and the New York Times, 1969.

DE SMET, Pierre-Jean, *New Indian Sketches.* 9th ed. Original publ., 1863. New edition, Fairfield, Wash.: Ye Galleon, 1985.

————. *Oregon Missions and Travels Over the Rocky Mountains in 1845–46.* New York: Edward Dunigan, 1847. Reprint, Fairfield Wash.: Ye Galleon, 1978.

————. *Origin, Progress, and Prospects of the Catholic Mission to the Rocky Mountains.* Philadelphia: Fithian, 1843. Reprint, Fairfield, Wash.: Ye Galleon, 1967.

————. *Western Mission and Missionaries: A Series of Letters.* New York: P. J. Kenedy & Sons, 1859; and New York: Kirker, 1863. Reprint, Dublin: Irish Univ. Press, 1972.

THWAITES, Reuben Gold, ed. *The Jesuit Relations and Allied Documents: Early Western Travels, 1748–1846.* Vol. 27. Cleveland: Arthur H. Clark and Co., 1899 [1906].

Secondary Sources

ANTREI, Albert (Manti, Utah, High School). "Father Pierre De Smet." *Montana* 13, no. 2 (1963): 24–43. Summarized biography, emphasis on winning Indian support of projected treaties, especially Fort Rice Treaty of 1868.

BURNS, Robert Ignatius, S.J. *The Jesuits and the Wars of the Northwest.* New Haven: Yale Univ. Press, 1966.

CONNETTE, Earle, "Jesuit Missionary Pierre-Jean de Smet Papers." *Manuscripts* 19, no. 4 (1967): 40–41. Washington State University Library has recently acquired approximately 550 letters written by De Smet to family in Belgium between 18 October 1921 and 15 January 1873.

CORNKER, Robert C., "Direct Successor to DeSmet: Joseph M. Cataldo, S.J., and Stabilization of the Jesuit Indian Missions of the Pacific Northwest, 1877–1893." *Idaho Yesterdays* 31, nos. 1–2 (1987): 8–12.

DAVIS, William Lyle, S.J. "Peter John De Smet: The Years of Preparation, 1801–37." *Pacific Northwest Quarterly* (1941), 167–96.

————. "Peter John De Smet: Missionary to the Potawatomi, 1837–1840." *Pacific Northwest Quarterly* (1942), 123–53.

————. "Peter John De Smet: Journey of 1840." *Pacific Northwest Quarterly* 35 (1944): 29–43, 121–42.

HARROD, Howard L. *Mission Among the Blackfeet.* Norman: Univ. of Oklahoma Press, 1971.

JADIN, Louis, "Les Soeurs de Notre Dame et Les Soeurs de Sainte-Marie de Nemur aux U.S.A., au Guatemala et en Angleterre sous Leopold Iᵉʳ" ["The Sisters of Notre Dame and the Sisters of Saint Mary of Namur go to the U.S.A., Guatemala and England under Leopold I"]. *Bulletin des Sciences de l'Académie Royale des Sciences de Outre Mer* [Belgium] 2, no. 3 (1965): 662–70. Relates history of Sisters of St. Marie de Namur in America after invitation by De Smet.

KILLOREN, John J., "The Doctor's Scrapbook: A Collaboration of Linton and De Smet." *Gateway Heritage* 6, no. 3 (1985–86): 2–9. Scrapbook of St. Louis physician Moses Lewis Linton detailing friendship in 1950–72 with De Smet. Contains information re. De Smet's missionary activity and his observations re. Western fur traders.

LAVEILLE, E., S.J. *The Life of Father De Smet (1801–1873).* Trans. Charles Coppens, S.J. New York: P. J. Kenedy & Sons, 1915. Reprint, Chicago: Loyola Univ. Press, 1981.

MCGUINNESS, Robert, "Missionary Journey of Father De Smet." *Alberta* [Canada] *Historical Review* 15, no. 2 (1967): 12–19. Account of De Smet's wanderings through Alberta for purpose of arranging peace treaty between Blackfeet and Plateau tribes.

MAGARET, Helene. *Father De Smet: Pioneer Priest of the Rockies.* New York: Farrar and Rinehart, 1940.

PALLADINO, L. B., S.J. *Indian and White in the Northwest, or, a History of Catholicity in Montana.* Baltimore: John Murphy, 1894.

PARSONS, John E., "Steamboats in the 'Idaho' Gold Rush." *Montana* 10, no. 1 (1960): 51–61. Biographical notes on well-known steamboat passengers to Idaho, Montana, Wyoming.

PFALLER, Louis L., O.S.B., ed., "The Golpin Journal: Dramatic Record of an Odyssey of Peace." *Montana* 18, no. 2 (1968): 2–23. Golpin, Fort Rice trader, served as De Smet's guide and interpreter on journey to hostile Sioux in S.E. Montana, to induce them to attend peace conference. Golpin's diary, discovered in Europe in 1929, includes verbatim reports of speeches by Sitting Bull, other prominent Sioux and on personality of De Smet.

SCHAEFFER, Claude. "The First Jesuit Mission to the Flatheads, 1840–1850, A Study in Culture Conflicts." *Pacific Northwest Quarterly* 28 (1937): 227–50.

SUNDER, John E. "Up the Missouri to the Montana Mines: John O'Fallon Delany's 'Pocket Diary for 1862' " *Bulletin of the Missouri Historical Society* 19, no. 1 (1962/63): 3–22. Delany in 1862 accompanies De Smet on trip up Missouri River and overland to Montana and the Rockies.

TERRELL, John Upton. *Black Robe: The Life of Pierre-Jean De Smet, Missionary, Explorer, and Pioneer.* New York: Doubleday, 1964.

CHAPTER 5: Henry Benjamin Whipple

Primary Sources

BRECK, Charles, comp. *The Life of the Reverend James Lloyd Breck, D.D., Chiefly from Letters Written by Himself.* New York: E. and J. B. Young, 1883.

ENMEGAHBOWH, John J. "Letter from Rev. J. J. Enmegahbowh." *Spirit of Missions* 39 (1874): 226.

JACKSON, Helen Hunt. *A Century of Dishonor: A Sketch of the United States Government's Dealings with Some of the Indian Tribes.* With a Preface by Henry Benjamin Whipple. Cambridge: Cambridge Univ. Press, 1885.

WELSH, William, comp. *Taopi and His Friends, or The Indians Wrongs and Rights (1807–1878).* Philadelphia: Claxton, Remsen and Haffelfinger, 1869.

WHIPPLE, Henry Benjamin. *Lights and Shadows of a Long Episcopate: Being Reminiscences and Recollections of the Right Reverend Henry Benjamin Whipple, D.D., LL.D, Bishop of Minnesota.* New York: Macmillan: 1912.

Secondary Sources

HANGAARD, William P. "The Missionary Vision of James Lloyd Breck in Minnesota." *Historical Magazine of the Protestant Episcopal Church* 54, no. 3 (1985): 341–51.

OSGOOD, Phillips Endecott. *Straight Tongue: A Story of Henry Benjamin Whipple, First Episcopal Bishop of Minnesota.* Minneapolis: T. S. Denison, 1958.

STIRLING, Everett W. "Bishop Henry B. Whipple: Indian Agent Extraordinary." *Historical Magazine of the Protestant Episcopal Church* 26, no. 3 (1957): 239–47.

ZANGER, Martin N. " 'Straight Tongue's Heathen Wards:' Bishop Whipple and the Episcopal Mission to the Chippewas." In *Churchmen and the Western Indians: 1820–1920.* Ed. Clyde A. Milner II and Floyd A. O'Neil. Norman: Univ. of Oklahoma Press, 1985. Pp. 177–214.

INDEX

Accommodation as cultural colonialism, 122
Addictions
  to alcohol, among American Indians, 117
  as evidence of Indian dysfunctionality, 118–19
Agriculture
  imposition of European practices, 53–55
  traditional, of the Yumas, 146 n.64
Alcohol, trade in, 86
  by the American Fur Company, 156 n.85
  See also Trade
Algonquin people
  cross-cultural communication of, 39–40
  and polygamy, 26
Alienation, 35
  imposed by Puritan theology, 41
American Fur Company, 82
  liquor trade of, 156 n.85
American School of Ethnology, 99
Anger, and revival of traditional ways, 3
Arikara people, 92
Aristotle, 129 n.28
Assimilation
  goal of, 109
  of Indian forms by missionaries, 114–15
  politics of, 102–3
Assiniboin people, 156 n.85
Astor, J. J., 82, 154 n.66
Audubon, J. J., 156 n.86
Augur, C. C., 105
Authority, impetus to, 17
Auto-genocide, 118
Axtell, J., 35, 38, 40
Azuaga, Pedro de, 146 n.78

Baptism
  of the Micmacs, 14
  surreptitious, 158 n.112
  See also Conversion
Beckx, Peter, Father-General, 74

Beeson, J., 103
Biard, P., 14, 92
Birth statistics, ratio of males to females, Osage, 77
Black Moon, 131 n.41
Black Elk, Nicholas, 128 n.23
Black Elk, Wallace, 166 n.22
Blackfeet
  De Smet's meeting with, 73
  interpretation of Christianity, 78
  liquor trade with, 156 n.85
Blackfeet Sioux, 130 n.36
Black Robe (De Smet), 91–94
Boff, L., 131 n.48, 163–64 n.3
Bowden, Henry, 129 n.32
Bozeman Trail, 163 n.58
Braeuninger, M., 125 n.7
Breck, J. L., 100
Bringas, D. M., 141 n.8
Bucareli, vice-regent of New Spain, 46, 63
  on mission segregation, 148 n.103
Buchanan, J., 96, 103

Calhoun, J. C., role in Jesuit expansion in the West, 70–71
Canonization as self-validation of Western culture, 66–67
Carson, Kit, 7
Catechetical examinations, Natick, 138 n.68, 138–39 n.69
Century of Dishonor, A (Jackson), 9, 107
Ceremony (Silko), 1
Chamisso, Adalbert von, 142 n.32
Chandler, Z., 109
Charity, acceptance of, and indebtedness, 84–86
Cherokee people, 163 n.3
Child, L. M., 106
Chittenden, H. M., 69, 89, 156 n.86
Chivington, J., 98

175

Disraeli, B., 113
Dress, style of
  and conversion, 26
  and culture, 101
  See also Hair style
Dualism, reciprocal, of the sacred, 131 n.41
Dysfunctionality, 126 n.8
  and continuing colonialism, 122–23
  of families, 1
  general, 111
  individual and community, 117–19

Economic dependency, 51, 155 n.72
  and cultural change, 138 n.60
Economic functioning of Indian settlements in
  California, 145–46 n.63
Economic power, 144 n.52
  and conversion, 50–56
  cultural bias of missionaries toward, 16
  and cultural genocide, 7, 10–11, 32–33,
    79–81
  and dependency, 155 n.72
  and Eliot's mission, 21
  and European domination, 116
  loss of, in expropriation of Indian lands,
    60–61
  military support for changing, 65–66
  in the Sierra Gorda, 48
  and social structure, 77–78
  versus sovereignty of the nation-state, 164
    n.10
Economic rewards to missionaries, 137 n.46
Edmunds commission, 110
Education
  achievements among American Indians, 117
  government-imposed and church-imposed,
    143 n.40
  by missions, in the U.S., 129 n.32, 150
    n.12
  government support for, 50
Eliot, J., 4, 10, 21–41, 66, 80
  economic benefits from exploitative
    policies, 17–18
Encomienda system, 51
  attack on, by Las Casas, 18–19
  basis in white superiority, 9
Enmegahbowh, 101
Episcopal church, Indian members of, call to
  acknowledge dysfunction, 110
Escandón, José de on integrated pueblos, 148
  n.101
Evangelization
  Christian, of Indian people of North
    America, 2
  legacy of, 117
  politics of, 43–46
  process of, 9–10
  See also Theology
Evolution, cultural, 99–100

Exploitation
  by fur traders, 86
  missionary complicity in, 17–18
Extermination, as de facto policy, 126 n.10
  See also Genocide

Fages, P., 62
Fages expedition, 145 n.63
Family
  ideal of, and cultural values, 8
  Native American and European, 26
  nuclear, traditional Indian, 52
  See also Kinship system
Family resemblance categorization, 127 n.14
Famine
  following disruption of traditional
    agriculture, 145 n.57
  and the economics of conversion, 50–56
Finley, J. B., 160 nn.13, 18
Flathead people, mission to, 72–73, 151 n.28
  failure of, 73–79
Flesche, J., 14
Folwell, W. W., 159 n.7
Font, Fray Pedro, 59–60, 145 n.62
Forbes, J., 112
Fort Laramie Treaty, 104, 163 n.58
Franciscans, 42, 140 n.2
  California mission system of, 46
  reduccion system of, 19
Fur traders, support for mission, 81–86

Galvez, Joseph de, 47
Garces, Fr., 60
Garraghan, G. J., 69, 72
Geertz, C., 113, 164 n.4
Geiger, M. J., 67
Genocide
  by Christian missionaries, 4
  definition of, 126 n.9, 127 n.11
  evidence from the Caribbean and Mexico,
    126 n.10
  by the military, and by missionaries, 98–99
  in the Puritan colonies, 24
  See also Cultural genocide
Ghost Dance, 7
Gila people, 145 n.62
God, concept of, 39
Gonzales, J., 120
Gookin, D., 31, 33, 133 n.11
Gospel
  versus cultural values, 113
  and culture, 129–30 n.31
  and economic exploitation, 83–84
Government
  missionaries as functionaries of, 86–88
  mission support from, 17
  reforms in Indian affairs, U.S., 96–97
  relationship with missions, 27–28